BROKEN BIRDS
THE STORY OF MY MOMILA

BY JEANNETTE KATZIR

ISBN#978-0-615-27483-6

FIRST EDITION

Cover art work by Alisa Lapidus

This fiction, which is based on true events is a product of the author's recollections and is thus rendered as a subjective accounting of events that occurred in her life.

Dedication

"A coward dies a thousand deaths
.....a brave man only once."
These are the words Mom has been telling me
since I was a young girl.
I wished that they were wrong, but try as I might,
those words have been proven right more times than I
wish to remember.

Channna towered over the Poltzer clan like a giant tree that could provide the troubled and the weary with shade from life's harshness. The downside was that in that shade nothing or no one could grow, as Channa demanded that she and she alone soak up not just all the heat, but all the light as well.

A mixed blessing if there ever was one.

DHM

TABLE OF CONTENTS

INTRODUCTION 9

TWO SIDES 11

CHANNA ALWAYS HATED STRANGERS 13

THE BOY FROM UZHGOROD 44

CHANNA GETS HER MAN 71

THE POLTZER CHILDREN COMETH 85

COMING TO LOS ANGELES 95

THE HOUSE ON LA JOLLA 98

RUM, VODKA & GIN 106

THE POLTZER LET IN STRANGERS 113

THE NEXT GENERATION 119

THE HOUSE AROUND THE CORNER 130

A CHESTNUT GELDING 144

TO THE TRADE ONLY 147

THE EMERALD ISLE 155

A BUSINESS FOR SALE 158

A DRYSDALE MARRIES A HILLBILLY 163

A COWARD DIES A THOUSAND DEATHS 167

CHANGES 181

A STAG ON THE HILL 199

BAD CELLS LINING UP 206

POLTZERS CAN'T BE QUIET 214

THE POLTZERS MINUS CHANNA 231

TOVAH 249

EMAILS, PHONE MESSAGE AND FAXES 255

BACK TO UZHGOROD 272

TIME TO END THIS MESS 303

HER FIVE FINGERS 329

MACARONI AND CHEESE 337

OTTA BIST MEIN JACLYN 339

EPILOGUE 340

A PHOTO OF CHANNA'S MOM 342

INTRODUCTION

My momila, Channa, had five children, which was quite a feat because she had "weak uterus muscles" and was supposed to limit herself to only three.

Mom insisted on having more children for several reasons:

For one thing, she was chronically disobedient and defiant when it came to medical instructions. When prescribed any medications, she never took the recommended dosage. "The doctors just want to make money off you, Jaclyn," she'd tell me.

Second of all, my parents were "sloppy," a term we used when we messed up in matters of importance. Birth control was clearly trivial.

Lastly, Mom and Dad were trying to rebuild the family they had lost in the war. Ultimately, I feel that this need to create life was the true reason they chose to have so many children.

This is the story of my parents, my four siblings and myself. Although this group has rarely all gotten along for any length of time—as you will soon see—these people made me who I am.

TWO SIDES

I quickly finished my breakfast, grabbed my purse and waited by the door. Shirley, my younger sister, was due to arrive any minute to pick me up. This was an important morning and we wanted to arrive early. When she pulled up, I hopped in beside her and we drove downtown. We parked in the parking lot across the street from the courthouse and walked together into the imposing City building and through the metal detectors. Our names were printed on an informal sheet of paper pinned to a board on the outside of a ninth-floor family probate room. We pushed the double doors open and made our entry.

The walls of our courtroom were covered with wooden panels and the floor was decked with the standard government-issue marbled vinyl tile. A long wooden conference table with six wooden chairs upholstered in black were set up for the attorneys and their assistants, and a wall clock displayed the time. At the head of the room was an elevated judge's desk, which was flanked on both sides by flags, one for the United States and one for California. Filling in the balance of the room were permanently installed stadium seats with walking aisles on both sides and in the center.

Shlomo, the eldest among the siblings in the Polzter family, was already seated in the first row. A bundle of frayed nerves, he had devised a method of handling his anxiety by placing a large, thick rubber band around his hand, which he planned to snap whenever he felt the need to scream. I wished he had brought an extra one for me.

Our attorney, Ken, walked in, exuding confidence. A few moments later, Nina, the youngest member of the family, arrived. She came over to us and said a quick "good morning." She was overflowing with information to review with Ken, so she took a seat beside him up front at the conference table.

Steven, the last member of the Poltzer family, was also already seated. He had brought plastic containers filled with files and paperwork. His laptop was turned on, but at the moment, he was busy reading some documents with great concentration, his finger resting on his temple. He had not looked up or acknowledged our arrival in any way.

Five grown children on two opposite sides of the aisle: Steven wanted it all.

CHANNA ALWAYS HATED STRANGERS

Channa Perschowski was born on November 27, 1929, in Baranavichy, a small rural town in what was then Poland. Picturesque with its red-brick houses, Baranavichy was nestled amid thick woods that thrived in the country's moist, dark soil. Beautiful blue lakes dotted the landscape and rivers wound their way past ancient castles dating back to the eighth century. Russian Orthodox Church turrets competed with Jewish synagogues, but only in the contest of old-world charm. Today, the area is in the eastern part of the Republic of Belarus, sandwiched between Poland and Russia.

When Channa was born, her mother, Rachel, was overjoyed. A few years earlier, Rachel had had to bury her young daughter Sonya, who had been born with a hole in her heart. The fragile girl suffered from shortness of breath and weariness, and had spent most of her time in bed. Rachel was a dutiful mother, never straying from her daughter's bedside. Rachel spoon-fed her bowls of hot, sugary cream of wheat with large dollops of butter that slowly melted around the sides of the cereal. Despite her mother's tender care, Sonya died in her mother's arms at the age of eight.

Her death was extremely hard on Rachel. She blamed herself incessantly, wondering what she had eaten or done that could possibly have caused her precious little daughter to lose her life. She would visit the graveyard often, spending much time sitting on Sonya's grave.

Rachel's only joy in those dark days following Sonya's death was Sonya's older brother, Isaac, who was two years older. Isaac had grown into a healthy lad with boundless energy. He had dark features and had inherited his mother's worried eyes and prominent Jewish nose. He was a little short for his age, but was solid as a rock and strong as an ox. Even at his young age, he had a tender side and loved his sister Sonya dearly, always treating her with gentle kindness. Sometimes he would capture small lizards as they scurried through the yard and brought them into the house, cupped in his hands, for Sonya to admire and touch with her little fingers. They would giggle until Rachel came into the room. "Isaac, get that out of here!" Rachel would scold.

Sonya's death was as hard on Isaac as it was on Rachel. But neither Rachel nor his father could give him the answers he sought or help him express the tremendous sadness he felt. So he kept as busy as a young boy could, fending off the pain he held in his heart.

In the years that followed Sonya's death, Rachel suffered miscarriages and feared she would never have any more daughters. But after eleven years, she finally carried a baby to term, and when Channa arrived, Rachel's heart filled with joy. A few years later, Channa had a baby sister whom they named Jetta.

Rachel was tireless and bestowed a great deal of affection on her three children. She would sit on the cold wooden floors and play games with them for hours, ignoring the cooking and the cleaning. When the weather kept the children inside, she would bake sugar cookies with them, carefully guiding their small hands while they pressed various shapes onto the floured dough. Then she would patiently show them how to sprinkle sugar and cinnamon onto the warm cookies as they cooled on the counter.

Shlomo, the children's father, was less patient. He worked hard and when he came home, he demanded serenity. He had little tolerance for the children's noise and energy, and at times he could be quite harsh. "Sit down and be quiet!" he often yelled. "Why don't you go outside to play—and stay there a while!" When the children did not obey his demands for silence, he banged his fists on the table, causing them to run and hide under their beds.

Luckily for the children, Shlomo traveled extensively for business. He was often away for very long periods of time, which made Channa angry. She constantly feared he had abandoned them. Neither she nor her siblings ever developed a close bond with their father. He had never tried to earn their love and they could sense their mother's indifference towards him.

While Shlomo might not have been the best father, he was an outstanding provider. He was in the *schmate*, or garment, business. He regularly journeyed to America with clothing patterns, which would be turned into blue jeans and shirts to be sold to the American public. He would save up all the money he made and bring it back to Poland and his family. With each homecoming came a bundle of cash, which was spent on a variety of things. Fences and windows needed to be replaced and the children always seemed to have outgrown their sweaters and shoes.

Channa loved the family home. It had originally been built for Rachel's mother as a gift from her father, Yonkel, to his only daughter. The one-story wooden structure had a single fireplace in the kitchen. A metal roof kept the house water-tight, although the rat-tat-tat was loud during the rainy season. The house was large for its time, with three bedrooms and maid's quarters (although the family had no maid). There was a covered porch and a charming white fence separating the house from the dirt walkway in front and the neighbors' houses on both sides. In the back was a garden where the family grew their own vegetables. Towards the rear of the property stood a number of mature plum and apple trees that bore sweet fruits that Channa devoured as soon as they were ripe.

Channa's grandfather, Yonkel, had made his money inscribing and selling Mezuzahs. A Mezuzah is a tiny parchment scroll. On it, written in black ink, are two passages from the Torah: *Shema Yisorel* ("Blessed are you, Lord, our God, sovereign of the universe") and *Vehaya* ("Who has sanctified us with His commandments and commanded us to affix the mezuzah"). These two passages declare a family's faith and unity with God and obligate the bearers to observe Jewish beliefs in and out of the home. The parchments Yonkel inscribed were placed in small protective cases and nailed to the right door post of all doors leading outside.

Life was good for Channa and her family. The town blossomed as several large Jewish-owned textile mills opened and brought prosperity to many. The streets were filled with merchants, shoppers, and children. Electric lines flanked the streets on both sides and horse-drawn carriages, weighed down with bundles of fabrics, rolled down the street.

Channa's brother, Isaac, married a woman named Freida, and they had two children, Samuel and Ruben. Isaac worked as a furniture builder for a man with a small shop. There, they hammered, sawed and stained wood furniture, filling customers' orders for tables, chairs and beds.

Isaac's children, along with her sister Jetta, provided Channa with an ever-present assortment of playmates. In addition to her human buddies, Channa had several animals. Her family's lop-eared goats provided milk for the family and sometimes newborn kids for play. One beautiful spring morning, Channa came out to their small wooden barn to discover that twin goats had been born during the night. Two wobbly-legged females stood on the straw with after-birth still hanging off their tiny bodies. Channa immediately fell in love with one in particular. She was reddish in color with large patches of white fur, big dark eyes and long, velvety ears. She named the tiny creature Rosa and carried her everywhere until Rosa grew too big. Whenever Channa entered the barn, Rosa would leap around joyfully. It was a happy time for Channa.

But happy times were coming rapidly to an end as World War II got under way. "Remember not to go to the park!" Rachel told Channa as she walked out the front door. A decree had recently been made that Jews were no longer allowed in parks. The atmosphere around the house and within the small town of Baranavichy changed seemingly overnight. Rachel became anxious whenever any of her children were away from her side and her daughters could feel her panic. While outside playing, Channa often spotted grownups huddled in groups and speaking in hushed tones. More and more people seemed to be out of work, and more police were suddenly present. Rachel tried to keep dinner discussions off the subject of what was happening, but Channa couldn't help but overhear disjointed tidbits. There were frequent mentions of someone name Adolf Hitler and talk of fires and killings.

The list of warnings from Rachel grew longer. "Don't tell anyone where we are hiding the money," she told Channa as they buried a stocking filled with cash beneath the house. (Banks were no longer available to Jews.) "Don't leave the house without wearing your coat with the star on it!" Channa was told as she headed for the front door.

"Why?" Channa asked, a little irritated.

"Because it's the law." Rachel answered.

Everyone was nervous and on edge, and everyone was busy hiding things. Although Channa couldn't make much sense of it all, she could feel that something was deeply wrong, and the home Channa had felt so safe in was beginning to feel less so.

A few weeks after this uneasiness had set in, someone banged on the front door one evening. Standing on the porch were two heavily armed German soldiers. Shlomo was told he would need to go with them immediately. He asked over and over again what he had done wrong and questioned where they were taking him, but they just repeated for him to come with them. Rachel pleaded and Jetta and Channa cried, but within moments, Channa watched her father leave without so much as a good-bye.

The house was in an uproar and Channa couldn't stop herself from nagging her mom about what had just happened to her father. Where had he gone? When would he be coming back? Why did they take him? Would the soldiers return?

Rachel stood for a moment, gathering her thoughts and absorbing the shock. She already knew in her heart that her husband wouldn't be returning, but she didn't know what to say to her daughters. After a long pause, she replied, "Don't worry, he'll be back." Channa tried to believe what she had been told. After all, it was so much easier for her eleven-year-old brain to think that her father was just away, rather than dead.

The turmoil inflicted by Hitler continued for several months. Jewish-owned businesses now had to display a yellow star in their windows. Physicians could no longer tend to Jewish patients. A seven o'clock curfew was instituted and entire

17

families started to be forcibly removed from their homes in broad daylight. Then suddenly one day, the mayhem appeared to stop. The authorities assured the Jews that no further restrictions would be imposed. An odd, hesitant normalcy returned to the town. For a time, Channa slipped back into her comfortable childhood.

But Isaac was skeptical. Life was not easy under the current restrictions. Since he could not find work building furniture, he had plenty of time to speak with other young men who were also out of work. They agreed that Hitler was not done with the Jews yet and that it was time to leave Baranavichy.

Isaac hurried home, eager to speak to his mother. "We must leave here," he told her as she stood by the kitchen sink washing dishes. Even while standing in his mother's kitchen, he found it necessary to glance around the room to see if anyone was listening. "Things are going to get very difficult and we had better get away while we still can," he said in almost a whisper.

"No!" Rachel replied adamantly as she scraped the remnants of the afternoon meal off the plates. "Why should we uproot the family when everything is quieting down? What if we go somewhere else and it's even worse? The neighbors aren't leaving and if they don't think it's time to go, why should we?" It was typical of Rachel to use the neighbors as a kind of barometer of what her family should be doing. "Just wait. Things will get better."

"Mom, please listen," Isaac implored her, hoping she would come to her senses. "We shouldn't wait."

"The neighbor across the street heard that the Red Army is getting close. We will be safe here," his mother said as she dried her hands on a towel.

Isaac shook his head sadly. He knew in his heart that he should insist they all leave, but he did not know how to convince her. He could not leave without her. So he kissed his mother goodbye and walked home to his wife and children.

For a brief time life was indeed better. Then, abruptly, things took a turn for the worse. Channa watched, confused and scared, as areas were cordoned off, bails of barbed wire were unrolled and secured to posts, and places that had been accessible just the day before suddenly were not. Street signs were torn down and replaced with new ones in German. Since not everyone in the town was fluent in German, people accidentally entered restricted areas and were severely punished. One day Channa saw Rachel leave the house carrying the family's radio. Then suddenly, she was no longer allowed to attend school. She was now home all day, which should have been a treat, but somehow wasn't.

Then one day, as Rachel was walking home, she saw a group of people huddled together around the bulletin board where all the decrees and edicts were posted. She made her way to the front of the crowd and read the newest posting:

> ### ALL FARM ANIMALS ARE TO BE TAKEN TO THE TRAIN STATION IMMEDIATELY

She hurried home. As she approached the house, she spotted Jetta playing with Channa. This time, there was no way to sugarcoat the news. "Channa," she said, "In the morning, we must take all the animals to the train station."

"No!" Channa said, spinning away and refusing to make eye contact with her mother.

But Rachel would not relent. She put down her bags and held Channa's face roughly to look in her eyes.

"We need to stay invisible to the Germans!" she said in a tone Channa had never heard before. It was the sound of genuine terror. Channa knew she had no choice.

The next morning, Channa walked into the barn. Rosa hurried over and Channa stroked her head and velvety ears. Sadly, she slipped a rope over the mama goat's head and led her away with the twins following close behind.

As they approached the station, Channa heard the sound of sheep, goats, chickens and geese filling the air. All had been brought to the station. A number of trains waited with their doors open, and a mass of people were handing their livestock to Germans who were haphazardly placing them into the windowless box cars. Tearfully, Channa hugged Rosa's neck, feeling her coarse hair against her cheek, and said goodbye. Her eyes were filled with worry as she looked up at her mother. Finally, it was time to leave.

Conditions continued to deteriorate and Channa watched day after day as, all around them, families were being moved and homes were being emptied of Jews. One morning, as Channa played quietly in the living room, a German soldier walked into the family's home without even knocking and announced to Rachel that their home was to be converted into a Nazi headquarters. Channa was broken hearted. In her childlike innocence and ignorance, she had hoped she and her family would be spared, but all of a sudden, without any warning, it was her turn to move.

"But this is our home!" Rachel exclaimed.

"You have no choice." The stone-faced soldier told them. "Grab everything you are able to carry on your back." He continued.

"And where shall we go?" Rachel asked, not quite believing this was happening.

"The nearest ghetto is a few miles away," he answered.

As they gathered the basic necessities and a few valuables, Rachel was forced to acknowledge that she had indeed waited too long to make their getaway. Now she and her two daughters would need to focus their energy on learning to survive. Isaac and his family had also been evicted from their home and they too, headed for the ghetto.

The ghetto was ten blocks long. Germans who happened to have homes in the newly designated Ghetto area had been asked to give up their smaller homes for the newly vacated homes of the Jews. Multiple Jewish families were forced to live together in single-family homes. German soldiers directed arriving families towards a home and then it was up to them to secure a place for themselves. Each family unit was allotted a room and everyone in the house shared the kitchen. The furniture was minimal, and drying laundry was always draped across the room. The windows no longer bore draperies as that fabric was now needed for a variety of other uses. Strong drafts blew into the rooms, and it was impossible to keep warm. Isaac and his family had a room down the hall and they derived comfort from being together.

Channa had brought very little with her to the Ghetto, just some clothing, shoes and a few of her favorite toys. Seated in the room that would be her home, she could not help but mourn the bedroom someone else would be sleeping in, the home someone else would be living and playing in, and the sense of security that was now lost to her forever.

Because quarters were so close and they had so little, Jetta and Channa began fighting about just about everything. Their fights were so noisy that the family in the next room often banged on the wall, threatening to call the Jewish Police. One afternoon, the woman from next door even burst into their room. Although there was much to fear, Rachel wasn't especially scared —this woman surely wouldn't want to create trouble for herself.

Rachel and her two daughters did their best to maintain some semblance of normalcy. Food provisions consisted of small portions of bread and meat, sometimes horse, once every two weeks so the search for food was relentless. Each day, Rachel and her daughters dressed warmly and headed out to begin their search for ways to supplement their meager diet. In the middle of what was now a carless street, vendors, mostly women, placed their meager saleable possessions on makeshift tables or spread them out on blankets or sheets on the ground. These vendors had acquired their surplus of food from black marketers who had smuggled the food in.

Buyers crowded around them, arguing about the price. Negotiating the price of a potato could take quite a while. When Jetta and Channa grew bored of the negotiations, they would run and join other children who were out playing or investigating new fencing the Nazis had recently put up. With Jews disappearing weekly, these new fences systematically shrank down the size of the ghetto. Channa stopped and stared at the coils of razors that rested on the ground. How small her world was becoming.

Rachel made sure nothing was wasted of their precious purchases. She carefully saved potato peels and other scraps that would until recently have been saved for the goats. Clothing, although tattered, could be sewn almost new again. "Remember not to throw anything away," she repeated to Channa and Jetta so many times that Channa even heard those words in her sleep.

One afternoon, Channa and Jetta went out into the sunshine on a cold, clear day. Everyone was wearing hats and some had donned blankets to ward off the chill. On one side of the town square, a man in a long, black wool coat watched a parade of people wearing yellow stars walk by.

On the other side of the street stood a German soldier, his collar was stiff, his jacket was heavily starched, and his boots were gleaming black. As the sisters walked by, he called out to them. "Halt!" He pulled Channa aside. Startled, she held her breath as she looked up at him. He towered over her. His eyes were cold and steely. "Can you sew?" he asked her in German.

"Yes," Channa answered quickly.

"Wait here," he ordered her. She could have run, but he frightened her so that she didn't dare.

It felt like hours as she remained frozen in position. She feared for her little sister, but dared not send her away. Finally, the soldier returned, spilling a load of dirty, stinking, hole-riddled socks into her arms. "Mend them and bring them back to me tomorrow," he ordered.

As Channa walked home with Jetta, she was careful not to drop a single sock. Jetta pushed open the doors to their home and they ran into the kitchen to tell Rachel what had happened. "What should I do now?" Channa asked her mom as she dropped the socks onto the table.

"Well, you're not going to give them back!" her mom told her sternly. "We'll give them to Isaac. And make sure you are never seen by that soldier again!" she warned.

Channa obeyed her mom's instructions and never ventured anywhere near that part of the ghetto again.

One morning, the sounds of gunshots and windows being smashed down the street awoke Rachel and her daughters. They ran to the window and knew instantly what was happening: a Pogrom. They then ran out the back door and sought entry to a hiding place beneath the house that they had scoped out for such a moment. They crawled on their hands and knees and then on their bellies until they were deep inside. It was small, dark and dank; the earth was cold and wet, and the floorboards above them left little space for movement.

Channa and her family spent a long, cold, hungry, bathroom-less day and night there, but it was the darkness that frightened Channa the most. "I'm afraid to die," she confessed to her mother while they waited.

"Don't worry," Rachel told her, holding her hand tightly and bringing it close to her heart. "If they come for us I will lie on top of you and the bullets will not go through me and you will be spared." It was an uncomplicated answer, and to a young and frightened Channa, it was sufficient.

Suddenly, they heard the floor boards above them creak and small amounts of dirt dislodged and sprinkled down on them. It was the sound they had dreaded. Perpetrators were inside their home hunting for them, and because they found none, they decided to trash the house. They broke what little furniture there was and smashed the windows and any other breakable items. They sliced into bedding, allowing the feathers to disperse in a giant cloud. On their way out, they grabbed anything worth stealing.

All the while, Channa and her family did not move or say a word. It seemed like hours until they finally heard the house doors slam and trucks drive off. They cautiously crept out. They stepped over the smashed glass and saw the feathers of their bedding catching a ride on the wind. What a mess! But nobody cared. Shaky but alive, they knew they were lucky to have all made it.

These Pogroms and indiscriminate shootings became commonplace, but cruel and unlikely as it seemed, daily life somehow continued to march on relentlessly. Channa was amazed to find that you could actually get used to almost anything. One time, while foraging for food at the ghetto market, she suddenly saw people become agitated. Children were being collected up by their parents who hurried away. The Nazis were on their way again. Rachel, Channa and Jetta would of course have preferred to return to the safety of their hiding place at home, but there was not enough time, so they ran to a bunker next to where an aunt was living. A vegetable cellar of sorts, it was very small, and everyone inside was crammed together like sardines. Women placed their hands over their children's mouths to hush them up. The bunker had no lights and there was little fresh air, but any safe haven was a blessing.

However, that day when Rachel and her daughters arrived at the bunker, the door was already closed and bolted from the inside. They pounded on the door and Rachel called out, hoping that the aunt would intervene. But the door remained shut.

Rachel grabbed her daughters' hands and spat out a curse as they ran off. A moment later, they spotted another group of people, so they followed close behind and sought safety with them.

It turns out that Rachel and the girls got lucky. The Nazis accidentally stumbled upon that first bunker where the aunt was hiding. A soldier, as casually as one would throw an empty soda can from a car window, tossed a hand grenade into that bunker and the aunt died. Also tucked away deep inside that bunker was Isaac's wife and their children.

The news traveled back to Isaac in the time it took for Rachel to bring her two children back home. He was in shock. He had just seen his wife and children earlier that day, and suddenly, they were gone. Isaac, like many others, learned to bury his feelings so deep inside that they vanished from view. He never spoke about them again. Unlike Isaac, Channa did cry for them and thought about them a great deal, but in order to go on she developed a mantra: *If thousands were being killed, she could bear it.* It didn't make any sense, but it somehow gave her some solace.

Channa's days of staying home by her Mama's side came to an abrupt end one afternoon when a man named Herr Becht walked onto the ghetto grounds and pointed at her. "I'd like her to begin work at my factory tomorrow morning at seven," he instructed a soldier. She was only one among many that he singled out that afternoon.

Herr Becht was one of the many German factory owners who were taking full advantage of the plentiful and free labor available in the ghettos. He owned a garment factory nearby where they made uniforms for German soldiers. He preferred to hire children because they were easier to control and he needed those tiny fingers to perform his intricate work.

And so Rachel sent her young daughter off to work each day, not daring to hold her back because Channa's name had already been added to the list of workers. Fortunately, Herr Becht was kinder to his workers than most employers. In addition to feeding the children in his care the customary single slice of bread with watery soup, he sometimes placed a thin slice of meat product on the open sandwich.

One day Herr Becht learned through his own sources that there was going to be yet another Pogrom or Skita (organized killing) that night. He gazed out at the sea of young innocents and decided he would try, in his own way, to do a good deed. "You kids who have been here all day need to stay here tonight. Stay here to live," he told them and explained the news he had heard. Most all of them stayed, huddled together for warmth, one eye scanning for soldiers and the other for Herr Becht.

Time dragged on, bit by bit, and many times throughout the night Channa wanted to take her chances and return to the ghetto. "I'll be careful and stay out of sight." she cried to him. But he shook his head and blocked her way. Finally, morning dawned and she decided she could wait no longer. Once one youth started home, they all raced back, running as they had never run before, each praying for the best.

Channa ran up the front steps to her home and threw open the front door open. She rushed inside, calling out to her mother, sister and Isaac. Ruin was everywhere. The furniture that had been put together from the remnants of the last Nazi attack was smashed again, and no glass remained in any of the windows. She ran from room to room yelling out as loud as she could, but the house was empty. When she stopped searching, it was quiet, very quiet. But then she heard a sound and her head snapped around. A neighbor lady from another house walked in tentatively and looked about.

"I'm sorry, Channa," she said as she looked at the jumble. "They came yesterday and took everyone away." She waited a moment and then slowly walked towards Channa. "You are welcome to come and live with me," she offered, placing a gentle hand on Channa's shoulder.

It was a kind, generous offer considering everyone's situation, but Channa did not hear a word the woman said. She was trying to absorb the news that she was an orphan now. Her mind went to that black place where you cannot think and you do not know what to do, where to go or what to say. She took refuge on her bed and after a while fell asleep. She slept all day until sometime around midnight, when she awoke to the sound of a voice calling her name softly. Was she still dreaming? Through the shadows, she strained to listen. "Channa?" the voice called out again, closer and louder. Her eyes focused through the darkness. The figure was familiar and understanding finally dawned on her. Her mother had returned and her sister was by her side. They all embraced, unable to let each other go.

"Jetta and I waited out the Skita somewhere else and we couldn't return until we were sure it was safe," her mother explained as she held Channa close. "I prayed that you and Isaac would keep out of sight." Finally, in the safety of their mother's arms, Jetta and Channa slept. The room was cold and the bed was broken, but they had their mother, and it was a good sleep.

The next morning, Rachel was cooking a warm meal for the girls, who were seated at what had until recently been a recognizable table. The house was unusually quiet because the family in the next room had been taken away. The front door suddenly opened and a pair of boots could be heard entering the house. The girls jumped up and ran over to Rachel. Everyone held their breath as the sound of the boots came closer. And then a face came into view. It was Isaac! All had been spared.

Isaac did not waste any time with pleasantries. "I'm leaving!" he told his mother. "I have been talking with a good friend who recently joined the Partisan movement. I am going to join him, and I'm taking Channa with me!"

"Why just me?" Channa asked, holding her mother's hand more tightly.

"They won't take anyone your or Jetta's age." he said to his mother. "You have to be able to fight and Jetta is too young." They all turned to stare at Channa. Things were happening quickly.

Rachel sent Channa and Jetta out of the kitchen so she could speak with Isaac alone. Channa and Jetta ran over to the bedroom. They held hands as sisters sometimes do when they need assurance, but didn't say a word to each other. Then they heard Isaac calling. The girls quickly returned and found Isaac seated beside their mom, who was now in tears

"Channa, I've talked with Mama and you're coming with me," he stated.

"But why can't everyone come?" she asked.

"I can only take you."

"Why should I leave Mama and Jetta and go with you?" Channa asked.

"Because they won't let Mama or Jetta join the Partisans," he explained. "If we stay here, we'll all die." He was frank and direct, and Channa recognized the frightening, foreboding truth in his words.

Because Isaac was so much older than she was, he was more like a father to her than a brother. She respected and trusted him, knowing he would take good care of her. So she told Isaac she would go, perhaps not yet fully understanding that once she left, there would be no turning back.

Once the decision was made, Isaac and Channa had to hurry. They planned to leave the very next evening and Isaac still had much to do. The next day, he headed out to collect guns from sources that were willing to part with them for money or gold. He planned to use the weapons as a bribe to get them to accept Channa into the group despite her young age.

Having safely hidden his stash in the synagogue to be picked up later, he headed home, but on his way he ran into a Nazi officer. The Germans had issued a decree forbidding Jews from going to Temple any longer and Isaac had broken the law. He was lucky not to have any guns in his possession, but he was nevertheless hauled off for a few days of *questioning*.

Meanwhile, Channa and her family waited anxiously for his return. Rachel had prepared food for them to carry, but by midnight, it was clear that they were not going anywhere. Days passed, but there was no one they could ask for information. They all began to fear the worst. Thinking her brother had been killed was an indescribable loss for Channa. She grew fearful of leaving her mother for even a moment, but life in the ghetto demanded that she carry on.

Three nights had passed and they had resigned themselves to never seeing Isaac again. Channa and her sister were eating a supper of hot soup and bread. As Channa watched the steam rise up and into the air off her bowl, she thought how lovely and circular the swirls of steam were. They heard the front door open. There was nowhere to run, so they just held their breath, waiting to see who it was. Then a face peeked in. Isaac had returned! He was a little bruised and battered, but their joy was immense. After warm embraces, Isaac made it clear that he was not here to stay.

"I have come for Channa and we're leaving tonight."

"But I've changed my mind!" Channa said, wrapping her arms around her mother's waist.

Isaac pulled up a chair, told her to sit beside him and spoke to her calmly, but firmly. "Channa, you don't know what I've seen or what I heard while I was with the Germans," he began. "They promised they're going to exterminate the Jews like rats. Leaving is our only chance," he continued. "And so we're leaving—tonight!"

There was no time for further discussion. Rachel now had a few precious hours to impart to her daughter as much survival advice as she could. She crammed Channa's mind with all the guidance she could. Then Channa packaged some pieces of hard bread in a torn remnant of a shirt and selected a couple of family photos to take along. She couldn't believe this was actually happening, and yet she kept putting one foot in front of the other. Finally, Isaac threw a large, heavy bag on his back and they were ready to go.

Isaac and his mother and sisters headed for the fencing at the ghetto boundary. With a makeshift box cutter Isaac snipped the bottom of the wiring just enough to create a small crawl space. Channa went first. She knelt down, her face virtually in the dirt, and pushed with her legs. Her clothing occasionally snagged on the metal protrusions, but with the help of Isaac and her mother, she finally emerged on the other side. The reality finally dawned on her. "I don't want to go!" she cried, knowing that she must.

She kissed Jetta goodbye through the fencing and told her, "I love you!" Then she hugged her mother awkwardly through the barrier, the wires preventing her from the warm embrace she wanted.

Channa breathed her mother in as one does a beautiful flower, trying to absorb her very being. Then she stared at her hard, searing the image of her mother into her brain. "Don't worry Mama, we'll stay safe." She said, trying to convince herself, as well as her mother. "And we'll be together as soon as this is all over."

Stretching out her arm through the fence, Rachel then ripped the yellow star from Channa's clothing. To the world outside the Ghetto, she was no longer a Jew.

As Channa walked away with Isaac, she felt numb. She was heading into an unknown, uncertain future. Her childhood was over.

Isaac and Channa walked in the shadows, trying to blend into the surroundings. The town was almost deserted; only stray dogs, cats and rats were out searching for food. It was cold and she could see her breath in the night air. They had barely walked a half hour when their worst nightmare materialized. A Nazi officer caught sight of them. "Wohin gehen Sie?" (Where are you going?) he called over in German. Isaac froze, but Channa thought quickly, and in her best German, she answered that they were going to the movies.

Movies? There wasn't a movie house anywhere in the area, but it seemed to be the right thing to say. The soldier smirked dirtily and allowed them to continue on their way, no doubt thinking they were a young couple on their way to a romantic interlude.

They still had a long journey ahead of them to get to the Partisan meeting place. Isaac decided that rather than continue pressing their luck on the public roads, it was safer to conceal their movements by utilizing people's yards as their route. So they walked beneath laundry lines, passing hostile dogs on the way. Often, the inhabitants of the houses they passed peered out of their windows but they dared not say a word. Instead they quickly closed their curtains, knowing it was safer to stay inside and pretend not to see or hear anything.

Finally, Channa and Isaac made it to the meeting place, a lumberyard, where they joined up with other escapees. Everyone shared that same face of fear. The brims of their hats were pulled down, almost covering their dark eyes and they were plump, not from being well fed, but from the multiple layers of clothing they were wearing in lieu of carrying luggage. Nobody spoke much as they all walked on, remaining in the shadows and vigilantly listening for the steps of soldiers.

For two more days Isaac and Channa walked with the others, mainly staying in the camouflage of the forest, until they reached the ultimate meeting point, the Zukov Partisan encampment. At first it reminded Channa of a town fair, abuzz with activity. Flags flew in the breeze and there were people all around. Men and women stood together in clutches conducting strategy meetings. Many wore their rifles on their backs. Over the previous two years, the band of rebels that Channa and Isaac had just joined had performed many acts of terrorism against the Nazis. They had sabotaged bridges, set fire to storage facilities, and destroyed numerous roads.

Channa had not expected to see so many women. Some had not one, but two bandoleers of bullets crisscrossed across their chests, and other groups of women sat on downed tree trunks, their heads covered by kerchiefs, slicing and chopping what would be the camp's meals. Much work was being done, but Channa could only think of her mother and sister.

"Hey you!" one of the leaders called over to Isaac.

"Stay here Channa." Isaac instructed her as walked over to the group.

"What is she doing here?" they asked. They all argued until one of Isaac's friends, Yitzchak, joined them and told Isaac to empty his bag. Isaac threw his duffle down at their feet. When it hit the ground, it made a distinct clank. No further explanation was needed; the rifles he had brought were the price for getting Channa into the Partisans.

Isaac and Channa were just beginning to get their bearings when Yitzchak approached them. "I have to go back to the ghetto tonight and pick up more volunteers," he announced. "I'll be back in a few days."

Channa seized the opportunity to get a message to her mother. "Could you take a note back to my mother?" she pleaded. "She needs to know we are safe." She scribbled something on a piece of paper she found on the ground, folded it carefully and handed it to him.

"Alright Channa, I'll give it to her," Yitzchak promised and took the note and stuck it in his pant pocket.

Days passed at the encampment and Channa quickly grew bored. She was too young to have earned the right to stand at the strategy table and had no interest in helping to prepare food. So she just spent much of her time seated beneath the trees, waiting for something to happen.

"People coming!" a scout called out, alerting the camp to new arrivals. Channa jumped up and looked in the direction of the voice. A young man, dressed in a light colored shirt, burst through the trees. He did not have a coat on and looked exhausted, but also exhilarated to have made it. More people began arriving, but Channa was searching for Yitzchak. Channa ran over to one of them. "Where's Yitzchak? Did you see him talking to my mother?" she asked. The escapee looked at her in disbelief. He had just run through the forest for days in the cold without any food and had little patience for this young girl and her questions.

"He's dead!" he told her bluntly as he walked over to a small fire. "Some big mouth spotted him and told one of the Nazis." Yitzchak had been no match for the soldiers. "They shot him, took his boots, and left him in the forest as a warning," the man told Channa.

Channa was distraught. Now her mother would never know that she had made it safely to the Partisan encampment. But as she stood by the fire, a woman who had just arrived recognized the devastation in her eyes and had pity on her. After a moment, she approached Channa. "I saw him speaking to your mother," she lied. Channa brightened instantly at the news.

While Isaac, Channa and the rest of the Partisans awaited the arrival of more people to fortify their numbers, Isaac noticed that even here in the forest, under these dire circumstances, men and women were forming hasty courtships, seeking out each other's company to soothe them during the long, cold nights. Isaac became concerned for Channa's wellbeing. At twelve years old, she was not yet a woman, but she was also no longer a child.

He decided the only solution was to do something about Channa's appearance. He took out his pocket knife and cut her beautiful long, wavy hair, leaving it uneven and scraggly. "Always keep your jacket buttoned all the way up and make sure you have your head covered." he ordered her.

Channa wept, but when Isaac walked her over to the edge of a group of trees and allowed her to listen to the sounds of men and woman romantically involved, she soon understood why the transformation was necessary.

With the new morning came a change of attitude in the Partisan encampment. Although people had few belongings, what they had was being packaged up for travel. The fires were put out and smothered so that no smoke would alert the authorities that they had ever been there. Although no roll call was taken, everyone began to leave at the same moment. The Partisans lined up two and three people abreast. Channa and Isaac stepped in line behind a couple of men who had several maps strapped to their backs. Aspen trees, which were now bare as fall was well underway, towered on both sides of the procession as the resistance fighters began to move through the forest, keeping their voices low and their ears open.

This was the beginning of a period of endless motion. The group never remained in one location longer than two or three days. That would be just enough time to set up an impromptu camp where they could calculate their next moves and dig shallow ditches to sleep in at night.

Channa was hungry and tired. She felt as if they did nothing but march. The temperatures were dropping, and the threat of snow filled the air. Late one afternoon, as the leaders were scoping out a good area to bed down, the group came upon a German soldier. His camouflage helmet rested on the ground along with his gun and auxiliary pack. Rifles were cocked instantly and scopes aimed straight at the sweet spot between his eyes. The soldier raised his open hands to the sky. "I am tired of fighting this war and have decided I can no longer be a part of this," he said in German.

Quickly, they kicked his guns away from him and tied up his hands. Then they forced him to march with them, hoping to disrupt any plans he might have in case the Nazis had sent him as a spy. When they reached an area of the forest they felt they could guard, they secured him to a tree and assigned a sentinel to watch his every move. "Shoot him if he tries anything at all!" the guard was instructed.

The Partisans leaders gathered to ponder whether it was mere coincidence that they had found him in their forest. "What if he was sent into the forest to tell us this story as a ruse just to learn where we are all hiding?" the men and woman questioned. "If we set him free and he tells them where we are, we could all be killed."

"We can't take that chance," the leaders finally decided. "He'll have to die."

Channa had watched the proceedings from a safe distance. She began to feel a little sorry for the soldier, who appeared almost pathetic, sitting on the cold ground with pine needles piercing his pants. So she walked closer and quietly said, "Hello."

"Hello," he answered back, "What is your name?" And soon they were in conversation. He told her he was married and had children close to her age. He did not seem cruel or filled with hatred; in fact, he reminded her of her father on those rare occasions when he had been in a good mood. She felt sympathy for the solider and decided to talk to Isaac about it.

"What are they going to do to him?" she asked.

"They're going to kill him," he answered her bluntly. "We're not going to take any chances that this might be a trick."

"But I have spoken with him and I really don't think he is a spy," Channa said. "Can't you convince the others not to kill him?" she pleaded. It felt so wrong to her to kill someone, even if this person was a loathed Nazi solider, particularly after she had spoken with him.

"What do you know of this war or of this world?" Isaac snapped, holding her gruffly by the arm.

"Then I'm not going to watch!" she told him and tried to hurry away.

Isaac grew angry. "It was a man just like this that murdered my wife and children!" he told her as he took her by the wrist. "These aren't people, but animals!" Seven months had passed since his wife and children had died, but he was only expressing his feelings now. "You will watch this Nazi bastard be put to death!" he ordered. "It is justice and you need to grow up, fast!"

They informed the soldier that he would be killed. The broken man sat on the ground and begged for kindness, but no mercy was showed. Channa shut her eyes and tried not to listen to his pleas for help. They did not even ask him to rise, but shot him there tied to that tree. Channa turned and ran away moments after the sounds of the gunshots echoed off the trees. She could not bear to look at the now slumped-over body of this man.

Dark moonless nights were perfect for conducting missions. Channa, Isaac and the Partisans disrupted communications by climbing up on telephone and telegraph poles and snipping the lines, and they set fire to resting convoy trucks.

They were in constant need of provisions, so when they came upon a farm, they usually paid it a visit. The farmer and his family would be forced at gun point to *volunteer* food, clothing and weapons if they had them. The farmers of course resented the intrusion and loss of provisions to a rag-tag group of forest-dwelling hoodlums. The farmers also suffered after the Paristans left, becoming suspect in the eyes of the Nazis. Although the farmers had no choice in the matter, they were often put to death for "assisting the Partisans," and their property was burned to the ground.

One day Channa, Isaac and their group were in a farm house when Channa spotted a lovely red wool jacket hanging by the door. It had four oversized buttons down the front, a stitched design that extended below the chest and a collar made of white rabbit's fur. "I want that jacket." Channa whispered in Isaac's ear. He pointed to the jacket with his rifle and the farmer's wife handed it over. Channa threw her old worn and torn jacket on the floor in a kind of trade and pulled on her new prize. It was a size or two too large, but she wore it proudly as a spoil of war, hoping it would do a good job of warding off the chill in cooler times ahead.

By the time Channa was fourteen, she had been a Partisan resistance fighter for a year and a half. And during that time she had grown hard. She had trudged through the forest and participated in many acts of sabotage. She had seen people put to death and walked past emotionally and physically broken people who could not fight any more. She had learned how to keep warm as she slept on the ground, which sometimes was covered by snow or, on a few lucky occasions, in sheds the group constructed out of little more than branches and fabric, and her beautiful hair had begun to grow back again. She had grown up fast, just as Isaac had wanted.

One day, the band was walking quietly through the forest. It was warm and the flies and biting bugs were out and about. When they came upon a stream, they all removed their canteens from their shoulders and immersed them under the fast-moving current.

Channa carefully hung her coat on a bare branch. It no longer had that beautiful apple-red color, having suffered through the winter rains, and its fur collar was no longer white. But she had grown into the jacket and it was still a cherished possession.

She went to the stream and knelt down to fill her canteen. Some of her companions were quickly dousing their hair with the clean water and rinsing their necks and faces.

Suddenly a scout came running back towards them. He sloshed through the water, yelling "The Nazis are coming! Run!"

Partisans scattered in all directions. Channa didn't waste a moment. She ran as fast as she could, matching Isaac stride for stride. They covered much ground, dodging trees and tearing through deep piles of leaves. Finally they stopped to catch their breath and take a look around. They had made it! There were no Nazis or dogs anywhere. But almost as quickly, Channa realized that she had left the forest without her precious jacket. And much worse, there on a branch back in the forest, in the side pocket of that once red coat, were her only photographs. Any personal possessions or mementos of pre-war life were more valuable than money or gold and very few people had been able to preserve photographs of family. She felt an unbearable sorrow. There would be nothing by which to remember the details of her family's features from now on, and she knew that their faces would soon fade cruelly from her memory. Nevertheless, Channa decided she must try not to forget her mother's and Jetta's faces.

But there was no time to mourn her loss. The Partisans began walking again, even as they were still catching their breaths and continuing to listen for sounds of danger. As she walked on, she placed one hand in a pant pocket and felt something. She pulled it out and there was a single photograph, folded in half. She had forgotten all about it. It was a picture of her mother seated on her sister Sonya's gravesite. Rachel's head was covered and her face sad and somber. Her skirt was long and her stockings covered her legs. Her left hand gently held the wooden post that bore her daughter's name written in Yiddish. The photograph was tattered, its black-and-white tones had turned to coffee brown, its edges were frayed, and a part of one corner was missing. But this lone snapshot helped ease Channa's pain and would help her refresh her memory.

After two years Channa and Isaac were still in the forest. The size of their group had dwindled greatly. Some missions had cost many guerrillas their lives, and now Channa and Isaac were called upon more often to put their lives on the line as well. While Channa was not really strong enough to handle a gun, she was often selected to sneak over to the edge of a bridge, place the wires for the explosives into a can, light the charge and quickly run back to the protection of Isaac and the trees.

One day good news arrived; the Germans had been forced out of their part of Poland. Baranavichy and the surrounding towns had been liberated. The partisan group quickly disbanded and everyone, including Isaac and Channa quickly headed for home.

They still had a long way to walk and they were still very hungry. Through the forest, they saw a plume of smoke. This mean a farmhouse lay ahead. Surrounded by an unfinished picket fence, the barn and house were connected. A chimney was busily pouring smoke into the sky. A tall tree provided shade to the barn and a flat board wagon with a loose dome of hay was parked out in front, seemingly awaiting its horse.

Isaac and Channa approached the house. His hand rested on the gun he had hidden beneath his coat. The farmer opened the door. He was a husky man, clean shaven wearing a pair of unbelted pants that seemed to be too large for him. His wife, who quickly joined him, was shorter and even huskier, with dark hair pulled back in a ponytail. She wore a short-sleeved floral dress covered by a large dirty white apron.

Isaac talked to the farmer while his wife quickly went to bring them something to eat.

"When you get into town they will most likely make you join the official Russian army, whether you want to or not. They need every able-bodied young man they can find to help fight," he explained. "If you'd like, you and your sister can stay here at my farmhouse," he offered. "To tell you the truth, I'm hiding my own three sons. I don't want them to fight either," the farmer added in hushed tones.

Isaac and Channa talked over his generous offer in private. Could they trust him? Did he have ulterior motives? If they went home too soon, there was a chance that Isaac might be taken away to fight and Channa would be left alone. Should they try their luck with this seemingly charitable man? "I say we stay here," Channa said, and Isaac nodded his head in agreement.

Channa and Isaac remained at that farmhouse for two and half months. They helped out with chores as much as they could and took up temporary residence in the barn. The accommodations were perfect for Channa because they shared the barn with the family's goats. Although they didn't look like the lop-eared Rosa, their tails swished happily and their stomachs bulged in that same familiar way. At night, as she lay in the hay with the goats sometimes bedding down beside her, Channa could think back to a happier time. Isaac kept a watchful eye on the farmer's three sons and the three sons kept a watchful eye on Channa, but he decided they would need to move when the farmer's wife approached Channa and asked if she'd like to marry one of her sons.

"It's time for us to go," he told her and Channa agreed. At breakfast, they expressed their gratitude to the farmer and his wife for their kindness. Then, two days later, on a clear morning Channa and Isaac collected their meager possessions, gratefully accepted some provisions and went on their way.

Leaving the safety of the farmhouse was dangerous. Isaac knew that he would be recognized as a young fight-worthy male. In order to avoid being called upon for service, he grew out his brown-and-white beard and didn't bother grooming it. With some clothing he had obtained from the farmer, he dressed up as an old man, wrapping a knitted shawl around his shoulders. When he and Channa arrived in the town of Slonim, he hunched over and Channa pretended to help him walk. The sham seemed to work and he was never taken for duty.

They had been away from home for three years and had traveled many miles, but geographically they had always remained less than twenty-five miles from home. They walked alongside a sea of homeward-bound partisan survivors and other displaced people for four days. A sad parade of tired civilians pushed hastily constructed push carts; women with babies joined the procession. All anyone could speak about was their hopes and dreams of having family alive to return to. As they traveled, they continued accepting *donations* from farmers, but many farmers and other town folk greeted them with sour faces. While Poles were obviously pleased that the war was over, many wished that those *Jews* would not return.

They obviously felt a sense of joy and relief, but it was tempered with trepidation. Yes, they had survived and could now finally walk down the streets without fear. But they remained anxious about their families and what was left of their past.

As Channa and Isaac entered their home town, they were astounded. They barely recognized the old familiar synagogue, and Jewish-owned businesses now lay in shambles, victims of fires or bombings. Mountains of rubble and debris sat in tall piles where buildings once stood. As they moved along among the other returning refugees, people gradually separated out from the crowd, going down side streets in search of the end of their own personal story.

Channa and Isaac were now just a block away from home. Empty shells of homes stood on their left and right. They quickened their pace, but said very little as they turned the last corner. Finally, the family home, Baronovitch 7, came into view. The fence that had once wrapped around their house was long gone, but from the outside, the house looked virtually untouched.

As they approached, they saw several children playing out in the front yard. There was a young girl with long blond braids and a couple of fair-haired boys. A light bulb clicked on in Channa's memory. Yes, she knew those children; in fact, she had played with them. She moved quickly towards the house, but Isaac stopped her.

"Channa, don't be surprised if they refuse to give us back our home. Many of the Goyim," he said, using the Yiddish word for Gentiles, "demand proof of previous ownership."

"Proof?" She asked in disbelief. But Channa was not ready to give up. She straightened her shoulders, walked past the children and knocked on the door.

The children's mother came to the door, holding an eight-month-old baby in her arms. As her eyes met Channa's, she did a double take, recognizing this now slightly older, though dirty and worn, girl of about fifteen. "Of all the Jews you had to survive. So what do you want us to do now?" she asked as she glanced around at her brood of children.

"This is our home," Channa answered directly and with conviction.

"Give us some time and we'll find a replacement," the woman assured Channa.

"Alright, but we don't have any place to stay." Channa explained.

"Come in, we'll make space for you in one of the bedrooms." Channa and Isaac picked up their bundles and walked back into their home. It looked the same, but different. Much of their own furniture was still there, but from the looks of it, the house hadn't been treated kindly.

It was now time for Channa and her brother to find their mother and sister. They headed back to the last place they had seen them alive: the ghetto.

Much had happened to the people who had resided in the ghetto these past few years. Himmler had ordered many ghettos to be liquidated, and most of the inhabitants of this particular ghetto had been taken to Auschwitz. Out of the many thousands who had once lived here, less than a thousand were still alive. Channa and Isaac were hopeful that Rachel and Jetta were among them.

They walked through the ghetto, street by street and house by house, calling out "Rachel! Jetta!" But no one answered back. Isaac and Channa asked everyone they could, but no one could provide any information on the whereabouts of their mother or sister. A search through governmental agencies also proved fruitless. The fact was that they hadn't made it.

As the realization began to sink in one evening, Channa gulped down the pain with sweet tea. She would always repeat to herself: *If so many people have died, then I can bear losing my family too.* As she sat quietly, holding her photograph to her chest, she dreamed of what life used to be like all those years ago. She remembered baking sweet sugar cookies, feasting on hot bowls of cereal with melted butter, and the glee of counting money that had arrived with her father from America.

Within a few days, they returned home. The truth was that it didn't feel much like home, but Channa and her brother attempted to resume some kind of normal life anyway. In the evening, Isaac would hit the streets, reconnecting with men his own age and with women who were out and about, anxious to begin new lives. One night, he was sitting outside the house when he saw a woman walk by. She was Jewish, fair-haired with blue eyes and a little on the heavy side. He started up a conversation with her and they hit it off quickly. After a very short courtship, Channa was surprised to hear that Isaac planned on marrying Leja right away. Channa was happy for him. Her family was beginning to re-form.

Although they managed to go through the motions of daily life, returning to any kind of real normalcy proved much more difficult than they could have imagined. The Poles were not particularly interested in having the Jewish population return. As a result, Jewish-owned businesses were slow to resume, as no one had any money and jobs were not being opening up. Unemployment was high and begging by Jews became prevalent. After about a year Channa, Isaac and Leja decided that they could no longer bear to live there. There was too much history, and they did not feel welcome.

Laws had been passed limiting the amount of money Jews were permitted to have. So when Channa and Isaac sold the family home, they were only able to get 32,000 zlotys, far less than the house was worth, but it would hopefully be enough to help them start a new life elsewhere.

Channa and Isaac walked through the house one last time. Somehow, it seemed important to say goodbye to their childhood home. Inside, Channa stared at the walls of the kitchen and the bedroom and even at the door, wanting to remember them forever. She was not merely saying goodbye to a structure; she was bidding farewell and rest-in-peace to her mother, father, sister and nieces. She was saying goodbye to her youth and her past and to everything she had known. Then she walked away and did not look back.

Channa, Leja and Isaac joined another procession of Polish Jews, this time headed for the sea port in Bremen Hafen, Germany.

The lines at the refugee migration office were long and they spent weeks waiting their turn. Travel by sea was not permitted unless your documents contained an official stamp. As they waited, they listened to people arguing and complaining, all telling their own sad stories of loss and near misses. Finally the three of them made it to the front of the line and Channa presented her "Certificate of Identity In Lieu of Passport" paperwork. On the right-hand side, toward the center of the document was a photograph of a now 17-year-old Channa. The official behind the desk studied the paperwork and stared at Channa to compare her to the photo. Satisfied with her likeness, he took a square, brown stamp with the number two printed on it and pressed it down on the paper. Then he inked another stamp and stamped the paperwork with the date "February 7, 1947." Only one thing now separated Isaac, Channa and Leja from boarding the United States Line passenger ship *Ernie Pyle*—an inoculation stamp.

"No!" Channa said, refusing to submit to the injections. There was no time to waste and so Isaac improvised.

"Leja, pretend you are Channa and you take them," he told his wife. Leja extended her arm, gritted her teeth and looked away. Despite their different appearances and the age disparity, no one seemed to notice. A few moments later, Channa received her embarkation card. The size of an index card, it was written in both English and German, and spelled out her name and place of accommodation, with a circular stamp denoting the date.

Channa, Isaac and Leja walked up the gangway and onto the *Ernie Pyle,* bound for a new life in New York, smuggling their gold coins in false heels Isaac had carved into their boots and shoes.

THE BOY FROM UZHGOROD

Nathan Polczer was born on February 7, 1926. He was one of twelve children. His father, Jeno, was a tall, lean man with thinning dark hair, a short mustache and piercing eyes. His mother, Jolin, was Jeno's second wife.

Jeno, unable to care for five children by himself, had remarried quickly after his first wife had died. This ignited great disharmony in the family. The idea of a new mother coming in so soon after Baila's death rattled the children. Irving and Malvina, Jeno's two eldest, were particularly angry and did not like the fact that Jeno's new wife, Jolin, was giving birth to new siblings at what they considered to be an alarming rate. They blamed it all on this "new woman," never acknowledging that she was not getting pregnant by herself. And yes, Jolin found herself pregnant quite often. First came Isidor, then Kalman, then my father Nathan, followed by Madga, Celia, Adell, and finally, Sanji.

Jolin was a large woman with very dark brown hair, which she hid beneath a patterned scarf. Her lips were thin, and her eyebrows were bare in spots, but her brown eyes projected a heartrending kindness. Her hands were those of a hardworking woman.

The family's small single-story home was located in what was then Czechoslovakia, in an impoverished section of a town called Uzhgorod, which means City by the Uzh River. The house's size was grossly insufficient for their large family. Its entrance door appeared to have been built for elves and the ceiling was unusually low. There was not much in the way of a kitchen and the family shared a single inadequate bathroom. The property's tiny yard allowed Jolin to grow a meager vegetable crop in the overworked soil.

By the time Sanji reached his second birthday in 1944, the crowded living arrangements proved too much for Malvina and Irving and they decided to leave for America. Although two fewer children did not provide much additional space, it helped somewhat.

Jeno operated a transportation business, which consisted of a horse and buggy. Unfortunately, he was not a very ambitious man and did not generate enough income to feed his brood of children. Instead of promoting his business, he preferred to concentrate on his religious studies. He was a fervent student of the Talmud, a set of books that spells out Jewish law and issues of ethics in great detail. Jeno and his fellow students could usually be found in Temple, deeply engrossed in discussion. The mundane tasks associated with providing for their families were left to the women.

Jolin picked up the slack by becoming the household entrepreneur. Twice weekly, barely after sunrise, when you could still see your breath in the air, Jolin and a few of her children would take the family horse and wagon to the marketplace. Upon arrival, she would caution the older children to make sure the younger ones never left the safety of the wagon or came out from under the blanket she had placed over them for warmth. She then climbed off the wagon and walked over to a truck that held multiple crates of chickens crowded together. The seller carefully lifted the hens beneath the breasts to demonstrate the fowl's high quality, and Jolin would nod approvingly … or not. When she had chosen seven or eight nice-looking hens, she placed them into her own enclosure, constructed of old wooden planks, and headed back home.

The children, now hungry, tired and cold, were relieved when they finally arrived back home, but she had her hands full with the chickens.

Jolin transferred the clucking fowl into the family's fenced front yard. She tossed the hungry birds some feed and hung a hand-drawn "Chickens for Sale" sign on the fence post. That accomplished, she went back into the house to prepare breakfast for her ravenous children.

Jolin made a tidy profit selling those chickens to her neighbors. Her clientele consisted of people who couldn't make it to the marketplace themselves.

But Jolin's real money-maker was sugar. Sugar was difficult to come by, but she had found a source through a minor network of black marketers. The money it generated made it well worth the risk.

While Jolin was busy taking care of her children and stepchildren, the house, the chickens and the sugar sales, and while Jeno was in Synagogue, wrapped in a prayer shawl, history was in the making all around them. The Munich Agreement was signed in 1938, dividing Czechoslovakia into three parts. Uzhgorod was taken over by Hungary.

Up until this time although the residents of Czechoslovakia had been noting Hitler's movements, they had not yet felt the full force the war. Shortly thereafter, the persecution of the Jews began. Deportations suddenly became commonplace, with entire families being taken away for no apparent reason. Jewish-owned businesses were turned over to the Czech population, Jews began being segregated from everyone else in town, and signs were put up restricting their walking to only one side of the street. Nathan tried to keep his mind on his studies, but everyone in the family was frightened.

It became more and more difficult to make money, and Nathan was told he would have to end his all-too-brief education and get a job. At only fourteen years old, he had never really given a career much thought. He tried his hand at re-treading tires, but really did not like the work. The tires smelled bad and he hated the tedium of it. His father then pressed him to take a job as a tailor's assistant, but Nathan did not like that either. Finally, he happened upon a hardware store that had a small "Help Wanted" notice in the window. The owner took a liking to the young lad and Nathan got the job.

Because he liked people, Nathan enjoyed selling and was good at it. He sold an assortment of tools, general house supplies and paint powder. Paint powder was considerably less expensive than premixed paint and his customers seemed to like it. Nathan continued working at the hardware shop for two-and-a-half years and was often left to watch the business when the boss was out.

One afternoon, Kalman, Nathan's older brother, burst into the store. "Nathan, come quick," he urged. "Isador is dead!"

Nathan locked the door to the business and ran home, where he found his mother crying uncontrollably and the authorities speaking with his father. He learned that Isador had been riding his bicycle near the town center. The open area was abuzz with pedestrians who were purchasing vegetables and nuts from the vendors. He had swerved to miss a woman, and his bike hit a stone. His bicycle went down, he slid out, and a bus, unable to stop in time, crushed him. He was buried soon after.

Life grew ever more difficult for Nathan and his family. Food shortages increased and long-hidden anti-Semitism suddenly surfaced everywhere. He and his family felt their future was growing bleak. News that the Germans were winning were only sometimes tempered by stories of small Russians victories. Through all this, Nathan tried to remain optimistic about his own family's safety, but the future didn't look good.

By 1944, the Hungarians decided that they had had enough of the Jewish population, and news spread that Jews would soon no longer be welcome in Uzhgorod. Nathan's parents heard the talk, but with so many children and so little money, they could not even broach the subject of leaving. So they did nothing.

Fortunately, sugar sales continued. Jolin sometimes had Jeno move the sugar for her. On one such occasion, Jeno was seated on his wagon behind his chestnut draft mare, moving slowly down the street with the sugar hidden from view under an old blanket.

"Stop," two Hungarian soldiers suddenly called over to Jeno, and he drew his horse to a halt.

"What are you carrying?" they asked.

Jeno did not know what to say. Since it was black-market sugar, he could not tell them the truth. The soldiers walked around the wagon. One of the soldiers handed his gun to the other and then lifted the blanket, exposing the sacks of sugar.

"Where did you get this?" he demanded.

When Jeno did not reply, he was gruffly pulled down from the wagon and taken in for questioning. The police were not interested in a small fry such as the driver; they were looking for the names of more important operators.

Jolin had no idea her husband was in peril. As the hours passed, she guessed that Jeno was probably still at Temple, but later that evening someone pounded on the door. She was startled to find two police officers. "Come with us!" they told her, refusing to explain anything further.

Jolin didn't want to leave her children, and her youngest ones, who had woken up, clung to her legs. The policemen pulled the children from her and dragged her from the house. Dislodged from their mother, the children now screamed and cried, not understanding what was happening.

Nathan came home shortly thereafter and found his brothers and sisters frantic. "We don't know what happened!" they cried.

At last, Jeno returned home. After a great deal of intimidation, he had inadvertently let it slip that the sugar belonged to his wife. Once they obtained that piece of information, they released him and he hurried home, but Jolin was already gone. He felt horrible, but there was nothing to be done.

While the police held Jolin for two weeks, waiting for her to divulge her sources, the Hungarian government announced to the Jewish population of Uzhgorod that they were being expelled from the city. They were instructed to turn themselves in to a holding facility (the town's abandoned brick factory) carrying no more than five kilos of personal possessions per person. The Jews who had money fled during the night, using anything they owned of value to pay for tickets out of town or for refuge in Gentiles' homes. But those who had no money, like Nathan and his family, had no choice but to turn themselves in. They had had no warning about their moving to a ghetto or what it would mean, but imagined that it would involve forced labor of some kind.

"What about Mom?" Nathan and his siblings asked their father as they gathered their belongings

"I don't know where she is or when she'll come back, but we have to leave," he told them. He created a small bundle out of clothing for the journey and took his younger children by the hand. They joined in the long line of men and women with children of all ages who were walking toward the holding facility. "She'll find us," he assured them.

Evening was falling and many women carried their infants warmly wrapped, while others walked sadly alongside their sons and daughters. The elderly needed assistance and cried.

At the brick factory, the soldiers directed everyone inside. They asked, again and again, "What are we doing here? What is going to happen to us?" No one answered. It took about two days to fill the facility and then the doors were shut.

The refugees were now left to worry and make do and the only word to describe it was: chaos. Each household needed to create a warm shelter, a small bastion they could call their own, and create a façade of safety for their children. Small make-shift tents appeared and every form of material found some purpose. Broken bricks were stacked to provide walls between neighbors as people attempted to create some minuscule amount of privacy. But with both adults and children crying, the noise was deafening.

Nathan felt beaten down. To block out the misery that was his life now, he put his head down and fell asleep.

Days passed, and finding food became the top priority. Many, including Jeno, had not adequately planned ahead. Food supplies were depleted quickly, and many nights they all went to bed hungry, having eaten almost nothing for days.

Meanwhile, under tremendous pressure and driven by a nagging need to return to her children, Jolin revealed the names of the people who supplied her with the sugar. She was released, not to the freedom she had expected, but to the brick factory. Her appearance was a great relief to everyone. Ever the enterprising provider, she quickly went about gathering what little food she could for her children.

They lived in the concrete and wood building without plumbing, solid walls or electricity for a little under two months.

49

There was nothing to do all day except dwell on stories they had heard and fantasize about when they would no longer be incarcerated. And there was the relentless search for food. Nathan was always glad when night came and they had all made it through another day.

Finally, one evening, the doors to the factory swung open and soldiers rushed in, yelling, "Get your things! You are being moved somewhere where you will be put to work!"

Everyone collected their belongings. As abrupt and unexplained as their confinement to the factory had been, their departure on cattle trains was even more sudden. Parents tried hard to keep their families together as they boarded the train compartments. But when the doors closed, screams could be heard as parents realized that someone had not made it onto the car.

When the doors closed, the flow of fresh air was cut off, and with no bathroom facilities, a stench soon filled the air. Those lucky enough to be able to see through the cracks watched the countryside and benefited from small whiffs of clean air.

They traveled for two days and then the train stopped and the doors slid open. Straight ahead, they saw a tangle of crisscrossing train tracks that all led to a single wide building with a tall tower. They had arrived at Auschwitz. Nazis with helmeted heads, stiff collars and red arm bands with swastikas ordered everyone to hurry up, get out and line up. The Polzer family stood together and Jolin held her younger children's hands tightly. They knew nothing about this place, having only been told that they were there to work.

"Women and children, on the left!" a soldier called out. "Men on the right!" Nathan's eyes widened as he was separated from his mother and younger siblings. He and some other men tried to cross back over to stay with the women, but the soldiers were intolerant and rifle butts swung hard.

Moments later, the Nazis yelled out something and the women and small children were led away. Nathan called over to his mother, but was warned to shut up. Jolin looked back at him and his brothers, her face fearful as she held on to her crying children. He watched in disbelief as they walked out of sight.

The men were then further divided, young on the right, old on the left. Nathan was young, strong and healthy, so he and a few of his brothers went on one side, while his father and the younger brothers were marched off. Again, he followed his family with his eyes until they were out of view.

Nathan was then instructed to strip off his clothing and ordered to march. He walked in the cold in nothing but his underwear. Being modest was pointless, so he just followed the line of alarmed but compliant men. A man with a razor sheared off his hair with little concern about inflicting pain. Nicked, bleeding and bare-headed, Nathan was then deloused. The powder that was flung on him got into his eyes, nose and mouth, but he had no choice but to continue living this unrelenting nightmare. He was then given concentration-camp striped pants, shirt and shoes. All the while, he kept scanning around for his family. Where had they gone? Even his brothers, who had been with him mere moments ago, seemed to have disappeared. He couldn't get over everything that was happening so quickly.

Having gone through the system, he was released into the camp yard. He walked over to a young man who was seated on a kind of stump. The stripes on the man's shirt were barely recognizable, hidden as they were beneath layers of filth, and his shoes looked almost comical, as they were a few sizes too big. Nathan took a seat beside him. "What is going to happen to us next?" he asked. "When will they let me see my family again?"

The man placed his hand on Nathan's shoulder and then pointed to a plume of black smoke that was floating skywards from a chimney located at the rear of the camp. "There are your parents and your brothers and sisters," he said sadly. Nathan did not understand at first, but then came the ghastly moment of understanding.

"To stay alive here, you have to fight every day!" the man told Nathan. "You must always hoard your food. Whenever they give out any food at all, take as large a portion as possible and then hide it beneath your clothing or in your pockets. Steal food from anyone who isn't watching," the man continued, as he gestured with intensity to stress his instructions. "When someone dies, get in there and take what you can. Those pieces of clothing will keep you warm."

It was a lot of information for a young man who had just arrived, but this big-hearted person was providing Nathan with life-saving information. "If you follow my advice, you might stay alive just a little bit longer," the man said as he got up. Then he walked away.

Nathan had listened, but he could not believe what he heard. Nathan walked over to the barrack to which he had been assigned, continuing to look for his family everywhere. As he walked, he saw just how huge this place was. It was filled with row after row of identical red brick Polish army buildings. The seemingly endless rows of structures were only differentiated by plaques stating each building's identifying number. It was the institutional version of what he and every other unfortunate soul was now – a nameless numeral.

Inside his barrack, resting against both side walls of the cement room, were chaotically constructed tri- and quad-level wooden bunk beds. Most bunks were not level and some barely cleared the floor. The windows that had once allowed light and air into the room had been partially cemented over and now the only light filtered in through a sliver of uncovered glass. A brick fireplace stood at the end of the room, but it was sealed shut. On the bare wooden rafters, the Germans had inscribed sentiments they hoped their prisoners would adhere to: ***Cleanliness Means Health*** and ***Be Honest – Keep Order***.

This horrible day had lasted forever. And when the sun began to set and the air turned cold, Nathan located a bunk, which he shared with three other new arrivals. The thin mattress provided no cushioning. Emotionally raw and exhausted, he put his head down and slept.

That night, all around Nathan, the sounds of the sick and dying rang out. As he looked around, he could see that some of the older and weaker prisoners had already degraded into living skeletons. Over the coming days, he saw them coughing up blood or vomiting up the poor excuse for soup they had been given. He overheard men whispering about the goings-on at the camps, and it was all incomprehensibly ghastly. "I have to get out of here," he thought to himself. "The longer I stay here, the shorter my countdown to death will be."

Each morning brought more uncertainty, more beatings, more scrounging for food and more stories about the Russians advancing. To keep themselves busy, the Germans enjoyed sorting people. They'd move men over to one side of the field, then to another.

After only a few weeks, Nathan felt as though he had been there for years. Every day, more people died or were taken away, never to be seen again. Nathan knew he had to do something ... and quickly.

One morning, a Nazi soldier opened the door to the barrack with a clank. "Everyone line up!" he yelled at them in German. Nathan had only moments to get up, get out and line up for the daily count. It was cold outside, and he was wearing nothing more than his concentration camp pajamas. The Nazi took his delicious time while everyone stood there shivering. "I need volunteers to go to work," the soldier announced after he finished counting them.

Nathan's ears perked up; it was the word "go" that interested him.

"We need carpenters and painters," the soldier stated and looked around at the men for raised hands. Nathan was no carpenter. The only thing he knew about carpentry was from what he had sold at the hardware shop. But it did not matter. He desperately wanted to go somewhere – anywhere – away from the dying and those smoke stacks that smelled of burning flesh.

He raised his hand and the Nazi instructed Nathan to follow him. There was no one to say goodbye to and he had no possessions to collect. He clung to the hope that something would be different, and maybe better, elsewhere.

Nathan and the other volunteers were marched to the entrance of the camp, and then walked beside the tangle of train tracks to a waiting cattle car. They sat quietly on the train as it rolled away from Auschwitz. Had they made a mistake by volunteering for this job? Was there a job at all, or were they on their way to be killed?

After several hours, the train came to a stop and a soldier slid open the door. A gun hung from the Nazi's hands arbitrarily, as if he knew he need not worry; these Jews would not try to fight. Nathan looked around, but the surroundings were unfamiliar. He saw many bombed-out buildings and prisoners working hard separating bricks from the debris. He had arrived at the Warsaw Ghetto, but it was a shell of its former self. The Germans had set the ghetto on fire to put an end to the valiant efforts of the Resistance fighters who'd fought in the Warsaw uprising.

Now Nathan and the others had been brought in to clean it up. They were instructed to put bricks in piles and then move the piles to pallets. It was mindless, backbreaking work, but Nathan continued to labor at the burned-out ghetto for three months. The accommodations here at the Ghetto weren't much better than those of the camps, but at least there weren't any crematoriums. Polish workers who had been brought in carried in news of the war, some good and some not so good.

His hands had gone from being cut and blistered to being hard and calloused, his stomach was always empty, and he had lost a great deal of weight.

One day at the end of winter, word suddenly spread like wildfire around the camp that the Russians were getting close and might be within sixty miles of Warsaw. The Germans had realized they had to leave, but what would they do with these "damn Jews"? They soon reached a decision.

"Everyone line up!" a soldier shouted. The workers stopped lifting bricks and formed a line. They were marched for three days and nights along a dirt road, staying mainly within the forest. They were given no food or water. They were already weak from the hard work they had endured and many perished on the way. The lucky ones, including Nathan, made it to the city limits of Kutno, a town in central Poland. There, the group waited for two more foodless, waterless and shelter-less days and nights for the transport trains to reappear. "Survive," Nathan repeated to himself over and over again. The Russians were supposedly very close and he hoped that maybe today was that wonderful day where he'd be liberated from this nightmare.

Nathan once again boarded a train, heading for destinations unknown, but always with the hope that the next place would be better. For two nights and three days Nathan and his unfortunate fellow travelers remained crowded in that cattle car. The air was stifling and the ammonia from the straw toilet area burned their eyes and sickened their empty stomachs. Unbeknownst to them, they were heading for Dachau, a town located ten miles northwest of Munich. The Dachau camp was a renovated munitions facility from World War I that had been turned into a prison for political dissidents. Now any Jew, Gypsy and homosexual fell into that category.

Eventually, the train came to a halt and the men were told to get out and line up once again. Dressed in their striped outfits, they were easily identifiable by their handlers, who marched them towards the camp entrance. Gentile residents of Dachau came out of their homes to watch the parade pass, holding their children by the hand to prevent them from getting too close. How envious he was of them. Their families were intact. They were free, free to go where they pleased and free of the fear of starvation. Free to know they'd see another day.

After a short walk, the wrought-iron gate to the camp, over which was welded *Arbeit macht Freir* or *Work makes Freedom*, was pushed open and they walked onto the grounds. Dachau was not all that different from Auschwitz. He was unsurprised but disheartened to find himself back in such a place. People walked, people cried, people starved, and a foul-smelling smoke rose from the rear of the camp. As Nathan's group arrived, Nazis assigned them each a barrack number. "You," a soldier said, pointing to Nathan, "Barrack number seven."

Nathan turned, walked over to the elongated wooden structure, and pulled open the door. Broken men were seated all about in their striped uniforms. Some had acquired hats, which kept their shaven heads warm, and a few had coats of a sort, which they guarded with their lives. He went over to the bunks. Carved messages of doom and foreboding were etched into the wood from the base almost to the ceiling. Nathan located a place to sleep in the upper row, which he shared with a two other men.

It wasn't very comfortable, but after the Warsaw Ghetto and the train, all he wanted was a place to lie down. These wretched circumstances were all too familiar, and he'd learned that his best option was just to tune them all out.

The air was thick with the smell of people urinating and defecating on themselves. Some were only hours away from death and a few had already crossed over and were in the beginning stages of decay. Laying in such close proximity to this many sick, dying and dead people provided the perfect breeding ground for lice, and within days, Nathan became infested with them. Although he scratched day and night until his skin was raw, he could not rid himself of them. The stink from what the Nazis considered a bathroom wafted over, too.

At daybreak, the Nazis announced that they needed volunteers for work once again. And again, Nathan raised his hand. This time, the train ride was very brief. He and the other volunteers were then marched through the deep forest. There, hidden in the tall trees, the Nazis were hoping to erect a hidden landing strip they called Muldorf.

Nathan was given the job of lugging giant boulders on his back to assigned locations. He performed his job day in and day out with no breaks and very little food and drink. He'd spend multiple days at Muldorf and on those nights when he was brought back to Dachau, he slept soundly. This was a blessing in many ways; he did not have time to care about the pain in his back or the blisters that covered his shoulders. He didn't have time to worry about the men who would not be joining him the next day because they had not made it through the night. Sleep was the greatest escape in his day, and it was a small but very real blessing to be able to shut out the world for a few hours.

One afternoon, he was hauling a fifty-pound sack of sand to the top of the landing strip hangar structure, following the instructions of a soldier who was leading the way, when Nathan noticed that the soldier had taken a small detour to have a smoke. The Nazi had turned his back. As Nathan reached the pinnacle of the structure, he stopped for a moment to catch his breath. He looked over the edge and saw a great opportunity for some payback. Below him, a chubby German soldier had fallen asleep. Nathan dug deep under his shirt and scooped out as many lice as he could. He glanced around, then opened his hand, allowing the lice to fall like tiny itchy flakes of snow on to the man below. It was a small triumph, but every act of revenge, no matter how minor, helped lift his spirits a bit.

The plans for the completion of the airport were unexpectedly scrapped one afternoon when American and British fighter planes began appearing in the skies above Muldorf. Bombs were falling, and it was clear that the end of the war was near. Nathan and the others were elated, but the truth was they were all still prisoners and needed to keep their wits about them. Just as before, the Germans now had a problem on their hands: what would they do with their workers? They could not let them go, so they decided to move them somewhere more secluded and dispose of them. Once again, Nathan and the other workers were loaded onto trains. But the tracks had been bombed out, so the Germans held their prisoners in the marooned box cars for three days while they tried to decide what to do with them.

With nothing to do but dream of escaping, some of the prisoners who were standing by the cracks in the doorways tried to peek outside the cattle cars.

"What are they doing now?" someone asked.

One of the men pressed his eye into the crack. "Some of the Nazis have abandoned their posts!" came the excited answer. Nathan and a few of his fellow prisoners discussed their options.

"Should we try to escape?" they wondered. They were terrified, but they ultimately felt they had no choice but to try. One of the men slid the car door open slowly, just wide enough for a person to slip through. But then, in an unforeseen moment of frenzy, everyone spilled out at once. They pummeled the one remaining soldier, beating him unconscious, and then all scattered in different directions.

Nathan joined up with Zolie and his brother Lejb, fellow prisoners whom he happened to recognize from his home town. Suddenly, just like that, after all their torment, they were free. As they ran off, they spotted a farm house off in the distance. Keeping the roofline in sight through the trees, they headed for it, ran up to the door and knocked. "Do you have anything we can eat?" they asked the farmer.

"Prisoners have already been here and taken our food," the man said inhospitably. "All we have left is potatoes."

"That'll be fine," Nathan told him and gratefully took some.

The three escapees quickly returned to the safety of the forest. They gulped down the unpeeled, unwashed, raw potatoes. However, only moments later, their silent meal and joyous taste of freedom came to an abrupt end. From behind every tree, German soldiers suddenly appeared, pointing guns at them.

"Halt! Put your hands up!" they commanded in German.

Nathan, Zolie and Lejb raised their hands. They were taken back to where the other escapees had been corralled, and soon everyone was marching again. After a quick hike, they emerged from the forest and began heading down the street. Signs indicated they were entering the town of Macht Schwaben and were en route to the local police station.

The police chief came out of the station. He was a short man with thin black hair and a receding hairline. His eyes were close set and he had a small Hitler-style mustache. He wore a dark pair of Jodhpur-type pants and his round belt buckle shone brightly. With a somber look, he began speaking to the crowd.

"The war is almost over, so we will be taking you to Sweden," he announced. "There are trucks waiting to take you."

Nathan did not believe a word the police chief said. Why would the Germans want to take Jews, whom they tried to kill only moments before, to the safety of Sweden? The police chief disappeared back inside the station and the Germans walked the group out of town.

Darkness was falling and a light drizzle began to come down. In front of them were a number of trucks. For the first time in a long while, they saw women. Screams could be heard from the young ladies, who were being told to get into the trucks. The truck beds were high and the girls were not able to maintain any modicum of modesty as they lifted their skirts to climb in. The Nazi soldiers chuckled as they watched the women stumble onto the trucks, occasionally lifting their skirts with the points of their rifles.

Nathan noticed a ditch on the other side of the street. If, instead of getting on the truck, he could hide beneath it, then roll down into the ditch and wait there until the truck drove away – all without being noticed – he could run into the forest and make it to freedom. He motioned silently to Zolie, who in turn mimed the message to Lejb. They walked forward, and then, while the soldiers were preoccupied, they ducked beneath the truck. They could see and hear the soldiers' boots on the gravel street around the vehicle.

So far so good, except that a few others had decided to join in. Nathan was worried that so many of them might be a problem, but he could do nothing but hope for the best.

They waited for the right moment. Then, slowly, one by one, they crawled towards the waterway, sliding down and huddling against the side wall. The ditch still held water mixed with sludge and dead bugs, but they did not care. The truck drove off. Nathan let out a sigh of relief. "Now we need to get into the forest!" he told the others.

"But what about our uniforms?" Zolie asked. "We'll stick out like a sore thumb."

"There's nothing we can do about that now," Nathan answered as he knelt down and crawled through the overgrown bushes toward the forest. He wasn't quite sure what to do next. He'd already learned that the forest provided insufficient protection.

The small band walked in the darkness, listening for soldiers and their dogs. Nathan, Zolie and Lejb remained together, while gradually the others set off in their own directions.

"I see a barn!" Lejb said quietly. And sure enough, at the edge of the forest, a crimson roof was visible.

They kept low and stayed silent until they reached the structure. Since they were still dressed in their stripes, they were not surprised when the farmer, alerted by the family dog, came hurrying out, pointing a large shotgun at them. There was no need for discussion; it was clear that this household would not be accepting visitors. The three turned and ran back to take cover in the forest as the farmer shot wildly into the air.

Only the moon illuminated their way as they continued their trek in the dark. Eventually, they spotted another home. They decided they would simply sneak into the barn and ask for the farmer's consent in the morning.

As they got closer, they were met by a large, black and brown dog barking wildly. But Nathan was not afraid. He approached the dog slowly and spoke to it soothingly. He extended his hand for the dog to sniff. Slowly, and tentatively at first, the dog's tail began to wag. The others walked past the dog, gently stroking it on the head as they approached the barn.

They parted the door slowly and stepped inside. After their eyes had become accustomed to the blackness, they located a wooden ladder and climbed to the upper reaches near the rafters. The hay there was dry and warm. Exhausted, they finally enjoyed a good night's sleep.

The morning light was just beginning to appear through cracks in the roof when Nathan heard the sound of a person's footsteps inside the barn. His companions awoke as well. Nathan peered down and saw a young girl standing beside a hay-cutting machine. In her hand, she held a container with some sort of powder that she was adding to the hay.

"I'll go down and speak with her," Nathan whispered to the others. "Maybe I can convince her not to tell on us, and maybe she'll get us some food."

The others nodded hopefully and Nathan gingerly crept down the ladder. The hay-cutting machine was making a fair amount of noise, so the girl did not hear him until he took his first step onto the ground. Her head spun around and she stared in disbelief.

"Please don't scream," he said, speaking to her in German. "We're Jews and we're running from the Nazis."

She carefully put down the box of powder. "What do you want?" she asked. He was surprised to discover that she, too, was a foreigner, a servant from Poland, it turned out. Nathan answered her in his best Polish mixed with Hungarian, explaining how he had come to be there.

"They've alerted everyone in town that criminals have escaped, so they are looking for you," she told him. "We are supposed to report anything we see."

"I'm not a criminal," Nathan said, "Just a man who doesn't want to die." He then pointed up to the rafters where she could just see two pairs of eyes and then two faces. "There are two others here and we are all very hungry," he said. "Could you get us something to eat?"

She hesitated at first, but then looked at Nathan's face. Finally, she nodded her head.

"I'll try my best," she told him and left the barn.

The others hurried down the ladder. All three held their breaths, hoping she would not betray them. As they waited, they strained to listen. They heard the sounds of cows and birds and then the dog started barking again. They feared that soldiers might be on their way.

Then they heard footsteps and voices approaching the barn. The door creaked open. An elderly man peered in without entering. Everyone's eyes met and no one spoke. Then the door was pulled completely open, and the light poured in. Nathan shielded his eyes from the blinding sun.

The Polish girl had returned and had brought the farmer with her. There had been no way for her to smuggle food enough for three people out of the house without being seen, and she couldn't afford to lose her job.

"We aren't criminals!" Nathan assured the farmer, opening his hands so that the man could see that he was hiding nothing.

"I understand, but I can't put my family in danger," the farmer replied. "Let me discuss the matter with my wife," he said and left the barn in search of her. Harboring Jews could cost the farmer, his wife and their children their lives if they were caught.

Nathan, Zolie and Lejb remained in the barn. Within moments, they could hear the farmer's wife approaching.

"Get out!" she began shouting in German. She had not even entered the barn yet, but the tone of her voice was clear. "I'm going to tell the police if you don't leave!"

"Please, we don't have anywhere to go," Nathan pleaded, trying to reason with her. But it was pointless.

Nathan altered his approach, speaking as the aggressor this time. "You and I know that the war will be over soon," he told her. "The Russians are almost here."

"If you report us," Nathan continued, "when the war is over we'll come back and *you* will be *punished*." This was unlike Nathan, but desperate times called for desperate measures.

The word *punished* seemed to do the trick. She became less hostile. The Polish girl ran back to the house and returned with bowls of cold consommé, which Nathan and his friends consumed quickly.

"We're willing to help out around the farm," Nathan told the farmer's wife. "We'll do any job you give us. We can clean up after the cows and do whatever chores you'd like."

"You can't come in the house and I can only spare scraps and potatoes!" she dictated. "And you must always stay out of sight!"

Nathan and the others agreed, relieved to consider the barn their new home.

They remained there for about three weeks, keeping out of sight and doing odd jobs. Nathan took over the job of mixing the powder with the hay, learning that it provided vitamins, enzymes and minerals to enhance the nutritional value of the feed. They repaired broken household items and worked on the family's trucks and tractors. Each day in the late afternoon, they hungrily awaited their daily bounty of leftovers and bread, and they slept soundly in the warm hay.

One afternoon, the three men had their heads deep within the engine of the family's obstinate hay-crushing machine. No one noticed when a Nazi soldier walked quietly into the barn. His lapels bore no shiny pins and he had no ribbons or fancy buttons. He was just a grunt soldier with light-colored eyes and a space between his front teeth. Somehow he had caught a brief glimpse of the escapees and had come to see them for himself.

Everyone panicked, but there was no time or place to run. "Don't worry," the soldier told them. "I'm running away from the army. I don't want to fight anymore."

"What do you mean?" they asked him, not quite believing him.

"The war will be over very soon and I am finished fighting," he said as he took his pistol from his side and placed it on the floor as a gesture of proof. Zolie grabbed the gun and he aimed it with a trembling hand at the tall stranger.

"Why should we believe you?" Nathan asked.

"If I wanted to capture you, I could easily have done so already," he said.

"We're hungry. Do you have any food?" Nathan asked the soldier, having changed his mind about the interloper.

The young man nodded. "I'll be right back."

As he disappeared out of view, Nathan and the others wondered whether it was a good idea to have allowed the soldier to leave. As they paced back and forth, their minds played out calamitous scenarios. What if a jeep was on its way with men carrying machine guns? Would the soldiers set the barn on fire and burn them alive? Or, would the Nazis take them outside, line them up against the wall and shoot them?

But before they could take any action, the barn door opened and the soldier reappeared alone, carrying a bag. He opened it and pulled out some hard cheese. Each one took a portion for himself, tearing pieces off a short, half-eaten loaf of bread.

"I need to ask a favor of you," the soldier then ventured. "I need to have someone sign a document for me."

Nathan and the others looked at each other uneasily. No one wanted to sign anything for anyone, especially a Nazi. Nathan looked at the piece of paper the soldier handed him and deciphered the statement, handwritten in German: *I state that Heinrich Freizlich did assist me in my attempts to escape from the Nazis.*

For the next two days, Heinrich tried everything he could, short of threatening the men, to get them to sign the document, but they kept turning him down. Finally, when the

63

soldier saw that it was a lost cause, he left in search of other Jews who might sign his statement.

At the end of their third week in the barn, in late April Nathan heard new sounds outside the barn. The family dog was barking wildly, a constant stream of motor vehicles seemed to be rolling by, and people were congregating outside and talking loudly. He went to the doorway and peered out, looking towards the town.

First, he spotted Nazi trucks and jeeps passing by on the road, adorned with white scarves and fabric signifying defeat. Shortly after, as Nathan continued to stare from the door, different automobiles drove slowly by. These did not bear swastikas, but stars and stripes. These belonged to American soldiers! The soldiers hung precariously from their door-less trucks, their army belts relaxed and their guns resting across their laps.

Nathan and his friends saw that it was—at long last—safe to leave the barn. They hurried out to the road. An African American soldier hopped down from a tank and approached them. He was the first black man Nathan had ever seen. "These are Americans?" he asked himself.

"You're free!" he shouted in English. Nathan did not need a translation to understand what he had said: the war was over. To say that he and his friends were relieved would be a gross understatement. Over the past eighteen months, as his family was ripped from him and his life stripped of all normalcy, he had repeatedly told himself that he would be alright. But now, as he stood there, a free man once again, all the suppressed terror spilled out and he could not control the tears of relief.

The American soldiers stared at Nathan and his friends in disbelief, shocked at their physical condition. They reached into their bags and tossed them cans of Spam. He was tempted to devour the meat. But it had been such a long time since Nathan had eaten any substantial solid food that he knew it would make him sick. So he stuck it into his pant pocket, saving it for later, just as he had been told to do that first day at Auschwitz.

Everyone then followed their new heroes, forming an odd parade of joyous survivors, most skeleton-like in appearance and some, barely able to walk, being assisted by others. The tanks rolled along unhurriedly, leading them back to Macht Schwaben. Germans came out of their homes and some waved, joining in the happiness. But many more looked sullen, disgruntled about their defeat.

The procession traveled to the police station, where the Jews had been told they would be taken to Sweden. But this time, no German police chief appeared. He had left while he still could and an elderly Good Samaritan had taken over. This woman had set up a soup kitchen to feed the survivors, using the police station as the dispensing center. "Come upstairs for hot soup," she announced.

Many were too weak to run, but everyone made haste as they entered the room and formed a line. There were not enough seats for everyone, but they relished the warmth of the chicken broth as they took a seat on the floor.

As everyone slurped and refilled their bowls, Nathan pulled the woman aside. "Schlofn?" he asked her in Yiddish, wanting to know if there was someplace for them to sleep. She told him they could stay in the police station attic.

After they had finished their meal, he and his two friends quietly climbed the stairs. They found a few blankets and slept for days on the wooden floor, replenishing their energy and allowing their bodies to finally enjoy that blissful slumber that only comes when there are no threats of torture or death hanging overhead.

A few days later, the woman came upstairs and spoke with Nathan. "I'm sorry, but you can't stay here much longer," she told him. "The building is being returned to the local police."

"I understand. Thank you for all that you have done for us," he told her, and he meant it. Despite his experience with Germans up to this point, he recognized that she had been genuinely kind.

There was no time to waste, so the three of them scattered, combing the town for new accommodations. It seemed an impossible task. Most apartment owners never even bothered to open their doors. "No rooms!" was the message they heard from behind closed doors. And on the few occasions when the doors did open up just a crack, one quick glimpse at a filthy, smelly Jew in concentration camp clothes clinched it: No rooms!

Tired and hungry, Nathan walked up and down many streets, growing increasingly despondent over their bleak prospects. He suddenly heard the whistle of a nearby train and his stomach churned. The sound brought back memories of a family lost, of trips to the camps, and of people who had died in the cattle cars beside him. He shook off the memories and willed his mind back to the street in Macht Schwaben. He turned a corner and came upon a three-story stucco apartment house, a plain building painted a manila color. The only hints of color were some flower boxes which held new seedlings just beginning to sprout in the spring sunshine. He stepped up two low stairs and knocked on the door, not holding out much hope.

A woman opened the door. She looked at Nathan and, before he said a word, motioned for him to come inside. Although she was slight, she was much sturdier than Nathan. Her skin was light and her hair covered with a kerchief. She wore a blue blouse covered with a tan sweater vest. "Are you hungry?" she asked.

"Yes." Nathan answered.

"You're from the camps?' she said, half-asking half-stating, and set a plate of warm food on the table before him.

Nathan nodded his head in the affirmative and gulped down the wonderful meal.

"Do you have a place to stay?" she asked, pulling up a chair opposite him at the table.

He shook his head, "No."

"Well, the man who lived upstairs was an officer and he went away in a great hurry," she explained. "He left some of his furniture and there are even some clothes in the closet. I can let you stay there."

Nathan could hardly believe his ears. He feared that his response would change her mind. "I have no money and there are three of us," he told her and waited.

"When you get a job, you and the others can give me what you owe me," she answered.

When Nathan met up with Zolie and Lejb at the police station, they had good news as well. "Nathan, we met some people who said they know where some of our family is," said Zolie. "We hope to be reunited with them soon."

Finding family alive was a blessing and a miracle. So many survivors were the only ones who remained of their entire families. And here, brothers Zolie and had stayed together throughout the war and were now fortunate enough to find even more family alive. Nathan wished that he could have had that same good fortune. "Come back to the DP camp and stay with us, Nathan," Lejb suggested, referring to a camp that had been established nearby for Displaced Persons," but Nathan refused.

"I'm happy for you that you have found some family," he told them, "but everyone in my family is dead, so I think I am going to stay in the apartment in Macht Schwaben."

Nathan was not sure what he would do later, but for now, in this small town, he had food, kindness and new accommodations. He possessed more than he had ever had in his life and knew that there was nothing waiting for him back in Uzhgorod

With no Zolie or Lejb to fill up the apartment, he began to fully experience the loneliness he had postponed for so long. He thought about his mother and father, sisters and brothers and couldn't help but wonder why he had been the only one lucky enough to stand in the right lane in the camps. Everyone else had been told to go to the left and now there were all dead. He felt guilty and often cried, aching with despair and solitude whenever he thought of them.

Even though he knew his entire family was dead, he still had to make sure. He visited the local DP camp and asked survivors if they knew of anyone who might know his family or neighbors from his home town, but he found no one. He checked with all the agencies available, he completed forms and posted signs everywhere, but no one ever responded.

It was time for him to put the past behind him and look for a job. This proved even more difficult than finding an apartment. He had no special training, and here in Germany, jobs for Jews were hard to come by.

After searching for work in vain for two weeks, which meant no money for food and no rent for the landlady, he finally turned to crime. He had seen a fabric store in the neighborhood that would be his mark. It was difficult for him to justify this, but he felt he had no choice.

One evening, well after midnight, when the street was dark and empty, he walked over to the shop. It had brick on both sides of the wooden doors and above these doors were windows Nathan could crawl through. Once inside, he soon felt badly about what he was doing and decided not to take too much, just a few bolts of fabric. He hurried back to the apartment with his ill-gotten goods and started thinking about who he could sell it to.

Underground businesses—which always seemed to flourish in the aftermath of war—made selling the material on the new black market easy. Tailors in the area were always in the market for gabardines and wool knits at a substantially discounted price.

For a short while, he made some money as a merchant of sorts, but not wishing to push his luck, he didn't return to the fabric shop and began acquiring saleable merchandise from other merchants in his line of work. By reselling these assorted goods on the black market, he eventually made enough money to buy himself some decent clothing. He had long since discarded those striped pajamas, but the clothes left by the German officer in his apartment did not fit properly. Finally, he was able to purchase his own gray trousers and a sharp-looking hat. His hair grew out and he gradually started to put on some weight.

Some of the inhabitants of his building were quite friendly, in particular a young German girl, named Lizalotte, who lived on the first floor with her family. Nathan and Lizalotte enjoyed each other's company. He found her likeable, down to earth, and non-judgmental about Jews. Before long, Lizalotte fell madly in love with tall, dark Nathan and they became an item.

But Nathan soon discovered that casually dating a German and having a serious relationship with one were different matters altogether. Lizalotte attended Catholic Church faithfully each Sunday and prayed hard about the predicament in which she found herself. How could she get Nathan to convert to the "righteous" way to God through Jesus? She could not possibly marry him as long as they were divided by faith.

One Sunday, following a lovely sermon, she approached the priest and spoke to him about her problem. "Don't worry, Lizalotte, I will go and speak with him," the priest reassured her. The Church was always anxious to gain another follower.

That afternoon, Nathan heard a gentle rapping on his door. When he opened it, he was taken aback. There stood a priest in a tan and black floor-length robe with crosses embroidered on his long flowing sleeves. He was clean shaven, wore round, wire-rimmed glasses and his blond hair was neatly combed to one side.

"Nathan?" the priest asked.

"Yes?" Nathan answered cautiously, wondering what this man could possibly want from him.

"I have come to speak with you about your involvement with Lizalotte," the priest began.

Nathan was puzzled. What business was this of the church? But he welcomed his visitor inside and they took a seat at the table.

"Lizalotte is a member of my congregation and wanted me to discuss the possibility of your conversion to Catholicism," the priest explained.

"But I am Jewish," Nathan replied.

"Many people with your background are finding God through Christ," the priest said. "And in order for your relationship with Lizalotte to move forward, she wants you to join our church." The priest fell silent and waited. Nathan was Jewish. His parents were Jewish. They had died in the ovens because they were Jewish. Even though he no longer believed in God, he was certainly proud of being Jewish. He would always be Jewish and nothing could ever change that. There was really nothing to think about.

Nathan politely escorted the priest to the door. "I'll think about it," he said, but knew the matter was closed. Germany had been a fine enough place to live, but in truth it was not his home.

He had recovered mentally and physically and now it was time to take a first step into a new future.

Nathan had recently made an acquaintance who had a girl friend who happened to know where his half-sister, Malvina was living in Brooklyn. His relationship with Malvina and his half-brother, Irving, had never been warm and it had been a long time since they had seen each other but he needed her help. In his first letter to her, he told her everything that had happened. He explained how he had searched for survivors, but discovered that no one in the family except him had made it. He told her that he wanted to leave this land and hoped she would help him come to America. At first, their correspondence was strained. After all, she had only lived at home with Nathan for a few years. But after his repeated requests for assistance, Molvina went to the Department of Immigration and started the paperwork that would allow Nathan to migrate to America.

Nathan was honest with Lizalotte, revealing to her his plans of leaving Germany for America, but she held fast and remained loyal to Nathan, hopeful that he would change his mind and remain in Macht Scwhaben with her.

A year and a half later, his documents finally arrived, featuring a new, Americanized spelling of his last name; Poltzer. Although Lizalotte was heartbroken, Nathan was thrilled. He packed a small suitcase and caught a ship named *Flasher* that sailed into the New York harbor on January 29, 1948. He was on his way to his new life.

CHANNA GETS HER MAN

Upon their arrival in New York, Channa, Leja and Isaac followed a herd of refugees off the ship and into the southwestern section of Brooklyn. They carried the gold they had made from the sale of their childhood home and a small amount of money, which enabled them to rent a small one-bedroom apartment.

Their new home was on the second story of a four-story building. It was a barely furnished apartment directly above a dress shop named "The Doris." The shop's selection was meager and the prices low. In its window stood a lone, headless manikin clad in a short-sleeved dress. Dual sets of metal fire escapes zigzagged down the side of the building, resting on the brick that separated the storefront windows from the lip of the apartment's windows.

The inhabitants of the building were mostly refugees. Multigenerational families often crammed into a single unit. Parked on the street were older-model Hudsons and Plymouths in dark colors, with running boards and once-brilliant front grilles. Elderly women sat on chairs on the sidewalk, watching youths playing stickball and dodging approaching cars. Obstructing the view of the sky was a seemingly endless cobweb of laundry lines.

Isaac, Leja and Channa had no one to help them learn the ropes in this new country, so they set about figuring out this new world on their own. Isaac's first task was to find work. Since his English was poor, he limited his search to his predominantly Jewish neighborhood.

Two blocks from their apartment was a furniture store owned by a man named Mr. Drenberg. The doors to his business were always open and chairs in need of repair or refinishing spilled out on the sidewalk, alongside tables missing a leg and other wood furnishings in need of mending. Most of the pieces belonged to affluent clientele that had trucked their belongings in for Mr. Drenberg to repair.

Isaac walked into the furniture shop and explained in Yiddish that he had been a fine furniture builder in the "old country." "Do you have an opening?" he asked.

He was in luck. "You can start tomorrow," said Mr. Drenberg, and they shook hands.

Isaac's pay for staining and sanding bed posts was minimal, so he took on evening and weekend jobs as a plumber to bring home additional cash. While the more pious Jews were at the Synagogue thanking God for the week, Isaac was repairing toilets and broken pipes.

Channa happily threw herself into the American life style. She enjoyed going to the movies and mentally cataloged all the fashions and hair styles she saw on her movie icons. She devoured any second-hand *Life* magazines she could get her hands on and memorized any pieces of movie trivia she heard or read. She attended night classes at the local high school, where she mastered conversational English. She was such a good student that she got a job at a nearby Woolworth's Department Store. Her job was to keep the shelves of cheap perfume, talcum powder, nail polish and lipstick fully stocked.

Channa relished the Fridays when her supervisor would hand her an envelope containing that week's pay. The money gave her a sense of independence and safety. She contemplated opening her first savings account, but Isaac wanted to manage the revenue for the family. "Give me the money you got from work," Isaac instructed her. "I'll hold it for you."

"No," Channa replied, "I can save it up by myself."

One afternoon, as she was counting the boxes back in the storage room, the manager approached her. "Channa," he began, "we're very pleased with you work and would like to promote you to store buyer for the woman's department."

It was quite a compliment, but Channa had not come to Woolworth's to advance her career. She wanted to find a man, and there were none in the women's cosmetics section. "Can I work in the cafeteria?" She asked.

The manager looked curiously at her—this young woman was going to refuse an elevated position to become a waitress? "No Channa, we'd like to keep you where you are."

Channa continued working at Woolworth's for another two months. Then, while shopping down the street at a dress shop one day, she was offered a job as a sales girl by the store owner.

Once a month, on Sunday evenings, she attended the Displaced Persons events organized by the local Jewish Community Center. She was attractive, petite, and sassy, with dark eyes and long, wavy, red hair. Since, at the age of twenty-one, she was of marrying age, Isaac and Leja dutifully attempted to get her married off to the *right kind of guy*.

"Channa, we found a nice man for you to meet," they would often tell her.

Her eyes rolled. "He's really old, isn't he?" she always replied, already knowing the answer. "If you like him so much, you marry him!" she would snap.

It turned out Channa had found a man to date all by herself. He was a handsome Polish man named Gershon, whose blond, curly hair and eyes had a slight wildness to them. He was good to her and wrote her love poems. She liked him well enough, but she was not about to get really serious about Gershon. She was still keeping an eye out for *"someone better."*

Nathan's entrée to life in New York and his much-anticipated family reunion did not go exactly as planned. Malvina and Irving always emphasized that they were only his *half*-siblings. They made no attempt to hide the fact that Nathan was being tolerated solely out of loyalty to a shared father. They did take him to meet some of his half-uncles and cousins, but the meetings were difficult, as these strangers who happened to be related spoke Bulgarian and other languages Nathan did not.

Irving's wife, Lanke, informed her husband that she was not going to allow a half-brother whom they did not know to stay with them for even a day, so Irving passed the responsibility for Nathan's housing to his sister.

Malvina and her husband allowed Nathan to stay with them in their small rented apartment and sleep on the living room couch for ten dollars a week, a monumental sum for someone who had just arrived with no means of support and no work prospects. He never even unpacked his suitcase, as Malvina had her house arranged exactly as she liked it and could not be bothered to move anything to make room for his things. Upon each piece of furniture rested a hand-crocheted doily, and upon each doily rested a glass-figurine collectible. They covered the entire apartment, some displayed in small free-standing curio cabinets and some in niches built into the stucco walls.

Eager to remedy Nathan's financial problems and hasten his departure from her home, Malvina obtained work for him at a large shoe factory owned by a distant cousin. He had only just begun to learn English so he was grateful for the work. For five months, he toiled away, handling leather and organizing boxes. Around him, sewing machines buzzed and hammers secured soles onto women's high heels and boots. The air was filled with cigarette smoke, and during the summer heat, they sweltered in the stagnant air.

He worked very hard, hoping to be promoted so that he could move into his own apartment and sleep on a real bed. But each time he mustered up the courage to go to the owner's office to discuss a promotion, he was put off. "Not yet," he was told by his cousin. So he continued sleeping on the lumpy couch for far longer than he or Malvina would have liked. His English had gotten much better and he was adapting quite well to his surroundings, but he felt frustrated and stifled at work.

Living with his half-sister made dating awkward, but he nevertheless began a relationship with a young woman named Rochelle. Originally from Hungary, she was attractive and trim, with shoulder-length dark hair. She enjoyed wearing brightly colored floral dresses and was waiting for the good life to arrive.

Rochelle had high hopes that Nathan would one day make more money and marry her. She prayed that the day would come soon and often asked him why his promotion was taking so long. "Isn't he your cousin or something?"

One afternoon, while he was moving a large bolt of uncut leather, Nathan was called into the main office. He felt optimistic; maybe the time had finally arrived for him to move up. When he entered the office, his cousin was seated at his desk, his short, thinning gray hair slick with pomade. The room stank of old cigar smoke. "Nathan, did you know that I have a granddaughter?" he began, squinting through his dark eyes. "Her name is Harriet and I'd like you to meet her."

Nathan was taken aback and a little flattered, but uninterested. "Thank you very much, but I'm already involved with someone," he said politely. "But I would like to speak with you about my willingness to come to work on Saturdays and learn some skills that could pay me more money," he ventured. "Your son, Mickey, has already agreed to teach me."

His cousin shook his head, still not looking directly at Nathan. He was not interested in training a new member of the staff; he needed a husband for his granddaughter, and so their meeting quickly came to an end.

Nathan continued laboring at the shoe factory for another four months. During this time, the issue of the granddaughter was never revisited, nor was a promotion. One morning, Nathan had had enough. He marched into his cousin's office and closed the door behind him. The cousin was so startled that he looked directly at Nathan. "Listen, I am a good worker and I need more money," he began, pausing for a moment as he waited for a positive response. But his cousin remained silent. "And if I don't get more money, I'll have to go to work somewhere else!" he added firmly.

"Well…." His cousin hemmed and hawed.

Nathan could see the writing on the wall and grew angry. "This is how you treat family members? It's disgraceful! I quit!" he said and marched out of the office.

From the moment he left the office, the phone started ringing. Malvina had already heard the news by the time he walked through the door. She was embarrassed and furious. "Who do you think you are to tell off anyone, you nothing!" She scolded. "You are the most unappreciative person I have ever met. You know you aren't going to be able to stay here forever!"

Rochelle was just as unsupportive. This development put a serious crimp in her wedding plans. "What is wrong with you that you can't move up, Nathan?" she demanded. "I know lots of men who are making a decent living. Why can't you?"

Nathan felt dejected. He had been living with his half-sister for almost a year. He had no place to call his own. Malvina didn't want him there, and now his girlfriend was unhappy. Self-doubt flourished.

Nathan looked tirelessly for work, but Rochelle grew impatient. "I have been seeing another gentleman who has a job and wants to marry me," she told him one day, catching him off guard. "So I am sorry, but this will have to be goodbye."

For the next few months Nathan's self-esteem suffered further. He found ill-paying odd jobs, but nothing solid. And, although he was a handsome young man, his attempts at finding a girlfriend were fruitless. With virtually no income, he could not even afford to take a date to a movie. So he decided to take a break from dating for a while.

One of the best places for men and women to meet was the boardwalk near Coney Island Beach, which was usually overflowing with young people who went to the ocean to see and be seen. Both sexes took turns strolling past each other, hoping to catch the eye and attention of a selected object of interest.

Channa enjoyed showing off her figure and had a favorite two-piece bathing suit that she felt accentuated her body beautifully. It had a bandeau top in black, white and blue and cupped her breasts in an attractive swirling pattern. The bottoms had a high waist, starting above her navel, and were a cross between shorts and a skirt. She pinned back half her long hair and painted her lips with the popular shade of the day, Red Majesty. Between her lips, she held an unlit Lucky Stripes cigarette; although she did not smoke, she liked the look. Fellows walked by, trying in different ways to catch her eye, much as male peacocks strut and shake their feathers. But Channa had not quite found what she was looking for.

It was Sunday afternoon and there was a Jewish Community–sponsored DP dance set for seven o'clock that night. One might think that Holocaust survivors would be thrilled to find fellow survivors, but this was not the case. In fact, there was a strange hierarchy among them. Partisans who had lived in the forest were the uppermost echelon. Those who had lived in ghettos were below them. And on the bottom rung were the concentration camp survivors. All three groups attended dances at the Jewish Community Center.

Channa began primping for the evening early. She combed her wavy hair over to one side and pinned the other side behind her ear with a sparkly hair clip. She wore gypsy hoop earrings and plucked her eye brows to create attractive half-moons over her dark brown eyes. She applied little color to her lids, but masses of mascara. She swept dark ruby lipstick over her lips, which matched her red blouse. This she wore with a dark, fitted skirt. Finally, she pulled on the high-heeled boots that she loved.

The DP dances were similar to school dances everywhere; some people hovered in clusters, while others walked around checking out the competition and contemplating possible conquests. Different languages could be heard around the room, all asking, *Where did you come from?* in Romanian or *Do you have any family still alive?* in Polish.

Channa strolled around, saying hello to this or that individual while the party goers listened to scratchy phonograph recordings of Dinah Shore singing *Buttons and Bows* and Perry Como crooning *Till the End of Time*. Over in a corner stood a table with refreshments, where bottles of pop with paper cups and plates of cookies provided men with excuses to chat with the young ladies.

A year had passed since Nathan's self imposed dating moratorium and he and he had decided it was time to try again. He arrived solo, sporting a well-groomed mustache. His hair was short and his eyes had an impish, though sad look about them. He still retained the strong muscles he had acquired in work camp, but he was lean.

He came with a purpose: he wanted to start a family. Neither shy nor bold, he strolled around the room and noticed the flashy, peppery Channa seated at a table with some girlfriends. "Would you like to dance?" he asked her.

Channa looked up and accepted.

"So what's your name?" Nathan asked as they moved across the dance floor.

"Rita," she lied, being a fan of Rita Hayworth.

They chatted a bit and danced through a number of songs. She thought him handsome enough and he thought her very fetching.

Time passed quickly, and when it was announced that the event would be ending soon, Nathan asked Channa whether he could take her home

She looked at him, uncertain what to say. She didn't know him and had never trusted strangers. "You'll have to take my friends home, too," she bargained.

"I will only take you home, not your friends," he replied, and so Channa refused.

"Good night then," he told her and the two went their separate ways, both in search of *"someone better."*

Rosh Hashanah, the Jewish New Year, fell on October 4 that year and, to celebrate the occasion, Channa, Isaac and Leja planned to go to Tompkins Square Park. It was a small neighborhood park, bordered on four sides by tall buildings. Wooden park benches dotted the walkways that divided the grass, and here and there, monuments carved from cement honored the park's namesake, Peter Tompkins.

Neither Channa nor Nathan had given any thought to each other since they had seen each other six months before, but when Nathan spotted Channa drinking from a water fountain, he came up behind her and tapped her on the shoulder. Mouth filled with water, she spun around, and, surprised, she spat it out, hitting Nathan and his freshly pressed shirt. "You startled me!" she said.

"Rita, I'm sorry, I didn't mean to," he apologized. "How have you been?"

Isaac and Leja were standing beside Channa. They looked at each other a little confused: Who was Rita?

Channa and Nathan took a seat on a nearby bench and could not help but laugh as Nathan tried to dry his shirt. The two sat there talking for quite a while as Isaac and Leja stood by, growing impatient.

"I think it's time to go home," Isaac finally interrupted.

Channa waved for them to go on without her; she and Nathan had seen something in each other's eyes.

"Come home quickly," Isaac instructed her and stared warningly at Nathan.

"I have to tell you my name isn't really Rita," she confessed. But instead of being angry with her, he found her white lie charming. They talked a little about their lives, but not in much detail. Nathan didn't want to divulge just yet that he had been in the camps.

When the air became chilly, they decided to walk back to Channa's apartment. They strolled slowly, passing bakeries and restaurants. As they walked by an eatery, a set of double doors suddenly burst open and out hurried a bride and groom. The newlyweds were in a blissful daze, all smiles and laughter. Following close behind them was a group of well-wishers dousing them with rice. Wayward grains rained down upon Channa and Nathan, striking them in the face and clinging to their hair. They looked at each other and grinned.

Nathan escorted Channa to her door, where an anxious Isaac was waiting. "So what do you do for a living and where are you from?" he demanded. His probing made Nathan uncomfortable, but he entered the apartment and allowed himself to be scrutinized for an hour. When they touched upon the subject of where he was during the war, he lied and told them he had been held in a ghetto.

"Can I see you again, Channa?" he asked as he headed for the door.

"Yes," she told him and they smiled.

As time went on and his affection for Channa grew, he knew he needed to tell her the truth about his war experience. Although it seemed a nonsensical lie to be so frightened about, he feared that this might cause her to turn away from him. She might be concerned that he had been exposed to disease or that he had been experimented on. Maybe his ability to have children had been compromised in some way. There were any number of possibilities, and he dreaded the prospect of this conversation. However, he knew he had to get the truth out sooner rather than later if they were going to get serious.

"I was never really in the ghettos," he finally confessed, "but went to the camps."

Channa's eyes widened.

"First Auschwitz, then Dachau," he continued.

This revelation caused Channa a great deal of consternation. Even though she had lied to him about her real name not being Rita, she did not appreciate his lying to her about something this important.

Was Nathan the right guy for her, she asked herself. He had no family and no money and could she really be sure he was physically fit to start a family? They talked a lot and after listening to Nathan speak so honestly about what had happened to him in the camps, Channa decided to take the risk of trusting him once again.

One evening, following a date, the two returned to her apartment. They were on the couch kissing with the lights off, when Isaac, growing concerned about his sister's safety, suddenly flipped on the lights. He knew perfectly well what happened when healthy young couples were allowed too much time in the dark. In the forest, and even in the ghetto, rules about intimacy had become more relaxed. *Live for today, tomorrow may never come* had become everyone's motto, and men and women were hooking up everywhere. But now that the future seemed more assured, Isaac believed that proper young ladies, which especially meant his sister, should keep their knees together.

"OUT!" he shouted, grabbing Nathan by the shirt.

"Isaac, stop!" Channa yelled, "I want him to stay!"

But Nathan was uncomfortable. He collected his jacket and began to leave.

"Meet me at the park next Saturday night!" Channa yelled. Nathan smiled in her direction and closed the door behind him.

"How could you do that!" Channa cried. She was livid; Isaac had overstepped the bounds of his parental duties. "I am an adult and I can take care of myself!"

"Channa, he isn't the right guy for you!" Isaac explained. "He doesn't even have a job."

"Well, I think he is the right guy!" she yelled as she ran into the bathroom and slammed the door behind her.

All that week, Channa wondered if Nathan would be at the park on Saturday. She fumed about the apartment, refusing to speak to Isaac and cried bitterly to Leja. "What if he doesn't show up?" she kept saying.

Perhaps because there was now a chance of losing Nathan, Channa had come to the conclusion that he was the *"someone better"* she had been looking for.

Saturday evening arrived, but Channa could not bear to go to the park and not find Nathan standing there. "Isaac, you go to the park and see if he's there, but don't say anything to him!" she commanded her brother. "Just come back and tell me!"

Isaac pulled on a hat and coat and walked the few blocks to the park. There, beside the fountain that had started this entire affair, was a lanky Nathan standing all alone, obviously waiting for his Channa to arrive. Isaac sadly shook his head. He had really hoped Nathan would not be there, but he returned home and told Channa the news.

"He's there!" he told a fully dressed and waiting Channa. She flew out of the apartment and all but ran over to meet him. When they spotted each other, they were both flooded with relief.

"Channa, I don't make a lot of money," he cautioned her, wanting to put all his cards on the table. Then he waited, wondering if she would send him away.

"Don't worry," she assured him. "We'll make it. I will not demand more than you can do."

"I love you and would love to marry you," he told her as he swept her up in his arms and kissed her. Channa smiled, flooded with joy and eager to embark on this next phase of her life.

They decided to get married in February, which was only two months away. Channa visited several wedding gown tailors in the area and selected a stunning white satin, long-sleeved gown. The bodice was lacy, but not sheer, with a smattering a sequins. The A-line skirt gathered at her tiny waist. The beautiful long train she selected flowed behind her, secured to a stiff fabric crown.

Time raced by and the big day finally arrived. Channa wore her hair in large curls. She had on dangling imitation pearl earrings with a matching necklace and she carried a bouquet of white roses. Nathan had donned a dark suit and black bow tie. A kerchief peeked appropriately out of his pocket and a three-rose boutonnière was pinned to his lapel. A Fedora hat, tipped slightly down in the front, completed the outfit. They were a picture-perfect couple.

Channa slowly walked down the aisle towards Nathan, Isaac on her right and Leja on her left. As they stood beneath the embroidered velvet Chupah, the Rabbi sang the blessings. At the appropriate time, Nathan stomped down on the wedding goblet, "Mazel Tov!" cheered their family and friends. On Channa's left ring finger now rested a beautiful rose gold band with alternating diamonds and rubies. Although it was not elaborate and the stones were microscopic, it was a lovely ring. Inscribed on the inside, was 2-25-1950, their wedding date.

There was no money for a honeymoon, so immediately following their wedding reception, the newlyweds returned to their newly rented third-floor flat at the Bedford-Stuyvesant apartments, the Brooklyn tenements of the era. The residents of the non-descript building where the Poltzers now lived were a mix of white Jewish and Italian families; the companion building next door was inhabited entirely by black families, but both shared the roaches and the rats.

Eager to provide for his new bride Nathan started looking even more diligently for a job. For several weeks, he was employed to carry bundles of fabrics to workers who sat at foot-operated sewing machines and added delicate finishes to scarves. Then he worked in the storage room of a men's store. But none of the jobs lasted long and he needed something with a dependable income, as Channa became pregnant shortly after the wedding.

He decided to visit an unemployment office, where he received a set of forms. The paperwork was difficult to complete because his English was not proficient enough, but with help, he was able to complete the form.

Nathan was placed as a grunt laborer in a small meat-packing house named Robert Lieberman Co., where he spent his days moving slaughtered baby cows' carcasses to refrigerated meat lockers.

His work days began at 4:30 in the morning. Channa would sleepily prepare a breakfast of eggs and rye toast with caraway seeds for her husband, pack him a bagged lunch, fill up his thermos with hot tea, give him a loving kiss good-bye, and return to bed.

Nathan took the city bus for the twenty-minute trip to the plant and entered the frigid building along with all the other early risers. Everyone dressed in company-provided white coveralls and wool hats and began their shift together. Nathan was instructed on the proper method of attaching the veal to giant hooks. He watched how they first split the sides of meat using power tools and how the more experienced butchers would cut the meat apart using sharp knives and cleavers. The work was hard and the pay was poor, but Nathan was able to learn all about butchering.

The plant closed unexpectedly after a few months. Not wasting any time, Nathan found a job at another meat-packing plant.

In his new job, Nathan learned to separate the meat from the bone. He would slip on a metal-mesh meat carver's glove, which shielded his right hand from the knives blades while leaving his left hand free to hold the slippery meat. The more talented the carver, the closer to the bone he cuts and the less meat is wasted. Nathan had found his secret talent; he was adept at the job. Soon he acquired his own assortment of knives, which he kept razor-sharp, and joined the Meatpackers union. This was a fortuitous move, for he was now being paid $75.00 a week, twice as much as before.

Nathan began volunteering for overtime. "Channa, what if the money I bring home just isn't enough once the baby comes?" he asked.

"Don't worry, Nathan, we'll make a good home for our child. Everything will be fine," she reassured him. Her faith in him gave Nathan confidence and she never complained when the many hours he worked seemed excessive.

With the baby's arrival only a few months away, Channa thought it was time to speak with Isaac about the gold he was holding for them. She did not know how much there was, but she knew that half of it should be coming to her.

"Isaac, I need you to give me my half of the gold," she told him.

"Why do you need it?' Isaac asked.

"Because it's half mine," she answered, not understanding what the problem might be.

"Well …," Isaac hesitated, sidestepping her request. "I'll get it to you after you have the baby."

THE POLTZER CHILDREN COMETH

On December 19, 1950, Channa realized that the baby was on the way. She had not given much thought to the actual process of giving birth, so when the first contractions began, she panicked. Nathan hailed a cab and told the driver to get them to the nearest emergency room.

Channa was quickly admitted after she was heard screaming out in pain. She was anesthetized and wheeled into the delivery room, while Nathan was sent out to stand by in the waiting room with all the other expectant fathers.

After many hours, a doctor came out and all the anxious fathers quickly stood up. Those who were smoking extinguished their cigarettes, expecting the doctor to call their name. "Mr. Poltzer?" the doctor asked, looking around, not knowing which nervous man that might be. "Congratulations, you are now the father of a beautiful baby boy," he announced after Nathan identified himself.

Nathan smiled happily. Hitler had not won; the Poltzer lineage would continue. Abandoning the other men to their anxious vigil, he hurried down the hall to his wife.

Channa was holding a small bundle, wrapped in a blue cotton receiving blanket. The baby was not making much noise, just some quiet gurgles. His head was covered with a blue cap, leaving only his face visible. "He's perfect!" Nathan gloated, touching one of the baby's tiny fingers.

"I want to name him Shlomo, after my Father." Channa said. Her choice of name was odd, as she was never very close with her Dad, but she wanted to honor him just the same.

"And I want his middle name to be Harrias, after President Truman," she continued. Channa spoke English well enough, but to her English-as-a-second-language ear, Harry S. Truman sounded a great deal like Harrias. The new mother and father both failed to understand that their son would carry that error with him his entire life.

Saint Mary's Hospital was a Roman Catholic institution, and since Shlomo Harrias came into the world a mere six days before Christmas, the nurses set up a tiny Christmas tree beside Channa's bed. Channa and Nathan said nothing about the small aluminum evergreen or the olive wood Crucifix that hung over the bed and were never impolite to the nurses when they continually brought up the suggestion of religious conversion, but they agreed to make sure that for their next child they would select a more appropriate hospital.

When Channa and Shlomo came home after spending four nights in the hospital, the new parents indulged in the purchase of an expensive baby pram. They'd proudly stroll up and down the street with their newest family addition, stopping frequently to make sure he was warm.

Channa had her hands full – hand washing, drying, folding diapers and keeping house, but she was content. Yes, the baby cried and screamed and never allowed her a moment's peace, but he was also totally dependent on her for everything and Channa liked it that way.

Several months passed and Shlomo was learning to stand. Irving and Lanke came over to see the little lad and took a seat on the couch. Channa tried to straighten up the room, removing the many toys spread all over the floor. Just as quickly, Shlomo kept retrieving his favorites: a wooden bumblebee that twirled its wings and buzzed when pushed or pulled, and various building blocks. He sat down among his toys, his feet bare.

As he played, Lanke did not smile or seem remotely enchanted. All she could fixate on was the jumble. "Channa, is this how you take care of your child?" she began. "And this apartment is such a mess. Is this how they teach you to be a mother and a wife in Poland?"

Nathan could feel his wife's jaw tighten and her hackles rise, but decided that whatever came next, Lanke had it coming.

"Who told you to come over?" Channa rebuked her sister-in-law as she bent down and put the socks back on Shlomo's feet. "And did I ever ask your advice on how to raise my son? If you don't like how I take care of my baby or your brother-in-law, don't come over and you won't have to see it!" To Channa, Lanke was a stranger, not family, and really had no right to an opinion. The two women glared at each other until Irving and Lanke picked up their belongings and left in a huff.

Channa would have preferred not to socialize very much—she had her family and was satisfied—but Nathan enjoyed people so they continued trying to maintain some semblance of a social life, regularly attending dinner parties with other young couples.

These were elegant affairs, with the women arriving in beautiful dresses and jewelry, their hair styled to perfection and the men in suits and ties.

One night at such a party, there was dancing after dinner. Nathan enjoyed dancing, and being a gallant male, tried to make sure to dance with every female in attendance. It was harmless on his part, but Channa hated sharing his attention and time with anyone else, especially other women. She did not trust him and was positive he was a womanizer just waiting for the opportunity to leave her for *"someone better."* She seethed all evening, and even though she danced with the other husbands, she was not happy.

On the way home, Channa lit into him, repeatedly threatening to take her son, leave Nathan and return to Isaac. "Why couldn't you have just danced with me?" she cried. The argument dragged on for days. He yelled back that dancing with the other women had meant nothing to him, but no matter how much he tried to reassure her, she refused to listen, preferring to unleash her fury on him. Doors slammed and chairs flew, but Channa ultimately would never leave her Nathan.

Channa had an unwritten rule book that she kept in her heart and she expected everyone in her close-knit world were obliged to adhere to it. When Nathan broke her rule of loyalty, she started to write these infractions down, calling these notes her *Book of Channa* . Over the years, she jotted down an ongoing tally of Nathan's wrongdoings on anything and everything—the back sides of discarded envelopes, inside the flaps of books, anywhere she could find to keep a permanent record.

They attended fewer dinner parties once the fury of that evening faded, and life settled back down. Channa continued to keep herself busy with the house and her young son and Nathan worked hard. Life was quiet and good.

Two-and-a-half years later, the Poltzer family welcomed their second child into the fold. I was born on June 12, 1954. Named Jaclyn, after my paternal grandmother, Jolin, I had a full head of nearly black hair and enormous eyes with long eye lashes, and I had inherited my namesake's slender lips and eyebrows.

Following their disagreement over child-rearing and housekeeping, Lanke and Irving no longer came to visit. However, Malvina, and her husband occasionally came by. Malvina was not as overt as Lanke in her disdain for Channa. Although her sister-in-law's facial expressions caused Channa some irritation, she never said a word. Channa could see Malvina's disregard for her and hated it, but there was nothing specific she could take issue with.

"Where did you get this cake?" Malvina asked one day when they were together, pushing her plate away as she made a slight face.

"Why, is there something wrong with it? I made it."

Malvina said nothing, but conspicuously changed the subject. "Shouldn't you be putting the children to sleep already?" she asked as she watched Shlomo inhale the dessert with his hands. "You know we have these Japanese neighbors and when I baby-sit their children, they already know how to use a fork," she announced, staring at Shlomo, who was now wiping the frosting onto his hair.

Channa gritted her teeth. "So, you watch other people's children?" she demanded. "You have never offered to watch our children."

Episodes full of tension and underhanded recriminations such as these made Channa decide that Nathan's family would no longer be welcome in their home. This was frustrating to Nathan—after all, he didn't have much family left—but he felt there was little he could do. He called them every month or so. However, their exchanges remained permanently cool.

Around that same time, Nathan changed meat-packing houses yet again and got a raise. The family happily moved from the slums of Bedford-Stuyvesant over a few blocks to a slightly better neighborhood in Bensonhurst. They rented a lovely two-bedroom, ground-floor apartment in a brownstone that butted up to a small but lovely park. Channa and Nathan finally had a bedroom to themselves, without children, and Shlomo and I shared the second bedroom. Channa enjoyed setting up house, filling their new place with art.

While Channa had severed relations with Nathan's family, she remained close with her brother, Isaac. However, her discussions with him about the gold were not proving very fruitful. "Don't worry about it," he told her, "I am watching it for you." But his assurances did not do anything to ease her growing concerns.

Isaac had been working as a carpenter and plumber for years now and had grown weary of both jobs, routinely complaining about his boredom and frustration. From time to time, he considered other professions. He gave some fleeting thought to the idea of raising chickens, but dismissed it once he learned how much work was involved.

The next business Isaac decided to investigate was vacation bungalows. New Yorkers often traveled to the Catskills in upstate New York on weekends and during summer break for a little rest and relaxation, and Isaac had heard there was a small colony of bed-and-breakfast resorts that catered to these vacationers. After visiting a few possible properties that were for sale, he set his heart upon one in particular. The collection of cabins was relatively small, with only nine modest structures sitting on a good piece of land, nestled up against a national forest. The bungalows needed some work, but the price was right and Isaac saw great potential there. "Come up and see it with me, Nathan," he proposed.

Channa was suspicious, wondering where he planned to get the necessary capital. "Don't give him any money," she warned Nathan.

That night, when Isaac and Nathan returned home from seeing the property, Isaac was elated. "I got it!" he announced.

"The property?" Channa asked, fearing he had made such an important decision too quickly.

"Yes," Isaac answered.

"Did you have that much money?" Channa asked, afraid that Nathan had disobeyed her orders.

"I had money saved up," he said, hesitating before he finished his sentence. "And I used the gold."

"The gold! All the gold?" Channa asked, beginning to raise her voice.

"Channa," Leja interrupted, "you lived with us for quite a while. Don't you think you owe that gold to your brother for saving your life and taking care of you all that time?" As he said it, Leja walked over and stood beside her husband.

It really wasn't Leja's place to speak for Isaac, Channa thought. "And whose name is on the paperwork if you used *our* gold?" Channa asked.

"Don't worry, Channa, I will have them change it and put your name on it also," he assured her, but she knew in her heart that he would go through with it.

Most of that night and for the days that followed, Channa argued with Isaac. Leja and Channa came to verbal blows when she lectured Leja about demanding remuneration for what she felt was simply family loyalty. But it was all too late. Channa was now at an impasse with her brother. She felt deeply betrayed and kept her distance from Isaac and Leja for several weeks. Eventually, however, she realized that she needed to make peace with what he had done if she wanted to continue a relationship with her only remaining relative.

Isaac worked hard on renovating the property and, on alternating Saturdays and Sundays, Channa, Nathan and the children went up to the Catskills for the weekend. While Channa and Leja sat on white Adirondack chairs on the lawn drinking tea, Nathan and Isaac worked on the bungalows.

It took Isaac and Nathan about two months to get the cabins ready for use. Perschowski's Vacation Resort opened for business. Isaac's resort did well, and during the summer months, almost all the cabins were fully booked. When Channa, Nathan and Shlomo came for the weekend, Channa was happy for Isaac. She wanted him to be successful—so he could pay her back.

Three more years went by, and on August 25, 1957, Channa and Nathan's third child, Shirley, was born. With her wavy, auburn hair, she was the family jewel, as sweet and feminine as they came.

After the delivery, the doctors pulled up a chair beside Channa's bed, explaining that she had weak uterine muscles and advised her that it would be best for her not to have any more children. Nathan was happy to hear it and agreed that three was enough.

Three children induced the Poltzers to purchase their first automobile. Nathan got a 1950 green Chevrolet with loads of mileage and lots of rust. And so the Poltzers could now go to the Catskills in style.

Meanwhile, Isaac had decided that he needed a swimming pool on his property in order to stay competitive during the hot summer months. He asked Nathan to help him.

While the two toiled day and night on weekends, back at home, Channa was growing tired of Nathan's continued absence. Many weekends, reluctant to travel with three children, she remained behind in Brooklyn. "Your loyalties should be with your family," she complained to Nathan "Isaac can build without you."

"He is our family and he needs my help," Nathan responded, and soon enough, it was done.

But Isaac was not yet satisfied. "Channa," he began one afternoon, "I need to add a few more cabins and Nathan tells me you have a little cash saved up. Can I borrow it for my property?"

Channa was dumbfounded. Had he not taken enough from her already? She had scrimped and saved, cutting corners at every opportunity to save up a nest egg, and now he wanted that, too. She hoped to buy her own home sometime soon. And given what she had lived through, she was determined to always have a stash of cash available for bribes if it ever became necessary again.

"No Isaac, I can't. We need that money to give our children a home," she said. "Our apartment is too small and it's time for us to buy a house."

So Isaac waited until he was alone with Nathan and then broached the subject again. "If you tell Channa you've decided to loan me the money for the property, she'll go along with it," he told his brother-in-law, never mentioning that she had already turned down his request. Nathan, wanting to be a loyal family member, unknowingly contradicted Channa and told Isaac yes.

When Channa learned of Isaac's underhanded actions, their relationship changed instantly and irrevocably. All her life she had so admired him, counting on him to always consider her and her needs. But now she saw him in a new light. Back in the forest, it had been the two of them against the world, but here, away from death's door, it seemed to be Isaac for Isaac. She knew she could never trust him again.

Nathan had made a promise, so Channa had no choice but to *lend* Isaac the money. She nevertheless held back a small portion.

Nathan was now cast in the position of turncoat and Channa raged against him. "Why couldn't you have just stayed out of this?" she yelled. "He is my brother, not yours!" In her mind, if Nathan had been a good and true husband, he would have sided with her. In her mind, he had let her down and she would remember this.

The ill-gotten infusion of money allowed Isaac to add a few more structures and soon all were rented out for the summer. The money began coming in, but Isaac continued skirting the issue of the loan. "I can't pay you back right now because I need to have cash for repairs," he told them. He seemed to have an endless array of excuses.

Finally, Nathan, wanting to get out of the frying pan he had jumped into, told Channa he would confront Isaac.

"No, you won't," Channa told him. It was one thing for her to argue about this with her brother, but Isaac was not Nathan's brother and she would not allow it. "You made this mistake and now you'll pay the price for it," she chided him. "Just consider the loan a gift. I don't want to talk about it anymore!"

Meanwhile, Nathan had been speaking with his sister Malvina, who had since moved to Los Angeles. She sang the praises of nice weather and financial possibilities. Channa and Nathan began toying with the idea of moving to the West coast. Nathan was tired of the snow and felt it was time for a change. One afternoon a whistle blew in the plant where Nathan worked. He learned that a representative from Hebrew National, one of America's largest meat-handling companies, had come to his factory to recruit possible transferees to California. Attired in a handsome brown suit, the gentleman touted the facility's excellent working conditions.

Nathan paid close attention. He was anxious to see if this might be the job opportunity he and Channa had been waiting for. "Mr. Shoenfeld," Nathan asked the representative, "If I come to California, am I guaranteed a job?"

"I'm not promising, but we'll hire as many as we can," the man replied vaguely.

The following week, Nathan visited his meat-cutter's union to confirm that he would be able to transfer his benefits, status, and pension to California. They assured him that he would not lose his union status if he moved.

That clinched it; it was time to go to where the sun always shined: Los Angeles. They had heard houses were affordable and neighborhoods were quiet. California had all the makings of a better life for the Poltzers.

The timing of the move was problematic because Channa had just found out that she was pregnant again. Upon learning of it, Nathan was not particularly joyful. After all, the doctors had warned Channa that having more children was not good for her health. Besides, things were already tight for them financially. And now, with this move and the uncertainty of it all, this was not the most welcomed of pregnancies. But when Nathan even mentioned the possibility of her having an abortion, Channa refused to discuss it. The subject was closed.

Nathan contacted Malvina and Irving to tell them the wonderful news. Nathan was well aware that there was still a major rift between Channa and his siblings, but he hoped enough time had passed. *We want to move to Los Angeles,* he wrote to his sister repeatedly, but her replies lacked any enthusiasm about a reunion. *Please contact me after you've arrived,* she wrote back. But Nathan needed more of a commitment, so he called her and asked if he and his family could spend at least one night in her home.

The phone went silent for a moment while Malvina gave it some thought. Then she let out a sigh. "You and your family can stay here for one night, Nathan," she told him.

And soon enough, they were off.

COMING TO LOS ANGELES

In late May, 1960, on the day of my family's departure from New York, Dad worked a full shift at the meat packing plant. All of our household possessions were sold. Whatever my parents could not sell for decent money, they gave to Isaac.

Dad rushed home to pick us up and we barely made our flight. Dad sat between Shlomo, who was nine and a half, and me, who had just turned six, to prevent fighting. Shirley, who was going to be three in August, happily sat beside Mom. As we pulled away from the gate, Shlomo and I animatedly waved at no one in particular; it was our inaugural flight and we were thrilled. We had always turned our heads skywards when we heard the sound of a plane overhead, wondering where those people were heading. But today, we were the fortunate ones venturing someplace new.

Malvina and her husband had borrowed a friend's car to pick us up. Sol's eyes widened as he surveyed the mass of belongings and the number of people he would need to squeeze into the car. Malvina was polite and proper, but did not embrace us with much warmth. She and Mom said little, barely nodding to each other as Mom took her seat in the back.

Malvina's apartment in Boyle Heights looked just like her New York flat. Her prized collection of breakables had traveled with her and each was again strategically placed on a crocheted doily. Shirley and I could not tear our eyes away from the trinkets. Our mother spent what little energy she had repeatedly removing these small treasures from our hands and pockets.

We slept on the floor, and early the next morning, Dad found us a motel room and we moved in.

Later that day, Dad went to the meat-packers union to inquire about securing a job. But the news was bad. "Your status and pension are non-transferable," a California union staff member informed him. "And most Hebrew National positions are being given to our long-standing local members first."

"What?" Dad shouted. "But they promised me! I would have never left New York if this was the case!" He had unwittingly forfeited many of the important benefits on which he had counted. He had uprooted his family from a decent home, relatives, and a paying job with benefits … for this! He felt foolish for having believed the wrong people. But there was no time for wallowing.

Unable to get through to the head of the Hebrew National plant by phone, he ventured down there in person on the bus. After sitting on a folding chair for half the day waiting for him, he finally spotted the man and hurried over to him. "Mr. Shoenfeld, do you remember me?" he began, and, before the gentleman had an opportunity to answer, he continued, "The union said that they are giving your new positions to their regular men first. If you hire me, I will be your best worker. Just give me a try, please!" Mr. Shoenfeld, paused and looked at the humble, yet self-assured man before him and was impressed. He nodded his head. And Dad was hired … just like that. Dad took Mr. Shoenfeld's hand and shook it hard.

With the promise of a dependable paycheck, Dad found us a small rental home. It was an older wood structure with a minute front porch. The house had two bedrooms and a combination breakfast room-family room-living room in which we spent most of our time. My parents hoped this home would be temporary.

I had mixed emotions about coming to the West Coast. I was only six and I liked California and the warm summer weather, but I also missed New York. I missed the park that sat just outside our brownstone apartment's window. I missed the towering sky scrapers I had grown up staring at. My Uncle Isaac was sometimes heavy handed, but he was my Uncle and now we wouldn't be seeing him or my only and favorite cousin, Barry. But I was young and quickly adapted to the bright new world around me.

On August 30, 1960, three months after our arrival, Mom's labor pangs began and she was rushed to the hospital. A few hours later, Steven Poltzer arrived. A large baby with tight curly hair, his coloring was light like Shlomo's and Shirley's, who took after Mom; only I had seemed to have taken after my father's side of the family.

"Mrs. Poltzer, I'm sure they've told you this before, but it is our strong opinion that you should have no more children," the doctor told her bluntly as he looked over her medical record.

"My husband forced me!" she told them, "I had nothing to do with it."

The doctor, a youngish man dressed in white with a stethoscope hanging from his neck, smiled, thinking that she did not appear to be the kind of woman who would be forced into getting pregnant against her will. But that was Mom's way; when things were going well, it was her genius, but when things were not, it was Dad's doing.

Dad worked harder than ever, and with all the overtime earnings, Mom slowly was able to fortify their nest egg.

We lived in the house until Steven was a year and a half old. Then, Mom received a letter from the landlord stating that the owner needed the house back. Surprisingly, Mom was thrilled. Although she had learned her way around the neighborhood, she longed to leave this part of town, mostly to distance herself from Dad's half-sister.

They decided to follow the migration of other Jews to the Fairfax district, near Hollywood.

THE HOUSE ON LA JOLLA

After an exhaustive search, they bought a decent-sized Spanish-style residence on a street named La Jolla, with rounded archways, a clay tile roof, a fireplace and an ample backyard on a quiet street. The neighboring houses had children a-plenty to play with and schools were within walking distance. The Poltzer had found a home.

In Mom and Dad's bedroom, Steven's crib rested against the wall. Shlomo got his own room, and Shirley and I inhabited the third bedroom. We all shared the single bathroom.

There was a small guest quarters attached to the detached garage that they planned to rent out.

My siblings and I cared little about the house itself. What mattered to us was the wonderful backyard. It had a banana tree and an established lemon tree that we loved to climb. I sat in that tree for hours at a time, gazing at the rooflines and tree tops. I could peer into the neighbors' yards and listen in on the neighbors' conversations. I could watch my brothers and sisters play and I could hear the birds singing in the trees. The yard also featured a metal swing set and a driveway perfect for tricycles and roller-skating. It was our idea of paradise.

As soon as we moved in, Mom got busy furnishing and decorating our new home. She scanned the newspaper for furniture sales and found a gold-colored couch with a loveseat she liked. She kept them looking fresh and new by covering them in plastic, going so far as to have a permanent wooden fence built to separate the living room from us kids.

Nina, the last Poltzer child, was born on July 8, 1962. At this point, Mom allowed the plentiful supply of siblings to act as pseudo-mothers. Shirley especially relished taking care of Nina who, like her, was very beautiful with fair, wavy hair. She thought of her little sister as her own personal living doll, dressing her and wheeling her around in her carriage.

As the Poltzer family now boasted five children, Mom had to be creative about finding ways to keep us entertained. The Zoo was one of our favorite outings, as was Knott's Berry Farm. There was no entrance fee so we went there often and we learned how to make our limited attraction tokens last a long time. But the highlight was summer camp.

We were each sent away for one session, but they were staggered throughout the summer break with no two children attending the same camp or being away for the same period of time.

I was sent to a sleep-over camp located in Griffith Park. Each morning at seven, the other nine girls in my cabin and I woke to the recorded sound of a bugle playing reveille. We hurried off to the dining hall, where they fed us powdered scrambled eggs, bowls of assorted cereals and toast with jam. Our bodies fueled, the balance of the day was filled with swimming, non-stop activities, craft making and hikes. In the evenings, we sat around the campfire pit with our colorful lanyards and sang camp songs. It was heaven. There was something about being at camp I loved. Maybe it was the opportunity to be my own person, far from home and away from my siblings. But those seven days each summer are among my happiest memories. When the day came for me to be picked up and taken back home I often cried, wishing I could remain there longer.

Summer always ended much too soon for us, but just in time for Mom. She definitely needed a little break from us after a full house all summer and looked forward to the beginning of the school year.

Mom had never learned to drive so we all walked to school. I usually made it to my assigned seat just as the final bell rang. I had a small pencil case with my pencils fully sharpened and a rectangular pink eraser. My seat was up close to the front due to my poor eyesight. Like most children, I liked some parts of school and others not so much. I wasn't very good at math, but I enjoyed reading and writing. I was a bit of talker and often got into trouble for speaking during class. Although I wasn't especially studious, I always finished my homework well ahead of time—not because I was a hard worker, but because I enjoyed the satisfaction of having the job done.

During these early years in Los Angeles, Shirley and I were close. She was my shadow. When the Santa Ana winds came blowing through and the branches from our lemon tree scratched on our walls at night, she would climb into bed with me and we would fend off those night-time monsters together. When Shlomo would play unusually rough with me, Shirley would come up from behind and pop him one on his head. However, despite our closeness, the seeds of a sisterly sibling rivalry began to take root early.

When we first moved into the house on La Jolla, Shirley and I shared bunk beds. She slept on the bottom and I slept on the top bunk. But soon the beds were separated. I took the side of the room with the door to the hall and Shirley got the side with the window. Such close quarters were a fertile breeding ground for disharmony. In an attempt not to acknowledge each other's existence, one day we decided to split our room in half, each living solely on our own side of the room. We taped a blue ribbon down the center between the two beds. Shirley's side was neat and uncluttered, her bed sheets securely tucked in under the mattress, her stuffed animals arranged on her bed and her clothes folded and carefully placed in the dresser. My side, in contrast, was scattered with piles on the floor.

Dad was the disciplinarian in the family. Once, when I refused to allow Shirley out of the bedroom (which would have involved her crossing into my territory), I knew I was in for it. Dad wasn't home for more than a moment when I heard, "Jaclyn!" His voice was so loud it reverberated off the walls. I knew what was coming and my answer was chock-full of expletives.

"Don't talk like that!" he yelled at me. His foot steps were thunderous as he approached. Within a second, he pulled the belt from his pants, the whooshing sound it made as it slid through the belt loops filling me with dread. Then he folded the brown leather in half and snapped it as a warning.

The chase began; he was quick, but I was younger and faster. We started with a few laps around the dining room table. I had felt the sharp sting of that belt many times before and had prepared for this eventuality. Weeks earlier, after a previous altercation, I had removed the screen from my bedroom window. So when my father came roaring down the hallway, I simply flung the window open and leaped out and away. A quick sprint to my bike and I was off. I biked around the neighborhood for a few hours, and when I felt enough time had passed, I returned. My father was usually asleep by then and all was forgotten by morning.

Dad's form of physical discipline sometimes disintegrated into all-out violence. Chairs were knocked down and broken, doors slammed, and every once in a while, Mom appeared with a new black and blue bruise on a leg or foot. Mom also had her own ways of inflicting pain on us. There was the *Knip,* a pinch with a twist, or her method of hair pulling, which involved selecting hair follicles from the tender location on the backside of your head, nearest your neck. She would pull them, lifting you ever so slightly off the ground. It was very effective. But her most successful method was to cry, slowly pulling at her shirt in despair until the buttons popped off.

"NO!" we would cry out, stopping whatever we were doing immediately. Nothing was more terrifying than seeing our mother so out of control that she was tearing at her own clothing. She didn't use it often, but her special weapon never failed.

A few years passed and Shlomo graduated to Fairfax High School while I advanced to Bancroft Junior High. Shirley, Steven and Nina now attended elementary school together.

Shlomo reached the benchmark age of sixteen, when young people in California reached the first rung on the ladder of adulthood and got behind the wheel of a car. He studied hard and passed his written and driving exams for his California driver's license on his first try.

Before Shlomo became our extra driver, we had to walk two miles to the nearest Safeway supermarket, alongside Mom as she pushed the stroller with a young Nina, and then lug bags of groceries back home. Mom always tried to make the walk pleasant by singing camp songs and recounting humorous tales about her time in the forest.

"Mom, didn't you miss your mother?" I asked, trying to understand what that loss must have been like.

"Yes, but there were thousands of people who were killed," she answered. "And if thousands were being killed, I could bear the loss of my family."

"That doesn't make sense, Mom." I countered, knowing that that could not be true. "What else happened?"

We had heard plenty about the Holocaust in school and it differed greatly from what Mom had been telling us. Most of the time, her stories recounting her partisan experiences sounded almost fun. We knew she was editing her stories for a younger audience. Other times she'd change the subject, always carefully avoiding telling us about any of the wretchedness she had endured.

Now, whenever the family car was available, Shlomo would do the grocery shopping. His fee for this service was his own stash of food. With five children, our favorite snack foods went quickly, so he hid his collection of Twinkies, Snowballs and sugary cereals in his closet and ingested them in secrecy in his room.

Steven and Nina, in their first years in elementary school, tried their best to find their way. Nina was the one above-average student among all of us, but she and Steven seemed to have trouble with bullies on the playground. They were small, slender children, unable to fend off bigger kids who pushed the younger, weaker ones around just for laughs. When Steven and Nina began coming home and telling Mom that the bullies were shoving them around, it confirmed Mom's belief that family was everything, that the outside world was our enemy and could never be trusted, and that we needed to protect each other from strangers at all costs.

Shirley was small and not a fighter, so she was not much use in protecting her younger siblings and neither was Shlomo. Once we were on a family excursion, driving in our 1955 green Ford station-wagon, Shirley was seated up front, near our father while Mom was in the backseat with the rest of us. Shlomo was in the seat that was most easily reached by Dad's angry hand. Inevitably sometime during that drive, somebody in the car started an altercation by sitting too close to an imaginary boundary line or making a face that someone else did not like, and soon everyone was screaming or crying. First Dad yelled and when that did not work – as it rarely did – his fist, now tight as a ball, attempted to make contact. Shlomo, as usual, got the brunt of Dad's rage. This violence took its toll. Upon entering high school, Shlomo became more serious, quiet, and withdrawn.

Instead, he unfortunately became Mom's personal confidante. She routinely sat with him, spewing out poison about Dad—how he was never to be trusted, how he was a chameleon, willing to side with any stranger if and when the need arose. But in the same breath, she'd describe him as a clairvoyant, which in Dad's case wasn't a compliment. He knew, in advance, that when he loaned the money to Isaac for his property Isaac would never pay it back, causing Mom to forever lose her brother. However, she would often end her tirades by confessing how she could never imagine living without him.

Shlomo also got to hear about her troubles with raising children. She spoke of how stifled she felt and that she wanted to get a job to become her own person. But Nathan vetoed that idea. He was a traditionalist and demanded that his wife stay home cooking, cleaning and raising their children.

This was a lot for an adolescent son to hear and try to understand. A disproportionate amount of responsibility rested on his young shoulders and he took this role seriously. No longer a child, but not quite an adult, he found himself in an awkward no man's land.

Shlomo had long been put in a position to intervene on adult matters, even getting involved when Mom became pregnant with Nina. Even Mom had been unsure about whether or not to go through with the pregnancy. Already knowing Dad's opinion and having no girlfriends to talk to, she discussed it with Shlomo. "What should I do?" she cried to her young son. It was wrong putting him in that role, but Shlomo treated her question with full adult consideration.

"Keep the baby," he told her.

As a result of absorbing all those demands on his emotions, Shlomo became increasingly withdrawn, nothing like the boy in New York who chased Shirley and me around the park, threatening us and subjecting us to head noogies. Mom and Shlomo's close bond had not gone unnoticed by Dad, and he was made to feel like the odd man out sometimes. Mothers should not confide in their children concerning so many personal things, he thought to himself.

Since Shlomo and Shirley would not fight physically, I took on that role. Going to the playground after school to assault child tormentors became part of my job description in the family.

I left my school early one day and made my way back to my old elementary stomping ground, making sure I was there as the final bell rang. I located my siblings, who pointed out that day's perpetrator. "You can go home now, I'll fix it," I told them. Casually I strolled around the playground and when the teacher walked out of view, I grabbed the young delinquent and shoved him down on the ground, hard. The asphalt was hot and the small irregular surface cut into his exposed skin. "If you ever look at, smile at, talk to or touch my brother or sister again, I will come back and kick the holy shit out of you, and if you tell the principal or any of the teachers that I was here, I will come back and really beat the crap out of you," I told him quickly and then I was gone. It took a couple of visits, but the thugs moved on to other children and left Steven and Nina alone.

As Shirley and I grew older, we became too argumentative to share a room. It finally came time to enlarge our home. Three bedrooms for a family of seven simply wasn't enough. So Mom and Dad decided to renovate and add on another two bedrooms and a bathroom.

I loved the prospect of having my own room. I chose the stylish carpeting statement of the day: long, thick, shit-brown shag, the kind you needed to take a rake to so it would stand up tall. Lavender was my choice for tile for the bathroom walls and shower stall. The ceiling was made of the new, trendy, cottage-cheese texture, and Mom and Dad spent a little extra and ordered us the style with flecks of shiny stuff sprinkled on it. The rooms were painted off-white to start with, but about every six months or so, I would go to the local paint store, pick up some paint and cover the walls in a brand new color.

In lieu of a conventional bedroom set, I decided I wanted a kind of apartment feel, so I selected a convertible couch for my bed. It was sculpted, camel-colored Herculon. By day, it served as a couch for my friends and me, but by night, my dog Bella and I called it our bed. My parents then surprised me with a fabulous RCA console record player. It was made of solid oak and had built-in speakers. I never allowed anyone to use it except Shlomo. He instructed me that when you handled your albums you always held them by their edges, that you never stacked them on the turntable, and that it was imperative to change the turntable needle religiously. I coveted my collection of records, repeatedly listening to the Beatles, Three Dog Night and Credence Clearwater, but I often fell asleep to Blind Faith, whose music featured a series of vocals set against organs and drum solos that I especially loved.

RUM, VODKA & GIN

During all these years, Dad had continued working for Hebrew National. In between carving meat close to the bone and lunch breaks, he began a friendship with a Hungarian man named Morris. They were both tired of working in cold lockers and waking up before the sun rose while all the higher-ups made all the real money, so they decided to go into business together. As they began looking for an opportunity, Dad purposely avoided mentioning his discussions to Mom. She did not like change of any kind and would not have supported him.

After about two months of searching, Dad and Morris came upon a liquor store, listed for $69,000. It was a good business located in the heart of downtown Los Angeles, strategically positioned near a major university with a built-in clientele of young drinkers. The price was high, but otherwise, it looked like a solid bet.

"I'd take it for $36,500," Dad said in jest.

"Sold!" the seller told a flabbergasted Dad and Morris.

Now it was time to break the immense, life-changing news to his wife. "What!" Mom shouted in disbelief. "Who is Morris?" she yelled. "What do you know about running a liquor store?" she asked. Her mind quickly sailed to the land of catastrophe. She had been so happy with the way their life had been, and she hated the idea of this stranger becoming part of their lives. They argued about it for days.

Then one day the door bell rang and Mom went over to the window and peered out through the slated glass panes. "Can I speak with Nathan?" a man asked in a heavy Hungarian accent. She knew that this small, balding, clean-shaven man must be Morris. Not bothering to invite him inside, she announced his arrival to a slumbering Nathan.

From that point forward, Morris came over every day. And each time, Dad stepped outside to speak with him. Mom felt totally excluded. Of course, she could have corrected this by simply inviting Morris inside and listening to what they were saying, but she and Dad had not had anyone over for years.

They continued to discuss the liquor store issue the Poltzer way, with flying furniture and walls that trembled from arguments that could be heard for blocks. In the end, despite Mom's rudeness to Morris, her anger and hurt, she agreed to go to the bank, take out the money Dad had given to her, which she now considered "hers" and give Nathan the money so the deal could go ahead. In truth, Channa was less concerned about this stranger than she was about the possibility of Dad becoming successful and leaving her for *someone better*. By keeping him as a lowly foreman in a meat locker, she was assured he would stay with her. As a business owner, on the other hand, he would be exposed to people, more money, and the opportunity to meet someone else.

P & S Liquor Store, as they named the enterprise, became Dad's life. He prized that small storefront business. Dad blossomed there, greeting regulars each day and cracking jokes. He learned to speak fluent Spanish and even picked up Jive. He lovingly made sure that the shelves were neatly stocked and that the windows and the sidewalk out in front were sparkling. He finally had something that gave him a sense of pride.

He and Morris alternated night shifts, but on those evenings when Dad did not work, he would drag any family members who did not have plans for the night or were too young to stay at home alone back to the liquor store. There, Dad and his kin would sit in the car and watch the store. As happy as this partnership seemed, Mom and Dad couldn't get over their feelings that Morris might be stealing from them. There had been no signs of it, but, then again, Morris was a stranger—and Mom couldn't overcome her lifelong history of not trusting any strangers.

While Dad flourished as a result of his time in the store, Mom withered. She became increasingly insecure in Dad's absence. "I bet women come into that store" or "I bet Morris is talking Dad into leaving me," she would say to us almost daily. She felt isolated and lonely. Her children were growing up. We all had friends with whom we could spend time, but Mom had no one.

For a brief time, she worked at a nearby confection shop. She enjoyed the job, but two of her children were still young enough to need her at least part of the time, so it wasn't ideal. The house was often a mess and dinner was not always on the table. "Nothing to eat again?" Dad complained. Her working was not making it any more enticing for him to come home earlier, so she quit the chocolate business, and again became Mom, the lonely housewife, awaiting Dad's return at the end of each day.

When I turned sixteen, I found my own focus shifting away from family. All of us were in such different stages of our lives, and I related better to my friends than to my sisters and brothers. I was a social creature, lucky to have a tight-knit clan of friends, with whom I started to share and do everything.

The age schism between Shirley, Nina, Steven and me felt unbridgeable. When you are in your teens, how could you actually expect your infantile sisters and brothers to understand your issues and needs? My small, loyal clique of friends—Leah, Cheryl, Freida and Lorraine—understood me far better. I'd met Leah in gym class. We stood beside each other while our teacher, Mrs. Leonard conducted role call. As she painstakingly attempted to pronounce all the refugees' last names, the two of us struck up a conversation. Over the coming weeks, the other three girls were incorporated into our very tight-knit five-some.

Freida belonged to a Jewish youth group, named B'nai B'rith, and talked the rest of us into joining as well. It was mainly a way for Jewish girls to meet Jewish boys and it seemed proper enough that our parents were pleased for us. The various chapters, as we called them, were grouped together by sex, school affiliation and age. Our Chapter was called Fidelity, and we had meetings on Wednesday nights. During these meetings, we mainly discussed when and where our next social-- parties arranged between a girls' group and a boys' group—would be.

At sixteen I found Jewish boys totally unattractive, awkward and clumsy. I yearned for blond haired, blue eyed surfer boys. The socials were typical for our age: boys and girls glancing around the room, chatting awkwardly, with the more confident boys approaching the more provocative girls, thus providing the less adventurous participants with something to talk about. Although I never found what I was looking for, I always had fun with my friends.

In between these monthly socials, we spent our Friday and Saturday nights at Bob's Big Boy, a mecca for local teens, checking out the guys who were there checking out the girls. The parking lot was the most fun. We had done our homework and knew the models, the designs and the approximate monetary values of all the cars. Yes, we were superficial, but no more than the guys who cared only about cup size. Mediocre guys who drove hot cars graded as high as a hot guy with a mediocre car. Girls, I imagine, were graded on cuteness, bust size and reputation—the worse the reputation, the more dates she received. There was even a paper "Sex Test" that was passed around that inquired on all manner of lurid behavior.

> *Have you ever kissed the opposite sex?*
> *Have you ever French kissed the opposite sex?*
> *Have you ever gone to second base?*
> *Have you ever gone to third base?*

In those days, good Jewish girls did not do *any* of those things, but not wanting to be known as goody-goodies, we tweaked the answers to increase our scores – the racier the better.

Going to school and getting good grades was not important to Mom. College was never even discussed. It was understood that we were expected to be married by twenty. Mom's dated attitude put me in an awkward position.

"Mom, everyone is beginning to talk about college. What should I do?" I asked her one afternoon after school. My friend, Lorraine, had been going over college brochures and I was beginning to wonder what would happen to me after high school.

"Well, what are your friends doing?" Mom retorted.

"Most of them are going to junior college." I answered.

"Then do what they're doing," she answered. And for her, the issue of higher education was over. In her eyes, my education paled in importance compared to my marital status, or, in my case, lack thereof.

"If you want to catch a boy," she would tell me, "you need to look trashier." I gave her a sideways glance, uncomfortable about what she was proposing. "But never let them use you," she added. "Or, better still, just copy what your friends are wearing," she suggested. Mom really wanted to advise us, but seriously doubted her own decision-making abilities in this area.

After graduation, Freida and Lorraine left to spend the summer in Israel.

Leah, Cheryl and I remained behind and did little, except some high sierra camping while we waited impatiently for letters from our friends. We read and reread their flirtatious accounts of La Vida Loco and whirlwind romances.

> *Dear Girls, I have met a wonderful guy named Uri. He is everything I could have ever wanted. He tells me he loves me and I'm crazy about him. I am planning on returning next summer. Love Freida*

In the high sierras, we continued to have our own adventures, but black bears who pillage your food rations in national forests just do not compare with romances overseas with handsome strangers.

When summer was over, I still didn't know what to do with myself. Since my friends were all going to junior college, I decided to follow suit. I was toying with the idea of teaching school. During the middle of my first year, I met a man named Gal. He was casually dating Leah so I didn't really give him too much thought—at first. He was visiting America after finishing his stint in the Israeli army and was here to see what this country had to offer. He had light skin for a Middle Eastern man, with dark hair and green eyes.

As we spent more time around each other, it became increasingly clear that there was some spark. He spoke almost no English and in those early days, we conversed using a dictionary as our go-between.

At first, we got together to discuss the fact that we weren't going to be together—but it was clear even early on that this was just a pretext. During these meetings, we'd get a bite to eat and I'd help him decipher the menus. I explained to him how to cash his paychecks and sometimes helped him explain to the international operator that he wanted to call home to Israel.

Ever since I was little, I had helped others. I had fought my siblings' battles on school playgrounds and spoken on behalf of my parents when their English failed them. It was now Gal who needed my assistance and I slipped very easily into that role. The fact that he was handsome and virile had also not escaped my attention. This powerful combination fueled a mighty attraction on my part.

I was truly torn about Gal. I liked him a lot, but felt that only scum stole their girlfriends' boyfriends. But Gal was very insistent. Very late some evenings, Nina would run into my room, informing me that "That guy's outside in front of the house again!" I would pull the curtains aside and see him standing there beside his rundown car.

"Gal, please don't come here," I told him repeatedly, to no avail. I tried not to fall in love with him, but the chemistry was strong.

At first we dated secretly, while I tried to figure out how to break the news to Leah. But this kind of secret was hard to keep and she found out on her own. It was awkward and painful between us for a while, but the wounds eventually healed.

Once our relationship was out in the open, things began to move quickly. For the next few months, I saw Gal every day. After he finished work and I finished school, I'd hurry over to the apartment he was sharing with two other Israeli fellows. Over the course of the next two months, I got to see that Gal was a good man, a kind man—and someone I could see myself spending the rest of my life with.

It wasn't long before we started talking marriage and decided that a three-month engagement would be fine.

THE POLTZERS LET IN STRANGERS

We decided to get married in early June, which gave me little time to prepare. There was a location to select, a gown to purchase, a guest list to create, flowers to choose and many other incidentals to plan. And most importantly, Gal and my family began to spend time together. Dad liked him. He thought he seemed like a solid fellow who would work hard and provide for me, maybe reminding him a little of himself when he and Mom were young. Mom, on the other hand, was weary, speculating, "Maybe he's an Arab just trying to get a green card." I didn't pay any attention to her, as I knew in my heart that she was mistaken. My siblings seemed to like him. They made gentle fun of his poor, but slowly improving English and had endless questions about what life in Israel was like and what if felt like to shoot an Uzi.

Gal's parents congratulated us by telephone, but explained that they wouldn't be able to come out for the wedding, airline tickets to America being too expensive. This meant that the wedding planning fell entirely to my mother and me.

I had never even attended a wedding and had a lot to learn. The gown I selected was a traditional white, high in the neck and narrow at the waist with cap sleeves. It was adorned with tiny, white, appliquéd fabric flowers, which also lined the edges of my long veil. Gal rented a white tuxedo that was trimmed with a half-inch of black satin. His pants and bowtie were solid black, as were his shoes. He also planned on wearing a traditional white yarmulke or Jewish skullcap.

I did not have any hard and fast opinions on location, but knew that I did not want the ceremony to take place in a synagogue. Rather, I imagined my wedding procession taking place outside, with flowers and the sky above me. Finally, after much searching, we happened upon an older Hilton. The hall was just the right size and it opened onto a patio-styled garden. Beautiful magnolia trees spread their branches, and the rose bushes blossomed all around. Strings of twinkle lights were suspended above an elevated platform where I could picture us taking our vows.

The ceremony began at seven-thirty in the evening on June 9, 1973.

I carried my bouquet in my left hand and the white satin ribbons that bound the floral arrangement cascaded down the front of my gown. Mom and Dad walked me down the aisle. Then I was by Gal's side and beneath the wedding Chupah. No one uttered a word except the Rabbi. I stood there, not fully paying attention to him, looking around, first at Gal and then at my parents. Mom and Dad were smiling broadly. Gal smiled and gently squeezed my hand. I nervously smiled back.

Our ceremony was conducted entirely in Hebrew. I understood not a word of it until finally, the Rabbi turned to me. "Do you take Gal to be your lawful husband?" he asked in English.

I smiled. "I do."

The rings were exchanged and then Gal's foot came crashing down upon a wrapped glass.

"Mazel Tov!" everyone shouted and Gal kissed me.

At the reception, Gal and I made our way to the dance floor. I had selected for our first dance a favorite 70s pop song of mine that seemed very appropriate: Gary Puckett's *This Girl is a Woman Now*. Neither Gal nor I were very good dancers, but we swayed blissfully to the music without a care about how we looked to anyone else.

Our wedding ended sometime after midnight and we spent our first night as man and wife in the hotel's bridal suite. It was only then, with my ears still ringing from the loud music, that I realized I would not be returning to my room on La Jolla tonight, or any other night..

I walked around the room, looking at my gown as it lay on the chair, considering my new name and identity. Much as I loved Gal, I didn't want to let go of my role as a Poltzer daughter and sibling. As I sat there gazing at my new wedding band, I consoled myself with the idea that I wasn't giving anything up, but just needed to adapt to playing more than one role—that of Gal's wife AND second-born Poltzer at the same time. Little did

I know then how those multiple loyalties would be tested in the future.

Gal and I would have preferred to go somewhere exotic for our honeymoon, but money was tight, so it was Lake Tahoe for us. We drove there in an aged Plymouth four-door Mom had given me. She still feared Gal was a green-card digger and switched my newer car, one she had given me for my sweet sixteen for the older one.

We stayed at Tahoe's glorious Rolling Dice Motel. The rooms were decorated in a disheartening mix of browns and we could hear the neighbors having sex through the thin walls. I have always been extremely shy, and open sexuality was fairly new to me, so having to listen to that commotion all night was very unsettling. Hardly a romantic paradise, but we muddled through, and I was just happy to have Gal by my side.

We tried visiting casinos, but the experience did not go well. I was never able to fool the security into believing I was twenty-one, so I was evicted several times. But Gal made it up to me by cutting our stay in Lake Tahoe short and taking me on an unplanned detour through Yosemite for our two final nights. We had no camping gear, so we stayed in one of the permanent tents the park offered to vacationers. The white canvas tent contained a full-size bed with linens and wool blankets.

In the morning, when the sunlight hit the tall sequoias, the air filled with a piney freshness. The fragrance of fellow campers frying up bacon and eggs filled the air. Blue Jays were out searching for food, and a small band of deer gently strolled about. Granite walls towered all around us and the roar from Yosemite Falls echoed off them. The Merced River that ran through the center of the park enticed swimmers and inner tube enthusiasts to make their way into the water. We hiked and rented bikes and had lunch among the tall trees. It was the most beautiful setting in which to experience our first happy days of marriage.

After the honeymoon, we headed to our first home together, an apartment in Hollywood. I had decided there was no point in continuing my aspirations of becoming a school teacher since it would take me at least three years to earn my credentials, and by that time, I planned to already be a mother.

Settling into married life had its ups and downs. I had never lived on my own and all of a sudden I found myself the lady of the house, responsible for all the cleaning, cooking and laundry. It was a little lonely while I waited for Gal to come home, so I spent a lot of time on the phone with Mom and my friends. Gal didn't like my dependency on my Mom, but could do nothing to stop it. As we spent more time together at home, we slowly found our way to each other and I started to derive more strength from him.

Since I was not going to further my education, I needed to get a job. I visited an employment agency and was queried about my skills, which were few since I had only finished one year of junior college. Fortunately, I could type fast, so I managed to land a job as a receptionist at a noted mortgage banking company in the foreclosure department. I did not particularly enjoy dealing with the company's clientele – people who were bottom of the barrel and suffering from self-imposed insolvency – but a job meant a paycheck.

Gal worked hard, changing occupations whenever the opportunity presented itself. His first job was as a landscaper's assistant. He soon switched to something a little more promising; installing floors for a contractor he'd met. Almost effortlessly, he learned how to put in ceramic tile, linoleum and even hardwood flooring.

Gal worked with the contractor for two years before deciding he had made his boss rich enough and that it was time to open his own business. We had our business name, G & J Floor Covering Company, painted on the large picture window and filled the showroom with display racks of Congoleum and Armstrong linoleums and a vast array of carpet samples. And after covering the all-cement floor with a blue and white sheet vinyl, we were ready to open our doors for business.

Unlike Mom and Dad's business relationship, or lack there of, Gal and I decided we'd work together. I happily gave notice to the mortgage company where I had worked and, accompanied by Stella, a Doberman Pincher we had been given as a gift, spent many hours sitting in our store, doing the bookkeeping, legal work and general paper pushing. I welcomed customers who came in to look around, but it was Gal who brought in the bulk of the business. He was a natural sales person even with his limited English. G & J had a slow start, but the sales slowly picked up and soon enough, there were bound rolls of carpet lying across the floor with customers' names hot-glued to them.

Once employed, Shlomo decided it was time to move out of the La Jolla family home and into an apartment with a roommate. He returned often to visit Mom and Dad, often serving as an audience to their never-ending battles. He was hooked on the drama of it all and always felt that he could help *Juba* – or "pest" in Yiddish – as he lovingly called Mom, if she'd only let him.

Although Mom and Dad had a good life, they didn't seem to know it. Dad was always either at work or at home with Mom, but it was never enough for her—she remained convinced that he was always on the verge of leaving her. And she took all her angst out on him. Dad, for his part, poured everything he had into that business, leaving him little energy for her emotional outbursts. But they were both healthy, with the security of having money in the bank, and two children out of the house. It's only too bad they didn't get much pleasure out of the life they'd created.

One Saturday when Gal was off working, I drove over to La Jolla to see Mom. I was so young that I sometimes had trouble accepting what it was really like to be married. "He's always working Mom." I complained. "When I got married, I thought I would see him more, but it feels as though I see him less."

Mom, in her way, tried hard to counsel her children in all areas of life, love and marriage. I had much to learn and Mom always seemed to want to help me.

117

"First off, don't love him so much." She began, "Let him chase you." She looked around to make sure there were no prying ears. "You are hiding some money, aren't you? Because when you are old and fat, he will leave you and who will want you then?"

"Mom, that doesn't sound right." I questioned.

"Who is the chicken and who is the egg?" She countered. That was one of her favorite quotes. And I was left to make sense of her confusing, discouraging advice. Neither Mom nor I had any desire or intention of cutting those maternal apron strings. After all, I had known her much longer than I had known Gal. My husband was a recent addition to my life, while Mom was my blood. I just needed to keep learning how to dance in both worlds: that of loyal and dutiful daughter, always preparing for the worst, and that of my husband's equally loyal and loving wife.

But try as I might, Gal could sense my split loyalty and often questioned me about where I got my strange views on marriage. I never mentioned it was from my own mother, out of fear that he would hate her for her mistrusting outlook and strong influence on me.

THE NEXT GENERATION

One afternoon I ended my workday early so I could visit my mother.

"Mom," I announced while she busily prepared dinner for the family, "I'm going to have a baby!" I had already imagined her joy at my news and looked forward to her heartfelt congratulations—so her response came as a shock.

"No, you're not!" she shot back emphatically, continuing to press the metal blade over the outer skin of a russet potato. In her eyes, I was still her little girl and pregnancy was the realm of older, more mature women.

"Yes, Mom, I am!"

"No, you're not!" She announced emphatically again as she carefully cut away a dime-sized discolored bruise on the potato.

"Mom . . . I . . . am!" And this time I spoke the words more slowly.

She set the potato down on the well-worn wooden cutting board and looked at me. Then her eyes traveled south towards my belly, which did not yet show any hint of a bulge. "How do you know?"

"I went to the doctor and he told me."

A smile quickly blossomed upon her face. If the doctors had said it, it must be true. She grabbed me and gave me a kiss on my forehead. The next generation of Poltzers was on their way.

With our family on the verge of expanding, it was time for Gal and me to buy a house. "Be sure the house you pick is close enough for me to walk to," Mom instructed us. "I'll need to be able to come over every day and help you with the baby."

We searched for what the realtors called "a starter home," walking through scores of houses all around La Jolla's surrounding area. But the homes were small, without yards, and situated so close to the neighboring homes that I could often smell what was on their stoves for dinner. It appeared that a decent-sized house in Los Angeles was just going to be too expensive, so we expanded our search.

Sunday was the customary Open House day, when, without the accompaniment of a realtor, prospective home buyers were invited to open cabinets, peer into bathrooms and gawk at kitchens. During one such Sunday, Gal and I found a house that satisfied most of our requirements. It was a small but viable home with potential; it had a large yard and was located on a quiet street. But we were conflicted; it was in Encino, a suburb of Los Angeles, and about fifteen miles from La Jolla, certainly not within walking distance.

"Why did you look at houses so far away?" Mom complained, upset by what she considered to be an act of disloyalty. "If you buy a house in Encino you know you will be destroying the family. How can I watch my grandchild grow up if I never get to see him?"

Her statement had merit and I felt terrible. It was never my wish to destroy my mother's dream, but I simply could not deny the financial realities. "Just come out and *look* at the house we want to buy. It is so much bigger than anything we could get around you," I begged her, hoping that once she saw the house, she would understand our decision.

Our escrow instructions allowed us a final walk-through within thirty days of signing the final paperwork, so we asked my parents if they would please join us to take a look. "It's a long drive over and this is a weekend," my mother complained as we traveled along the freeway, heading towards the San Fernando Valley. "Do you have any idea how much longer the drive will be during the week?" she reminded us, already hating the house before she had even seen it.

As we pulled into the driveway, a grimace appeared on her face and stayed there for the duration of her visit. She and Dad looked into the kitchen and bathroom, sadly shaking their heads. Then they visited the backyard and their eyes fixated on the enormous untamed jungle of citrus trees that appeared not to have been trimmed in years. The weeds were knee high and partially obstructed the view of the property. "We don't like it," they said, plainly and simply. "Do you have any idea how hot it gets in the Valley in the summer?" Mom warned.

"Gal will fix everything up and he'll make it wonderful," I said, assuring both them and myself. Although I knew I could move ahead without her blessing, I desperately wanted her approval as we took this huge step. It would be so much easier for me if she could be supportive. Alas, no luck.

"Well, we won't help you with a dime if you get this house!" they threatened.

Back at our apartment, Gal and I discussed it, weighing all the pros and cons at length. "I don't understand why they are so upset," Gal said. "I am thousands of miles from my family; your parents are only a car drive away."

In the end, we decided we were willing to face Mom's wrath. So we signed the final paperwork, slid over a check that represented our life's savings, and closed escrow on the small fixer-upper.

The morning the house was ours, we brought in a rental truck and filled it with my camel-colored couch, prized stereo and our queen-size mattress. We stacked boxes containing all our possessions all around them. It took a full day, but we finally carried every last box into our new home and closed the front door. It was my first very own home and I was excited. Putting things exactly where I wanted felt immensely satisfying. Gal was a workhorse and I knew he would make it a wonderful home for us, and as I walked through the different rooms and hung pictures on the walls, I knew in my heart that those were my walls.

The house was a single-story California Ranch, with a porch and a bay window in one of the two bedrooms. The kitchen was prehistoric, still sporting a wall faucet that fed a white corner sink that matched the white painted cabinets. Both coordinated with a white free-standing semi-operable Blue Bonnet range. Unsightly cracked and chipped four-inch white ceramic tiles with blue corner trim represented the countertop and backsplash. Everything in the kitchen was due a remodel; in truth, the entire house needed lots of help.

Mom and Dad eventually relented and began coming over regularly. They never changed their opinion that we had purchased a fiasco, and since they believed that no one else in their right mind would ever want that house, they felt we were destined to be stuck there in the hot Valley for eternity.

With the assistance of friends, and occasionally a fifteen-year-old Steven, Gal replaced the existing cabinets with new ones of solid oak. He installed a new countertop of beautiful Italian ceramic tile with a matching backsplash that went all the way up to the cabinets. He brought in a new range and cook top and knocked down the wall that separated the laundry room from the kitchen, thus creating a viable cooking and eating area.

"What are you going to do about the dining room?" Mom asked during one of her visits, looking at the bare spot beneath the fabric Tiffany-style hanging lamp.

"Nothing yet," I answered. "We'll get something when we can afford it."

"Well, your father and I want to help you get your first formal dining room set . . . and don't you need bedroom furniture, too?" Mom offered. It was a generous and kind gesture, and one I accepted gratefully.

Much had transpired to change the Poltzer family over the past few years. With my marriage, a first grandchild on the way, Shirley's increasingly serious relationship with her high school sweetheart, and Shlomo's move to an apartment of his own, we were rapidly scattering in all directions. But we Poltzers still enjoyed spending time together and gathered regularly for special occasions of all kinds. Mom would cook up sweet Noodle Kugel with caramelized onions and raisins, warm Vichyssoise soup and Gefilte fish. On weekends, Gal and I had the family over for barbecues. These were relaxed and happy times, and even Mom seemed a little happier these days. Although Dad was still spending more hours at his store than she liked, she had other things to think about.

As pregnant women go, I was especially uneasy. There was a long list of things that could go wrong and I fretted about them all. One night I accidentally rolled over onto my stomach. I jumped up quickly, positive that the baby had been squished. I waited anxiously until morning to call my obstetrician and make sure everything was alright. When the dog jumped up on my belly another afternoon, I was back on the phone with the doctor, worried about the injuries the impact might have caused. Some people see a glass half full and some see it half empty; I see the glass shattered and feel the shards of glass cutting my feet.

In still more defiance of Mom's directives, Gal and I decided to go through Lamaze, a method of natural childbirth that touted pain management through relaxation and controlled breathing. I was terrified of needles and wished to bring my baby into the world syringe free.

"You won't be able to handle the pain of delivery!" Mom warned. She did not mean to frighten me, but earnestly felt that since she never had to endure the sober ache of delivery, I should not either. "Who told you about this . . . this nonsense? I was knocked out each time I had a child and you turned out alright."

"Mom, they do things differently now and I'm going to try and do this naturally," I answered back, trying to reassure myself as well as her.

Learning the gender of an unborn child was unheard of in the mid-seventies. So when it was time to ready the second bedroom for our new baby, we had no choice but to select an innocuous soft yellow for the room. A stuffed Pooh bear I had had since I had gone to Disneyland when I was about sixteen sat on a cushioned changing table, and we placed an unfinished wooden rocking chair by the bay window. Preparing the room for a little person I had yet to meet was an odd sensation. I already loved the child, even though I didn't know him or her yet. I tried to absorb what it would mean to be a parent— entirely responsible for another human being—but had no real idea what parenting would entail or how to prepare. I knew I could love, but hoped I would do a good job and give it all the love and nurturing I felt I had had at home. But the feelings were still so abstract, as the reality of the baby hadn't quite hit me….yet.

At night as I lay in bed, I stared at my belly. I often watched it protrude and retreat as my little soccer player ran laps and kicked imaginary balls. At eight months, Gal and I, armed with pillows, attended the Lamaze classes. We joined an assortment of women with bulging tummies, who slowly took their seats on mats scattered on the floor, and husbands, who seemed to be both excited and slightly embarrassed by having to practice breathing and back massages in public. As the next month and a half passed, our group of parents-in-waiting dwindled as more and more of them had their child.

The middle of July was just as hot as Mom had warned us it would be. It took a combination of air conditioning and portable-fan air aimed straight at me to help keep me somewhat comfortable. On one windless, stifling night, I tossed and turned, unable to shake the clammy feeling that hampered my slumber. To wash away the sweat, I took a quick shower and returned to bed. My stomach was bothering me and the discomfort seemed to have a rhythm to it, but I could not believe that this could possibly be what all the birthing hoop-la was about. Where was the unbearable pain I had heard about? So I did not say much to Gal ... at first. The next morning, after preparing him breakfast, I sat on the couch and gently mentioned in passing that I had been having pain all night.

"How often?" he asked, being a recent Lamaze graduate.

"I don't know, every hour ... hour and a half," I answered and started to give it more serious thought.

Gal quickly dialed the doctor's office and after speaking to a nurse told me that we needed to head to the hospital. I picked up my suitcase, and, suddenly, we were off. Upon seeing me waddle into the hospital, a nurse hurriedly came over and had me take a seat in a wheelchair. "First child?" she asked. I guess it was obvious from the stunned looks on our faces. "Then we'll have plenty of time to check in," she told us as she took a clip board out and began asking us questions. In the middle of providing my medical history, I started to feel a contraction coming. The pain grew, peaked and subsided. We completed the check-in procedure and I was assigned a labor room. So far, delivery was a breeze.

"I can handle this," I told myself proudly.

Hours passed. In between contractions, I watched a very young Nadia Comaneci tumble and flip her way into infamy during the 1976 Olympics. Infant monitors were hooked up to my body and I occasionally watched a red line zigzag across the screen.

The hours continued to tick by, and even though my contractions came and went like clockwork, I was not dilating very quickly. "I can't do this much longer," I admitted to Gal, having grown incredibly weary.

"Yes, you can, Jaclyn," he reassured me. I closed my eyes for a three-minute nap in between contractions and Gal stepped out of the room. A moment later, he returned and handed me a handwritten note that read:

> *Jaclyn, I am very gald you are going to give me a baby and I am sure you will be the bast Momy.*

He could have simply voiced his kind thoughts, but he wanted something that would lift my falling spirits. The spelling was a little off, but the sentiment was dear. I read it over and over, more confident than ever that he would be a terrific father. Then I carefully folded the note in half and placed it in my purse. Mom was wrong; Gal was a good man.

I had been in that hospital room since eight in the morning. Fifteen hours later, after an endless stream of contractions, I was drained. The doctor suggested that we do something to help move things along. "We can break your water bag and it'll jumpstart your labor," My eyes must have revealed my concern. "Don't worry, it'll be pain free," he assured me.

"Okay," I said, apprehensively.

Moments after breaking my water bag, the contractions started coming fast and hard. "Nurse!!!!!" I yelled, "I need drugs!"

A nurse hurried in, needle in hand, but by that time the contraction was finished and I reverted back to my plan to do this naturally. "I'm sorry," I told her. "No shots for me." She lowered her hand and left the room.

Another contraction overtook me and once again I roared, "Nurse!!!"

In she ran … again, and once again, I told her "No thank you."

I repeated my demands for sedation a number of times and finally begged her to ignore me when I called. "All right," she told me, "but I will keep checking up on you and if you change your mind I can give you something to ease the pain." Then she closed the door.

Several more hours passed and I could hear a woman down the hall pleading for someone, anyone, to take her out of her misery and kill her. I began to wonder if maybe she was going through premature labor and had not had a chance to learn any breathing techniques.

The hand on the clock struck three and the woman down the hall had long since stopped yelling. I felt alone, imagining that everyone had had their baby except me. Finally the doctor told me that the baby was in position and that I was sufficiently dilated. "It's time to have this baby," he said. The nurse whisked Gal away to be attired in a sterile hospital gown while an orderly pushed me in my rolling bed to the delivery room. On all sides stood shiny sterile machinery; the lights were blinding. They strapped me into position. I did not appreciate being tied down like an animal, but I was in too much pain to care. The contractions were coming almost continually at this point, and the urge to push suddenly became uncontrollable.

"Focus! Breathe!" Gal reminded me.

"Don't push till I tell you," the doctor told me sternly as he pulled on a pair of rubber gloves.

"It's coming out the wrong place!" I yelled out, feeling a strange sensation in an area of the body that I did not associate with delivery.

"Don't worry, the baby is just very low," he assured me. "Now we're ready. PUSH!" he ordered.

Each push demanded I locate some hidden strength in the bottom of my soul. When he said the head was coming out, I should have been happy, but, honestly, I was too tired. "Push!" he said again. All at once, the baby left my body and at 4:45 am,

July 9, 1976, a red-skinned, black-haired, little girl came into the world, weighing all of six pounds one ounce. The only sound was that of a new being bellowing out hello to the world.

I looked over at the tiny person and marveled. It felt strange – all of a sudden, just like that, I became somebody's parent.

Gal was ecstatic. After holding his daughter in his arms, he rushed away, quarters jingling in his pocket. He had many phone calls to make, regardless of the hour.

At about six o'clock in the morning, Gal finally went home to take a needed shower and to change his clothes. The baby had also left the room to endure a barrage of infant testing so I was left alone in the room. I should have tried to sleep, but I could not; I was wide awake, trying to come to grips with the fact that my life had forever changed.

"Little Mother, someone would like to see you," the nurse said softly as she came back into the room an hour or so later. I quickly looked around wondering *who she could be talking to*. Then I remembered: I was a little mother now! She handed me the little bundle and left the room. I held my daughter close and gazed down on her face. Her eyes were open and the noises she made were virtually inaudible. A hand had come loose from the receiving blanket and I studied her fingers. She was perfect.

"You belong to me and I belong to you," I told her. Everything was different now; I was forever bonded to this tiny bundle of pink and she to me.

Soon Gal returned refreshed and jubilant.

"What are we going to do about a name?" I asked. "Jennifer is a nice name, but it is so popular," I added. Gal was not paying attention; he was too busy staring at his daughter as he walked around the room in circles. "What do you think of the name Laura?" I asked Gal, repeating the name over and over again to myself.

"I like it, but I want her middle name to be Hebrew," he requested. "Hadar is a beautiful name in Israel." So Laura Hadar Bechor was the name we put on her birth certificate.

Ten o'clock was the beginning of visiting hours and my family had been waiting impatiently in the downstairs lobby since nine. At the stroke of ten, my door opened and everyone rushed in. Mom's face was euphoric. She kissed me, then gently took Laura and cradled her in one arm as she held one of my hands up to God with the other. Hitler had failed – the Poltzers had continued on!

Nina and Steven gently touched one of Laura's tiny toes. "She's so little," they kept repeating.

When it came time to return home a few days later, Gal drove especially slowly and carefully. We three were alone in the car now as a family for the very first time. "We're responsible for her now." Gal said proudly. Holding her on my lap (the infant car seat law didn't exist then), I marveled at how tiny she was. I was simultaneously thrilled and terrified by this adventure they called parenthood.

For the first few weeks following Laura's birth, the Bechor home seemed to have a revolving door. Many relatives and friends were eager to see her, but none were more in love with her than her grandparents. The simple act of watching her sleep innocently in her crib filled them with happiness. My mother even fought me for the honor of changing her.

I had been told not to take her outside until after her six-week check up. After that, though, Mom and Dad drove out to accompany me to witness Laura's first outdoor experience. It was almost September and the temperature tipped over a hundred degrees, but, somehow still fearful that the baby might catch a chill, Mom suggested that we dress her warmly. When almost every inch of her body was covered, the four of us braved the elements. Slowly and carefully, Mom pushed the yellow stroller a few blocks while Dad watched out for pot holes.

When we had exposed Laura to enough fresh air, we returned to the safety of my home. Tiny beads of perspiration covered Laura's face as we removed the multiple layers of clothing. Once she was safely tucked back into the comfort of her crib, the three of us plopped down on the couch, exhausted. I turned on the tea kettle and the three of us sipped sweet, weak tea and munched on cookies.

THE HOUSE AROUND THE CORNER

Having lived on La Jolla for fourteen years, Mom knew every walkway, window and door of every house within reach. She knew that homes in the neighborhood rarely if ever came on the market. But one morning, when she came to the corner of her block, she saw a "For Sale" sign in front of a home just three doors away from our family residence.

Shirley and her longtime boyfriend Eric had recently gotten engaged. Although most of us in the family weren't crazy about him, considering him dominating, controlling and intrusive, Mom was smitten. And after witnessing our move, Mom was determined to keep her other kids close by.

She hurriedly called Shirley, imagining that this would be a perfect home for her and Eric. Before they even had a chance to see it, Mom put down a ten thousand dollar deposit to ensure that no one else "stole" the house from under them.

She eagerly escorted them around the tiny house, studying their every facial expression. "So, what do you think?

"It's darling, Mom," Shirley exclaimed, and Eric chimed in enthusiastically.

Since Mom would never allow Shirley to live with Eric before they were married, Shlomo moved in temporarily.

As the wedding date approached, Shirley and Eric revisited the tiny house, suddenly noticing how full it looked with Shlomo's meager possessions. Sadly, they decided it was too small for them. Mom was disappointed, but decided that Shlomo would keep the house.

Eric and Shirley got married in late July. Although I was sure that Shirley could have found someone better, I knew how much she adored Eric and was genuinely happy for her. The service was long, but we all smiled as she welcomed the long-awaited wedding band onto her finger. Eric stomped on the covered glass as we all called out "Mazel Tov!" and then he kissed his bride.

A conspicuous absentee on this happy day was Shlomo. He could not stop feeling disquieted in his heart about his sister and her likely future. More than his other siblings, he had had a front row seat to Mom and Dad's dysfunctional marriage, and Shirley and Eric seemed to be living a re-run of our parents' lives. Mom, however, was overjoyed with Shirley's marriage to Eric, believing him to be a responsible and perfect match for her daughter. If Shlomo did not want to come, she was not going to try and stop him.

In the late seventies, housing prices went through the roof. Homes whose values had not moved in many years were now selling for three to four times their original price, and the climbing did not show any signs of stopping. Gal and I, recognizing the opportunity, put our house in Encino on the market. "Now is not the time to sell your home, Jaclyn," Mom warned us. "What if you sell your house for too cheap and can't get another? Just stay where you are; I'm used to your house," she continued. "Can't you be satisfied with what you have?"

"Why do you let her say those things to you?" Shirley asked me whenever she heard Mom.

"It's alright; I don't pay attention to any of it," I answered back, deceiving myself into believing I could allow her words to wick off me like water does off a duck's feathers.

"Yes, you do," Shirley informed me. Of course, she was right. Mom's words had made me begin to doubt our decision, but Gal remained confident.

"Don't worry, Jaclyn," he assured me. "This is the right time." As he'd predicted, the house sold within the month and we'd doubled our money within two years.

"I bet you sold it too cheaply," Mom scolded.

We raced to find another home. We finally found what we were looking for, another single-story ranch-style house, five miles farther out in the Valley, in an area called Woodland Hills.

Meanwhile, Shirley was trying to get pregnant, to no avail. She and her husband were both young and healthy and no one could understand what the problem was. It was during this time I learned I was pregnant with baby number two. While this was a wonderful moment in my life, I was torn about how to broach such a delicate and painful subject with someone who was having difficulties getting pregnant. There was no way of saying it without inflicting some pain on Shirley, but I wanted her to get the news from me and not Mom, and so I told her as gently as I could.

"I'm so happy for you," she told me in a voice outwardly happy, but barely masking the sadness and resentment beneath it. Shirley had always felt that she got the short end of the stick in the family. This had been true for years. When we were young and I received my first pair of reading glasses, Shirley wanted glasses, too. She was so eager to get her own that she lied at the eye doctor, ensuring that a pair of prescription eye glasses was ordered on the spot. This theme had come up time and again over the years in a variety of ways.

Months passed, and hope was beginning to fade, but Shirley finally got pregnant. Everyone was thrilled for her, and I was most of all, for it eliminated the awkwardness that I had felt for months.

While Shirley's first baby was not due for several months, I was nearing the beginning of my final trimester. Being pregnant the second time around was a much calmer experience. I no longer panicked every time I bumped my enormous belly.

Still dreading needles, I planned on having this baby naturally as well. When the time arrived they once again placed me onto the delivery bed and strapped my legs into position, but when they reached out for my arms, so they could be strapped down also, I pulled them back. "No!" I said, trying to suppress the urge to push. "I am not a cow!"

I pushed with everything I had and at 9:45 on the morning of December 4th, 1978 a five-pound, eight-ounce baby boy arrived. He was bluish in color with black, black hair and eyes.

We named him Ian. But his middle name was a major bone of contention. Gal's family originally migrated from Syria and he is what they call a Sephardic Jew. Sephardic Jews are permitted to name children after living relatives and Gal wanted to name Ian after his father, Jacob. But my parents were eastern European or Ashkenazi Jews, and naming a child after a living parent puts the evil eye on him and was therefore forbidden. "What about my father?" I asked. "That's not fair to him."

We came up with a compromise, Jay. It still sounded more like Gal's father's name than I liked, but it was the best we could do. Later I discovered that on any paperwork written in Hebrew, a language I could not read, Gal wrote "Jacob," so depending on the language, Ian's middle name is either Jay or Jacob.

Since the times of Abraham, male Jewish children have participated in a physical and religious bonding ritual, the Bris Milah (Covenant of Circumcision). The Bris signifies the link between God and his Jewish people, and in keeping with the Divine's specification, the Bris must occur eight days after a boy is born. I understood the issue about the covenant with Abraham and our commitment to God and all, but circumcisions are difficult. Although everyone assured me that the baby would not feel a thing during the entire procedure, the idea that someone was going to cut the foreskin off my precious baby's penis worried me. What if they were wrong and Ian in fact felt the pain? If the Moyal, a specially trained doctor's, hand slipped infinitesimally, my son would be marred.

Setting my concerns aside, I hurriedly located a reputed Moyal and began to work on getting my home in order for the event. There were many phone invitations to make and I needed to put together a brunch banquet to feed my guests.

On the scheduled morning, I was a nervous wreck. I made sure the dining room table was replete with platters of bagels, mounds of cream cheese and plentiful amounts of smoked salmon and whitefish. I set out a vast selection of Danishes and Rugulach and covered the Egg Challah that was yet to be blessed. I turned the coffee maker on and set out pitchers of orange juice and ice water.

Guests soon arrived and before I knew it the house was filled. Then a knock came from the door and the Moyal entered the house. Wasting no time, he began setting up, carefully placing his assorted medical tools by order of need. He called everyone into the area and the time came for me to hand off my little one to Gal. A chair was placed beside the Moyal for my father, who had been selected to serve as Sandek, or chosen person. It would be his job to hold my baby on a pillow while the rite of circumcision was performed. Within moments, I was whisked away to the bathroom by my mother and some others, hoping to be out of earshot of Ian's cries.

"This is the way it has always been done," Mom repeated as she squeezed my hand tightly. Then she excused herself to bear witness to the covenant. In reality the procedure took only a few moments, but it sure felt like hours. I could hear the faint sounds of my son's whimpers coming through the walls, and then, thankfully, I was called back in to retrieve my now official Jewish son. The sweet Manischewitz wine they had placed on the baby's lips in lieu of a numbing ointment must have done the trick because he slept through most of the party. My father regained his color after turning pale from watching the procedure up close, and Gal beamed, filled with fatherly pride.

With fatherhood on the horizon, Eric needed to start making more money. Up until that point, he had done a variety of odd jobs, drifting in and out of a variety of careers— working in his grandfather's liquor store, styling hair in a salon, and selling cases off illgotten cigarettes out of the trunk of his car— and had never really settled onto any one path. Now, he figured that since Dad and his own grandfather had done well as liquor store owners, he might as well give that a try as well.

A business broker showed Shirley and Eric a fairly successful liquor business in the Valley. It was located on a corner, and, according to the broker, had established a respectable presence in the neighborhood. Dad was of a different opinion. Fortunately (or unfortunately), a liquor store directly across from his business had also just gone on the market. "I don't know anything about the store you saw in the Valley, but I know that the one across the street from me is a real money-maker," Dad told them with authority.

Mom loudly countered the suggestion, as she intuitively knew Dad and Eric would not make good business neighbors. But Dad's judgment in this case bore more weight than Mom's sense of foreboding.

Eric was now a business owner and good sense would dictate that he would arrive at his business before dawn and leave late at night to ensure that everything ran smoothly. But that was not Eric's way. He felt that only stupid people worked their own businesses and that it was smarter to have assistants do all the grunt work. Angel, Eric's appointed manager worked an obscene number of hours. He not only ran the store, but also busily took inventory and filled out order forms for additional merchandise. Meanwhile, Eric spent virtually no time behind the cash register.

Late spring came, and on May 20, 1979, Shirley gave birth to a sweet baby boy. He had platinum blond hair and crystal-blue eyes – very un-Poltzerly physical traits – and she named him Garth. She had learned her lesson from my Bris and decided to have her son circumcised in the hospital to avoid the stress. And since Eric was only half Jewish, he agreed to her choice.

As nervous a first-time mother as I was, Shirley was that much more so. Prior to being allowed to hold the blond-haired boy, Shirley and Eric insisted that everyone wear hospital gowns and masks, which they had permanently *borrowed* from the hospital. But no one was allowed to hold him for very long.

Ian and Garth were only five months apart, but they could not have been more different, physically and in temperament. Ian had bone-straight black hair and dark eyes. He stood up and walked at nine-and-a-half months and was climbing on everything soon after that. Garth had creamy white skin, fair as could be, and curly blond hair, and refused to crawl. He found it was so much easier to motion towards something when he wanted to go and have others carry you there.

Shirley and I had a glorious time with our almost twin-aged children. I came over often and we'd sit and talk about everything baby as our children played on the floor. She was not bored when I spoke about feeding schedules and diaper rashes, and I was understanding when she talked to me about issues such as sleeping through the night or theories on dealing with colic. We'd often go to the Zoo together, me pushing a carriage for two children and Shirley pushing her precious baby boy.

Since the economic upturn was still in progress, Gal decided to try out his business wings once again. Although we lived in the San Fernando Valley and did most of our work there, we were still driving into the city every day to G & J Floor Covering. Tired of sitting in endless gridlock, we decided to close the strictly flooring business and open a total home design shop closer to home. Ever the pessimist, Mom cautioned us against trying to expand, and once again asked why we could not be happy with what we had. She had no confidence in me or Gal, figuring we had made it as far as we had out of sheer luck. In her eyes, expanding was tempting fate.

We decided that our new business would be set up differently. Instead of spending hours on his knees, eyes filled with sanding filament, Gal would sell and subcontract others to do the labor.

We found a good spot nearby and Gal set to work renovating it, creating out of plywood, nails and sweat a two-story showroom with two staircases, one leading to the plumbing department where we had round ceramic sinks and square hammered brass bowls, kitchen and bathroom fixtures and an assortment of toilets with regular and elongated seats. The other staircase led to the window and wall covering section, where an immense library of wallpaper and fabric books were available. He finished off the showroom by erecting a cherry wood, traditional-styled kitchen cabinet display in the front window, fully equipped with oversized sink, faucet, instant hot water spout and a built-in soap dispenser. We called our new endeavor Bechor's Home Designs and opened for business.

At first the liquor store Eric owned generated a very acceptable income, but then Eric began noticing inconsistencies creeping insidiously into his daily cash take.

Dad, on the other hand, had been paying close attention to Eric's business activities. He made it a point to wander over constantly and was disgusted at how that business had been allowed to deteriorate. When his words of wisdom continued to fall on death ears, Dad called Shirley.

Shirley grew tired of being the recipient of Dad's repetitive and intrusive phone calls and his incessant complaints about Eric and lashed back. "Dad, what do you want me to do?" she yelled back. "You know, this is really all your fault!" She scolded, no longer willing to be the victim and having transformed into the aggressor. "I wanted him to have a store out in the Valley, remember? That one on the corner, in the nice neighborhood – but you stopped us and convinced Eric to buy this loser!" Dad slammed down the phone, bouncing the receiver off the hook.

"I hate it when Dad comes over and yells," Shirley told Eric after Mom and Dad had left. Shirley was positive that Dad would now use this as excuse not to visit so often.

"I don't feel welcome," Dad told Mom, after she again asked him to drive her back over. "And I hate seeing Eric lying around the house when he's supposed to be at work."

In the meantime, Shirley had begun to get involved in real estate and pressed on with these ventures, doing what she needed to do to bring money into the household. She placed notes in the mailboxes of homes that appeared to be in need of a little refreshing, asking them if they would be interested in selling their property privately. One such letter paid off when the owner of one home, wanting out of that community, sold it to

Shirley for far below market value. The house sat on a huge lot and showed loads of possibility.

Shirley was gifted when it came to real estate and it was the money that she generated in the buying and selling of homes that ultimately provided her family with their true income. I was proud of her and her ingenuity.

Having children so close in age came with many fringe benefits; Ian and Garth had a built-in best friend in each other. Each time the major toy stores sent out their mailings of multi-page advertisements, Ian and Garth sat huddled together for hours, discussing and circling the many toys and video games they would be asking for when the next birthday or Chanukah arrived. There was always available space on a bed for an impromptu sleep-over, and these took place most weekends. A place setting was always quickly added to the kitchen table for meals and when one child went on a day trip to a fair or movie, the other one would surely be invited to come along.

One afternoon Garth, Ian and Laura were reclining on my family room couch watching cartoons. The kids watched intently as the animated fair-haired, over-muscled hero in skin tight male panties repeatedly vanquished the evil Skeletor, who looked pretty much as his name suggested. I had taken a moment away from preparing dinner to speak with Shirley on the phone. Garth stood up, taking a momentary break from the television show, and begin twirling. "Be careful that you don't get dizzy from spinning so much," I called over to him and continued my conversation.

Garth stopped his whirling, but the room continued rotating and in a split second he fell, striking the edge of the wood and glass end table with his head. "Shirley, come over NOW!" I told her, "Garth's hurt!"

Shirley came through the door in what seemed like moments, and when she saw her son lying there on the couch with a bloody towel hanging from his head, it took her breath away. "Why did you let Ian push Garth down!" she screamed as she gathered him up, intending to head straight for the emergency room. "Why didn't you do a better job of watching him? You've always let Ian pay too roughly with him!"

"Shirley, I was on the phone with you and I was watching Garth the whole time!" I answered back, a little indignant at the accusation. "Ian never got up from the couch; he was in a *He-Man* hypnotic trance. No one pushed Garth; he simply twirled around, got dizzy and fell down on the edge of the table. It's no one's fault!" But it did not matter what I said, she would never believe me. In her mind I had always turned a blind eye when it came to Ian and Garth's horseplay.

It took three stitches to close the wound. They attempted to keep the face scar free by bringing in a plastic surgeon to do the suturing, but Shirley could not get over the fact that I had allowed this to happen.

December arrived and it was time to celebrate Ian's fourth birthday. We could not have a party without Garth – he was Ian's other half – but Shirley was not sure she wanted him to come. Fortunately, Mom decided to intervene. "Shirley, Jaclyn is sorry. You need to bring Garth to the party. It's not good to hold a grudge against your sister," she told her, and Shirley apprehensively agreed to show up.

Ian's party was held at a pizza parlor that was popular with kids. When Shirley walked in with Garth, I could feel a cold blast coming from her direction. She hovered over Garth as he rode the black and white coin-operated hobby horse and stood beside him as he wolfed down the chocolate birthday cake. Garth had forgotten all about the accident, but even his curly blond hair could not hide the fact he was sporting a band-aid over his scar. Time would heal Garth's gash, but I began even back then to become concerned that nothing would ever fully heal Shirley's and my relationship.

Meanwhile, times had changed and Nina, unlike me, had headed off to four-year college, where she excelled academically. But it was not her brilliant grade point average that gave Mom great joy – it was the young man she had become involved with. She met Jeremy one afternoon while she was out shopping at a vintage clothing store.

Jeremy was the Jewish son of the heir to some substantial aluminum money. Their mutual chemistry was instantaneous and Nina was happier than she had ever been; she was young and beautiful and had this wonderful fellow in her life.

Although Nina was crazy about Jeremy, she thought that now might be a good time to attend college in Colorado. "It's only for one semester," she informed Mom and Dad.

"Are you sure now is a good time to go?" Mom asked. "Colorado is so far away and now you have this boy interested in you. I don't think this is a good idea!" But Nina felt confident about Jeremy and hoped that this separation would turn out like Shirley and Eric's love story. According to Shirley, when she and Eric broke up for a short time, the separation caused Eric to realize that there was a real possibility he might lose Shirley forever. This caused him to drive like a fool to Palm Springs, where she was vacationing, ring in hand, where he begged her to take him back. Oddly, that is not how I remember it happening. As I recall, Mom drove Shirley insane with all her talk about how she had made a huge mistake letting such a prized catch go. Shirley panicked and begged him to take her back – which he did. But from that day forth Shirley no longer held any power in the relationship. Clearly, we all choose to shape our memories to suit our own needs. In any case, Nina had high hopes that Jeremy would wait for her, and pursued her plan to move to Colorado for a few months.

September arrived and it was time for Mom and Dad to drive Nina to Colorado. Jeremy spent the night, on the couch of course, to ensure he would be there early enough to wish his sweetie farewell. His eyes welled up with tears, and as he held her close, he placed a letter into her hands. He had written about his deep feelings for her and how much he would miss her. "Don't read it until you're on your way," he bid her. Nina promised to call him weekly and then she got into the "Jew Canoe," as she called the family's Lincoln Continental, and left.

The sun had set by the time they drove through Utah and it was late evening when they finally pulled into the campus in Boulder, Colorado. After helping carry in Nina's luggage and kissing her goodbye, it was time for Nina to start studying and for Mom and Dad to head back home to Los Angeles.

For the first few weeks, Nina called Jeremy every night. She told him about Colorado, college life and how much she missed him. She also called Shirley as the close relationship they had formed while growing up had not been altered by distance. "So how's everything going between you and Jeremy?" Shirley asked.

"Every night he tells me how much he misses me and when I left he gave me the most beautiful love letter," Nina replied.

"Very sweet. Just remember that being apart and missing each other worked wonders for Eric and me."

When Nina first started dating Jeremy, she brought him around to visit Shirley and Eric often. Eric quickly recognized that here was a boy whose family had a great deal of money, and he became increasingly unwilling to share him with Nina.

As soon as she left for college, Eric began a telephone barrage. He got all chummy with the lonesome Jeremy and set about sabotaging their relationship. He casually but constantly discussed Nina's fidelity. She was far away, far away with boys, and perhaps a particular boy.

"Do you know something?" Jeremy asked Eric after being properly primed. "Is Nina dating?"

The fish had bitten the bait. "I don't know," Eric answered, utilizing well placed silences. "What do you think?"

Jeremy was not going to be made a fool of. He was young and handsome and decided that odds were good that his girlfriend was seeing someone else, so he made up his mind to begin dating, too.

Nina, totally unaware of what was happening back home, waited patiently in Colorado for the Shirley plan to pay off. Although she was being asked out constantly, she remained loyal to her Jeremy. But after a while, she began noticing that there was something different in Jeremy's voice when she would call. She had no idea what it might be or why she was sensing this.

Thanksgiving break was approaching and she was planning on coming home to join in at the family feast. It would be an excellent reason to see what was going on with Jeremy. "We'll pick her up from the airport," Shirley and Eric offered.

As Eric crammed her luggage into his trunk, he asked if she would mind if they stopped at the mall on their way home. "It's on the way," he explained.

"Sure," Nina answered, not thinking too much of it, although she found it strange that they were headed for a shopping center that was, in fact, very much out of the way.

They rode the mall escalator to the second floor and Eric strode out with purpose holding Shirley's hand. When they arrived at Theodore's, a trendy establishment which had cute clothes for men and women, they stopped. An especially pretty girl who was busy folding a batch of sweaters asked if they needed any assistance. Eric said no and then they just left. It was a peculiar detour, but Nina was too busy thinking about Jeremy to notice.

When Nina arrived home, she quickly dialed Jeremy's phone number. "How about we meet for dinner? I can't wait to see you," she told him, but Jeremy did not mirror her exuberance. She brushed his lackluster response aside, showered, perfumed and carefully dolled herself up. When Jeremy picked her up, she was perplexed by his aloof demeanor. "Hey, you're wearing a Theodore's shirt," she told him, trying to break the tension. "I was just there this afternoon."

"You were at Theodore's?" he asked suspiciously.

"Yes, why?"

"Nina, while you were gone, I began seeing someone," he stated, matter-of-factly and not particularly kindly. Nina went silent. Had she missed something? Was this not the guy that was

142

crying when she left? Wasn't he the guy that had written that beautiful love letter telling her about how wonderful she was and how much he would miss her? What could have happened to change his mind so drastically, so quickly? "You probably saw her at Theodore's today," Jeremy explained.

"Eric," Nina asked when she got back home that evening, "Did you know about this girl Jeremy has been dating?" She waited for a moment and thought. "Did you have anything to do with it?"

"With what?" he answered in an innocent tone of complete denial, averting Nina's gaze. She was devastated; she had had such high hopes for the two of them and now was totally blind-sided.

"See, this is because you went and left him!" Mom scolded Nina. "What makes you think you will ever get another man now? Men like young women and you're getting older each day." Nina now felt doubly bad; she was reeling and could have used a sympathetic shoulder to cry on, but Mom was not about to *reward* Nina for making what she considered to be bad decisions. In her heart, Nina began to panic.

The band-aid had long since come off Garth's head, and Ian and Garth slowly returned to their pre-injury routine. Ian again went on outings with Shirley, and Garth resurrected his weekend sleep-overs beside his cousin. Shirley and I did not speak about the occurrence. There was no need, as I knew she would never change her belief about what happened and I remained hurt that she doubted my honesty. We simply pushed the matter under the rug, hoping it would fade away.

Shirley had baby number two on April 16th, 1984, during the Passover holiday, and they named him Jeremy. It was an inappropriate choice, but Shirley felt that the Jeremy/ Nina issue was dead and it was such a nice name. Although Shirley had hoped for a girl this time, she was thrilled with her baby boy.

A CHESTNUT GELDING

Meanwhile, Bechor's Home Designs was doing well, and I continued doing the bookkeeping while the children were in school. With nobody in the family scheduled to get married and no babies on the way, there seemed to be a lull in activity and I decided to do something special for myself. I had been in love with horses since I first saw a dark bay horse run across the screen on television back when I was in a little girl. In my young teens, I had forsaken my classes more than once to run off with my girlfriends to the stables wedged up against the famous Hollywood sign. We would rent some poor overworked quarter horses and ride through the Hollywood hills bareback, trotting and galloping beside freeways and up and around mountains. Finally, I decided that it was time to get my own horse.

Anyone who has ever purchased a horse without the good sense of getting some experienced help can tell you it is a recipe for disaster, and my first experience was no better. I had gone to a horse trader who had been recommended by the National Arabian horse association. I was honest with the fellow, which was a huge mistake, admitting to him that I was an advanced beginner. I had read all the books and knew what I was supposed to do, but the horse trader had read his horse trading book also. He hand-walked a gorgeous, although totally unbroken, chestnut Arab with a white star and stripe on his face past me to a small pen and unlatched his halter. The horse raced free, carrying its tail high. He ran around and then stopped short, snorting and tossing his head. And (what a surprise), this horse just *happened* to be in my price range. Then the horse trader did not say another word. He did not have to—he could see the look in my eyes. I could not wait to give him my money and take this magnificent creature home, or rather, to a boarding facility in Griffith Park.

This beautiful Arabian gelding, which I named Cayenne, proceeded to buck me off weekly whenever I tried to ride him in the stable's enclosed ring. He particularly enjoyed stopping short and spinning away quickly. "I hate coming to see you ride, Mommy," Laura told me. "All you do is fall off."

I got the message and decided to place myself and my young horse into full training with the boarding facility's trainer. Each month I wrote a check to this gentleman who had been riding horses since he could walk. He would then ride my horse five days a week. In addition, he had his young protégé, a lad in his early teens, work my horse at a walk, trot and canter. Neither man had any trouble, but whenever I stepped up into the saddle, a few times weekly under their tutelage, I failed. The horse knew I was up in that saddle. He could sense my fear and took full advantage of me, bolting off, spinning and refusing my simplest of requests. This horse was much too much horse for me, but still I persevered.

Eventually, when I caught myself thinking up excuses why I should not come and ride, and after hitting the ground for the umpteenth time, I knew it was time for this horse to go. I put Cayenne on the market.

I did not ride again for a while, questioning whether horseback riding was in the cards for me. Mom had always hated it and reminded me constantly about all the injuries I was bound to sustain if I continued this nonsense, but horses were in my blood and a few months later, I decided to give the equine world another chance. I found an instructor who specialized in frightened beginners.

Cliff was a retired stuntman. We worked together for some months and on those days when terror had me in its grip he would tell me jokes – some clean, some not so clean – or point to the red-tailed hawks in the sky and distract me with facts about them. When the time seemed right, we began discussing getting me a horse.

Cliff and his wife Jean journeyed to New Mexico each spring armed with a list of needed horses for customers and my name was now on that list. "I found you one," he told me by telephone after returning from New Mexico. "Come to the barn and take a look." Cliff was a big believer in never selling clients more horse than they could handle and he felt that a trusty quarter horse gelding was exactly what I needed.

I walked to the back of the property and spotted a number of horses nervously milling around. "He's in one of the stalls on the side," Cliff told me as he walked into the cluster of horses to locate my horse.

Sunday Cody Spirit was the registered name of my chestnut gelding. He was just turning five, had soft doe eyes and had been broken in such a way that a beginner would be able to ride him. As he came out of the stall I smiled. He was long-legged, with a tail shortened by younger horses who had munched on it.

Cliff did not pressure me to purchase the horse, feeling that when the time was right, I would know. Each morning I would arrive at the stables and Cliff and I would ride out into Griffith Park, which butted up against the Santa Monica Mountains and was filled with small bands of deer and coyotes that scurried away whenever we saw them on the trails.

Although Mom outright disapproved, claiming owning and riding horses was a gentile sport and that I was wasting my children's inheritance, I loved my new acquisition. Riding was something that belonged exclusively to me —not my siblings, children, or husband. Horseback riding was something I could excel at and since I hadn't finished school excelling at something, even if it was only riding a horse, was important to me. Escaping to the safe haven of the stables became an increasingly important ritual for me over the years.

TO THE TRADE ONLY

Gal's business had done well for a number of years, but the prices for kitchen cabinets and carpeting were getting too competitive with the discount stores that were popping up everywhere. At the same time, wood flooring was becoming very popular and Gal figured that more and more contractors and installers needed a source for their supplies in the San Fernando Valley. Having watched housing trends for years, he saw that the good money was in selling hardwood flooring, so he decided to open a small, side-street, *to the trade only,* hardwood flooring facility in 1984. He stocked the small warehouse with a number of pallets of wood flooring and an assortment of moldings and adhesives. Not wanting to hire strangers to watch over our material, we approached Steven, who was between jobs and gladly came to work for us in our new endeavor. We called the business Global Flooring Supplies and Steven was in charge of accepting the incoming inventory and closing the sales that Gal led his way. Everything proceeded smoothly and the business soon began to break even.

Shlomo's life, in contrast, was not as happy. His career was not providing him the feeling of accomplishment he wanted. He was one of those rare people who truly wanted to help those in need, but department heads did not appreciate his spending so much time on each call. With each call, he imagined Mom's face on that unknown person calling in for money after Dad died.

He was directed to spend no more than ten minutes per call and if he went over he was to take their number and call them back later.

Shlomo had a conscience and refused to do this to them, and so he was constantly being called into the office where he and the supervisor would battle it out.

As Shlomo's thirty-fifth birthday approached, he told Mom he was thinking of quitting his job working for the government. He hoped she would support him, but she didn't.

She warned that if he quit no one would hire him. "What about your retirement package? Your medical coverage? You'll lose it all! Just stay there a few more years and, when you're sixty-five, you can retire with all the benefits. No one is happy with their work." When she made pronouncements like these to her children, it was hard not to take them as an incontrovertible statement of fact. "Who is the chicken and who is the egg here?" she added for good measure, just in case we dared not listen and were in need of an extra reminder. Shlomo had chosen this occupation and now had to stay with it until the end. "Better to stay and be miserable than try something else and lose … and you *will* lose," she emphasized.

Shlomo's emotional tie to Mom was strong and without her encouragement he dared not make a move. He decided that if he was not going to be permitted to truly help people, which had been the reason for his chosen occupation in the first place, then he wanted a transfer to a position in the government where he did not interact with the general population. In this way, he hoped it would not dishearten him if he were not helping mankind as he had always envisioned.

After putting in his request for a transfer, still within the Department of Social Security, Shlomo was assigned as an assistant to an Administrative Law Judge. His new position placed him in a two-person cubical with a view of an opposing office building across the street. A computer sat on one desk while multiple overflowing piles of files filled with documents rested on his second desk. A non-descript beige telephone rang often with inquiries from persons who were checking the status of their request. It was Shlomo's job to organize and analyze pertinent facts, such as whether the applicant had ever filed for benefits before and what the results of those earlier filings were. He needed to ascertain what their sicknesses or ailments supposedly were and how well they matched up to the doctor's reports. A copy of Shlomo's report was then placed in the Department's files, while two other copies were sent to the Judge and the case attorney. Then Shlomo would move on to the next applicant. He worked hard at his new position but the piles never seemed to lessen. The job was a little more to his liking, but he remained unfulfilled.

Shirley and I both had heard and believed in the fallacy that a woman could not become pregnant while breastfeeding, but as she learned, it was nothing but a myth. More quickly than she wanted, Shirley found herself expecting baby number three.

Although Shirley desperately wanted a girl, Adam was born in February. He was a gorgeous baby with dark brown curls and sad, puppy-dog eyes. A gloom hung over the child like a dark cloud; it was as if, straight out of the womb, he knew that his mother was disappointed he was not a girl.

Down the street from our home was an area of untouched wilderness, a slightly hilly expanse full of old-growth trees where we often took the kids on family walks. One day, a large sign appeared on the land; a developer had obtained the property and was planning to subdivide it.

Gal and I thought it over and decided the time had come to make our move. We would purchase one of the corner lots and build our home from the ground up. Of course it would be risky, since Gal had never undertaken such a large venture, and there was the question of whether the community would ever fill up, but we decided to go ahead and take our chances. My parents were predictable in their response to our news. "Can't you be happy where you are?" my parents complained. "What do you know about building? What if the area stays empty? You could end up being there all alone with the coyotes." They were sure we were destined to lose everything in our need to *show off*.

To remain within our construction budget, which was minimal, Gal did much of the work himself.

The entry foyer was circular in design, resembling a tall, wide tower. If it had included an open window, it would only have lacked Rapunzel and her long, fair hair. Straight ahead was our dining room, where double French doors led out to a future back yard. To the right was the living room with a walk-down fireplace conversation pit and upholstered seats, which led into our family room, kitchen and an octagonal breakfast room. The upstairs would be comprised of Jack and Jill bedrooms where the children would share a bathroom situated between them, an office for Gal, and on the other side of the hallway, was the master suite.

In the summer of 1985, we moved into our dream home.

Still predominantly devoid of homes, the community was wonderfully silent. Nightly bands of deer strolled down the empty streets and the coyotes came out and howled, trying to coax our dog, Stella, outside. Ian, Laura and Garth were free to ride their bikes the full length of the community, never worrying about cars. I actually found myself wishing the community would never fill up with homes.

While I enjoyed the absence of nosy neighbors, Mom and Dad were anxious for our community to fill up. Mom was also concerned that my yard was little more than a prairie home for the gophers and mice. "Why don't you have a fenced yard yet?" she asked on one of her visits. "And what about a pool for those hot summer days?"

"I'm out of money, Mom," I told her, knowing these things could wait. "We'll get one soon."

"That's nonsense," she said, "I'll lend you $10,000 for a pool and fencing and when you sell the property you can pay me back." As was Mom's way, she went from being unsupportive to finding a way to help us out. We accepted her off and Gal began chalking the outline of the pool he planned to construct.

After easily passing her final exams, it was time for Nina to graduate. It filled us all with great pride to watch the only Poltzer female to earn a college degree accept her diploma. Mom and Dad were elated with her nursing degree.

She returned to LA, found a job in a hospital, and worked hard, but she was not happy. Nursing was a noble cause; helping those in need was commendable, but she was a creative sort and yearned for something in the world of fashion.

Although Mom and Dad offered to help her out, Nina wanted to make it on her own. She appreciated their gesture, but she was eager for them to be proud of her. As the last child, Nina had always felt unwanted and forgotten. She was constantly being reminded that she was getting older and that men only wanted young women. Men, Mom told Nina, were not to be trusted. "Only children that come from your body are loyal," she explained. And then, to further cement her children's loyalty, she explained that Dad have never wanted her to have the fourth and fifth children and that she alone fought to have her and would always be there for her. But no matter what Mom's reasoning might have been, she hurt Nina deeply.

Despite my many efforts to connect with my sister Shirley, issues continued to arise from even the smallest transactions, causing bitter confrontations that no one could forgive or forget. When Gal was preparing to update the display room in the window of the showroom, Shirley, who needed to fix up her latest flipping project, approached me and asked if she could purchase it. I hesitated, explaining to her that it was missing some of the backs and sides and that it would therefore need some additional carpentry work. However, she insisted, and so we agreed on a price and Gal had it delivered to her home.

Since Eric was born with six thumbs, Shirley asked Gal if he could help her husband install it. So that Saturday, the two men pulled out the existing cabinets at the home. As the new cabinets were being put into place Shirley began complaining. "Where are all the backs?" she asked. "How could you sell me something without all the sides and tops?"

I reminded her that I'd explained this to her before.

"I don't remember you saying that! I had no idea they would be this incomplete!" she protested. Gal stopped his hammering as an argument began to rage back and forth between us.

Not wanting family discord, Gal drove to a hardware store and purchased some sheets of plywood. He carried them back into the house silently, too enraged to speak. He pulled out his electric saw and cut and installed the plywood where he was able, but it was not an exact match. Nor was it cabinet quality, but it was never supposed to be. "I've done all that I can do," he told them. "You're going to need a finish carpenter for the rest."

"Well, I'm not going to pay for them," Shirley informed us. "Then why did you let Gal work his ass off and finish the installation before you decided not to pay for them?" I asked angrily.

Gal flung his tools back into his tool box and we left.

A volley of phone calls immediately ensued, as each of us tried to get Mom and Dad to take their side. Meanwhile, Gal was furious. "Don't ever ask me to do business with Shirley again," he told me emphatically. "And I don't want them coming over any more!" Mom tried to remain impartial, but I sensed that she considered Gal to be the villain. I was given the classic Potlzer speech: *Always turn the other cheek when it comes to family. Gal is merely your husband, but Shirley is your sister and family comes first.*

I convinced myself of the benefits of looking the other way. We were going to get rid of the cabinets anyway and Shirley was my sister. Gal tried to bury his hurt deep inside, but I knew he felt alone and ostracized. We all just pretended to forget the episode—but the truth was that, in this family, none of us ever forgot any slight or injustice.

Shortly thereafter, Gal decided that there was more potential in the wood flooring business than in home décor. Although it was a gamble, we closed Bechor's Home Designs for good and focused exclusively on building Global Flooring Supplies. The housing market was still booming and the community where we had built our home was doing well. Opulent houses were going up everywhere. Gal, always the entrepreneur, was convinced that, if he could get his hands on a piece of property, he could build a house for speculation and earn some of that money. He brought in a money man who agreed to front the money for the land if Gal would obtain the loan for construction and guarantee the house would be completed within an agreed-upon time frame and budget. We needed to move quickly since no one really knew how much longer this housing boom would last. The plan was to put the house on the market within one year and split the profits. Gal worked extremely hard and breezed through the construction. The house sold quickly and the money was phenomenal.

We were overjoyed by how the deal had worked out, but again, my mother couldn't help but see the glass as half-empty. When I told her the news, she only commented on how well had the partner had made out. Ignoring Mom's thoughts on the subject, we decided to roll the dice one more time and build again –except this time, we would do it alone. We took all of the money we had made and purchased a lot next door to ours. Seeing our community grow and prosper, Eric and Shirley decided they wanted a piece of the action. There was still a decent selection of lots available and they purchased a nice-sized piece of property three blocks from ours. I was thrilled at the prospect of having my sister just down the street. Yes, we'd had our differences, but we'd also had many good times together. I loved the idea that I could borrow sugar from my sister just down the street and hoped that the proximity would lead our relationship onto friendlier ground.

Eager to begin, Shirley visited an architect and designed the home of her dreams. However, when she submitted her blue prints to the builders, they discovered they couldn't afford it. Shirley and Eric then suggested that Gal build their house. He had a good track record and, since he was building another house anyway, there were sure there would be lots of cost savings.

Gal had forgiven many things. He had rescinded his declaration prohibiting Shirley, Eric and their family from coming over. They had even started coming over on Friday nights to watch *Dallas* and Gal always welcomed them warmly.

But this whole plan made Gal very nervous. He simply did not want to gamble with Shirley and Eric. What if they changed their minds about window placements or did not come up with the payments for deliveries on time? What would he do when Eric used his favorite ploy of *The checks in the mail?* Our construction loan clock was ticking and Gal simply could not forget the kitchen cabinet fiasco. Finally, we had to tell them we could not help them.

Shirley erupted like a volcano. "You just don't want me to have what you have! You have always wanted to keep me down!"

In their eyes, we were being spiteful and selfish. They could only see it as an act of betrayal.

Without Gal's help, it was impossible for Shirley and Eric to get their new house built. And since their bank clock was also ticking, they decided to sell the property, blueprints and all, laying the blame for that busted dream on us. No matter how hard I tried to improve our relationship, the list of grievances between us grew longer every year.

THE EMERALD ISLE

I was now in my mid thirties. Although Gal and I had
frequently traveled abroad to Israel to visit his family (despite
my mother thinking it was a total waste of money), I finally
decided the time had come for me to embark on my own travel
adventure. I learned about a seven-day horseback riding trip in
Ireland, and knew that was what I wanted to do. It would be my
first time leaving the country on my own. I managed to persuade
Gal to let me go, but that was only half the battle. How would I
tell my parents I was going off on a horseback riding vacation
without my husband? I could imagine them asking, "Why are
you going with a bunch of marriage-destroying gentile women
on a self-indulgent trip?" In the end, I took the cowardly way out
and simply didn't tell them.

Nina decided to join me. While Gal was not thrilled
about letting me go by myself, he finally gave me his blessings
and put me on the plane with Nina and my friends.

We were as giddy as children as the plane took off and
Ireland was more than I could have hoped for. I fell in love with
the magnificent landscape as soon as landed.

We rode for hours that first day, jumping over the stone
walls as we made our way through the sheep-filled pastures.

We stopped mid-day at an abandoned castle for lunch.
Even though I was used to riding, my body had begun to ache a
bit. As we pulled the saddles off, we could see the steam rise
from the horses' sweaty bodies.

After lunch, we strolled around the exterior of the castle.
It had obviously once belonged to someone of great importance,
but now it sat vacant, a memory of days gone by. Short hunched-
over Irish women, carrying what appeared to be the makings of
dinner in plastic bags, passed by. They nodded politely and kept
on walking down the road. After two hours, we once again
mounted our trusty steeds and began heading toward the hotel.
We passed houses set close to the street and mothers who had
come out of their homes carrying their little ones to wave at us.
We finished the day with one last long gallop along some train

tracks and then turned back into the enclosed field the horses called home.

When we got back to the hotel, we released the horses. The sun was low in the sky and shining directly at us, transforming the horses into silhouettes. I saw Nina standing by the fence, watching her horse as he rolled off the day's ride. It made me happy to see her light of heart and having a good time.

On one rain-free but blustery day, we were told to strip down to our bathing suits. "Today we are going to ride our horses into the sea," our guide announced. I opted not to ride since I wasn't feeling well, but I watched from the beach. Nina hopped up onto her horse bareback, holding on to the long mane. Following the leader, Nina and the others rode into the blue sea. The afternoon had scattered clouds against the turquoise blue sky and the water was cold, but the warmth of the horses beneath them kept them warm. They sloshed through the small surf farther into the sea until the water lifted them up and the horses began swimming.

Nina was clearly elated. "It's as if you are riding a dolphin that is bobbing up and down with the current," Nina later described.

I was happy for her, glad that she was having this moment of bliss.

That night, we feasted on hot soup, fresh bread and Irish coffee with whipped cream at the hotel's pub. Its walls were all dark red-stained wood and a mirror covered the entire back wall. The bartender had a thick, proper Irish brogue, which was almost as proper as his white pressed shirt and black tie.

After dinner, I called home to make sure all was well. To my surprise, Dad answered. "What are you doing, Jaclyn?" he asked me, his voice taut with anger. "Gal can't be expected to take care of a business and watch the children too! The minute we found out what you did we came right over to help the poor guy. This is not the way a responsible mother and wife behaves. How could you leave your children to run off and play like this?"

I wanted to die.

"Why didn't you tell me!" my mother yelled, having torn the receiver from my father. "Who taught you to lie to your mother? It must be that horsy set. They have poisoned your mind!"

I was paralyzed, the phone glued to my ear. Despite the fact that I was a full-fledged adult, I simply allowed them to continue yelling at me like I was a child. And I responded as they hoped I would—overwhelmed by guilt.

What had started off as the trip of a lifetime was now a miserable ordeal, and the rest of the vacation was little more than a sad blur. When I got home, Gal and the kids were happy to see me, and that eased my feelings of guilt. Of course, they all looked healthy and well, and after seeing them all in such good spirits, I wished I'd been allowed to just enjoy this one little adventure without my parents' interference and judgment.

Having arrived safely back home, I finally phoned Mom and Dad. Slowly, reluctantly, I dialed the number. "I'm home!" I said, making an effort to sound cheerful.

"Never do that again!" Mom ordered. But then suddenly she eased off. I realized that maybe my absence really rattled her. Maybe she was speaking out of fear more than anger. And when I thought of her past, I wondered whether this was just another example of how she had never recovered from losing almost everyone near and dear to her during the war.

A BUSINESS FOR SALE

Shortly thereafter, there was big news in Dad's life. His partner Morris wanted to retire and gave him the option to retire or buy him out. Dad still loved having that business. He relished going to the store and speaking with all those people every day. It gave him a reason to be, and it was the only place where he felt entirely autonomous and competent. However, Mom was adamant that Dad should not pay Morris for his half. "Why should he get the money so easy," she stated, seemingly unaware that that was simply standard practice.

Having reached an impasse, he and Morris sought legal counsel. Threatening letters from both sides' attorneys flew back and forth. But neither Dad nor Morris was really willing to spend the money to take this matter to court … just yet.

Meanwhile, Eric, upon learning that my father's liquor store was probably going to go on the market, approached Morris and Dad and offered to buy their business. Of course, they would have to carry the paperwork for the loan, as he could not get a real bank loan. Surprisingly, after some discussion, they accepted Eric's offer.

"No!" Mom yelled upon hearing the news. "Sell the business to a stranger!" Although Mom adored Eric, she knew in her heart that this odd partnership would never run smoothly. But Dad felt it was his best option.

Mom sadly shook her head as everyone signed the paperwork. Eric was now the owner of Dad's pride and joy, and Dad was forced into retirement.

When Steven heard about a fledgling Submarine sandwich franchise, he approached Shlomo as a possible partner, but Shlomo refused the offer, not wanting to mix family and business. Eric, however, was still looking for deals and was very interested in pairing up with Steven. In no time at all, the deal was done.

Steven got trained for the job, learning about the nuts and bolts of the business, as well as how to calculate the franchisor's cut of the profits. He was quick and learned everything he needed to know easily. Eric, however, could not be bothered. He rarely showed up to work, but had plenty of opinions about the business's finances.

Owning a business as part of a chain organization involves jumping through many hoops. Rules and regulations abound and inspectors are ever hovering, assuring franchisees are abiding by their standards. Steven understood this and knew how to maneuver, but Eric would not cooperate. He wanted to introduce additional food products, cookies and sodas that had not been approved by the chain, to sell for additional profit and Steven constantly had to tell him "No."

Their store's inspector repeatedly told Steven and Eric that their location was in jeopardy of being closed, as she did not like the way they ran their business.

One day, Mom very suddenly informed me that her brother Isaac was coming to California. She had only visited him a handful of times after moving to California, feeling it was best to keep her distance from the brother who saw her as a walking wallet. Leja, his wife, had run off with another man, and his sons had moved away. At eighty-five, he was now old and ill, suffering from diabetes. He needed constant care, and he reached out and asked his only sister if he could come to California and live with her. "I've already made the travel arrangements and have a ticket in my hands," he announced. Mom was stuck.

And so a short time later, she and Dad found themselves waiting at the airport as he was wheeled off the plane in a wheelchair. Mom was happy to see him, but having Isaac there also stirred hugely complex emotions in her; she loved this brother-father-mother figure, but felt that he came with an aura of foreboding.

She saw how thin, sickly and weak he had become. He told her he did not expect to live many more years and again asked her if she would nurse him until he died. This little old man was the reason she was alive today. He was the person who walked with her in that forest, holding her hand tightly, keeping her out of harm's way.

While Dad would not have objected to Isaac staying with them, Mom thought on a different plane. She worried that Isaac's runaway wife would get the money, the property and everything without having ever helped. No, Mom was not going to be used, not even by her own brother. "I'll make you a deal, Isaac," she finally told him. "Leave all the property, all the money to me, and when you die, I'll hand everything over to your two sons, but not one single penny, not one inch of land, will go to Leja." And in her typically paranoid way, Mom was also terrified that Dad would get some of his own ideas from this and that he'd end up doing the same thing to her.

Isaac still hoped Leja would return to him. He was not willing to rock the boat by demanding a divorce or signing such paperwork. And since neither Isaac nor Mom would budge, Mom felt she had no choice but to put him back on a plane two weeks later and send him back home.

A year later, Isaac died, most likely due to complications from diabetes. When Mom received the notification from Barry, she was heartbroken and guilt ridden. She did not tell any of us and swore Dad to secrecy. She never even returned to upstate New York for the funeral, merely allowing the day to come and go, but she suffered each hour of the day knowing her brother was being put into the ground without her being there to cry for his passing. None of us learned about his death until some years later, and to this day, since she also did not tell Dad where they took Isaac, we don't know where he is buried.

Meanwhile, Nina was still looking to break into the world of fashion. When a friend mentioned an unpaid internship on a nearby movie set, she jumped at the chance.

Dressing movie stars was a very methodical procedure. With each scene came a detailed list of everything that each actor was to wear. It was Nina and her girlfriend's job to make sure that the clothing was resting neatly in the dressing room trailer for the star or starlet to put on as they were having their hair and make up done. Then there was the final check, ensuring that all the buttons were buttoned the right way and that the cape hung correctly off the left shoulder and not the right. Once the filming resumed, Nina and her friend would then begin preparing the costumes for the next scene. Nina enjoyed working with the costumes, dealing with stars of all kinds, and journeying to movie sets far and near. In no time at all, she went on to become a paid employee.

   Shirley's need to have a little girl was intense. She had been doing research into having a child via gender selection and was willing, one last time, to carry a child if she was positive it was a girl. She had read all the articles on positions of conception and foods that promised to increase the odds of having a girl, and she had even contacted a doctor to find out the cost of having the sperm spun so that she could have only female sperm injected into her via turkey baster. But before she could get it all arranged, she recognized that familiar nauseous feeling. A pregnancy test showed she was expecting again. What to do? She did not want another child if it was another boy. Her doctor told her that there was a test that would foretell the sex of the child, but there was a catch – they would not perform the test unless the mother was over thirty-five. Although she was under the age barrier, I was not.

   "Jaclyn, I need to be you for a test I need to take," she told me. I rummaged through my purse and handed her my driver's license. I hoped that the laboratory would not notice that although we were both brunettes with brown eyes, I was a few inches taller and much heavier. A few days later, I got a call announcing that Shirley was expecting a girl.

   One afternoon, a few weeks later, Shirley's phone rang. "Hello, this is the medical lab, may we speak with Jaclyn Bechor"

   Shirley thought for a moment. "This is Jaclyn."

   "We need to inform you that the results of your pregnancy testing were compromised and we can no longer state with certainty that your child is a female," the technician informed her. Her jaw dropped. It was too late to consider an abortion.

The wait until October was interminable, but a phone ringing at my house in the middle of the night could only mean one thing: the baby had arrived. Normally one asks if everything went well, if the mother and baby are all right, but not this time. I did not even say hello, just, "What is it?"

"It's a girl!" Eric said proudly. "We've named her Amber."

That was all I needed to hear; at last Shirley could rest. She could be happy and live out her vision of dressing her pretty little girl up in pink things and fixing her hair with bows and ribbons. The family continued to grow.

A DRYSDALE MARRIES A HILLBILLY

For Poltzers, the urge to marry was not limited to the women in the family. Steven had found himself a serious girlfriend, a strong-willed woman named Brenda whom none of us liked. Despite our protests, he continued to pursue the relationship, determined to prove he could handle her. We knew we had no chance of changing his mind when her parents flew in from the East coast to meet Mom and Dad.

The encounter was awkward at best, even icy at times. They could not have been more different. Brenda's mother was very tall and slender, with a strong East Coast accent. She had her short, professionally colored hair done weekly and talked a great deal about her country club. She wore designer costume jewelry with diamonds on her fingers that matched her tennis bracelet. Her soft-spoken husband wore a handsome, golf shirt, tucked neatly into his pressed trousers, and an elegant pair of leather penny loafers.

And then there were Mom and Dad. In Mom's world, if a single color is good, then a flurry of loud reds, blues and yellows is always better. For this meeting, Mom chose a vibrant polyester button-down blouse with oversized flowers. Her polyester pants sort of matched and her sandals coordinated with her purse. Dad wore a short-sleeved, muted-tone shirt with his dark-colored pants and black shoes. He also wore his trusty camel-colored cardigan button-down sweater, in case the coffee shop where they planned on meeting had its air conditioning on too high.

Conversation was uncomfortable. Mom and Dad, having saved every penny they earned, were up against a couple who enjoyed displaying their success. Dad tried to be subtle, but Mom was her usual self, a bull in a china shop. "What are we going to do to help the children financially?" she asked, fighting off the urge to take the salt and pepper shakers and place them in her purse. "I am a firm believer that parents should help young married couples," she continued and waited for them to agree.

"We feel that children should be allowed to make it on their own," Brenda's mother said. "If they are old enough to get married, then they are old enough to take care of themselves. Brenda has been living in California without any financial assistance from us for a while," she boasted. Brenda's mother punctuated her statement by opening her small hand bag and reapplying another coat of Chanel lipstick.

Knowing that any other suggestions on the topic of financial assistance would fall on deaf ears, they changed the subject to discuss wedding arrangements instead. Brenda's mother implied strongly that Mom and Dad's involvement in this affair was not needed or wanted, but that they would be welcome to pay for the bar bill. The meeting ended cordially, but did not fulfill Mom and Dad's hopes for mutual cooperation.

The Poltzer women never pretended to be excited about the upcoming wedding. We never contacted Brenda about assisting her with party arrangements and we never reached out to her girlfriends volunteering our assistance with her bridal shower. We remained silent and just awaited the invitations like any other stranger.

The shower was being held at the house of Brenda's long-time friend Louise. She set up two round tables for ten; white banquet tablecloths were spread beneath light-colored plates. Pitchers of unsweetened ice tea with quartered lemons floating in them sat beside low-profile floral arrangements. A separate table was set up to display the standard luncheon faire: quiche, green salad and fresh fruit.

After milling around making casual conversation, mostly amongst ourselves, Mom, Shirley, Laura and I took our seats at one table and Brenda and her friends sat at the other table.

In attendance were a cross-section of women – some married and some divorced. It seemed that it was the collection of divorced women who spoke the loudest about marriage. As Mom listened, Shirley and I could see her nostrils begin to flare. Try as we might, we could not keep her quiet.

"Brenda," Mom blurted out, "you have to understand that in order to stay married, you must be willing to take a little abuse." Instantly, all chewing stopped and the room went silent. Eyes turned toward Mom and everyone listened intently.

"Abuse?" Brenda asked, her jaw tightening, wishing Mom would just eat and remain quiet.

"Yes. Jaclyn, Shirley and I are often hit by our husbands. It's part of being married," Mom proclaimed.

Shirley and I froze and our eyes opened wide. We were stunned, mortified and shocked. "Mom," I interrupted, "Gal's never hit me."

"Eric's never hit me either, Mom," Shirley chimed in.

But Mom would not be challenged. "Maybe you won't admit it in front of all these people, but I will. Your father hits me and I'm used to it." She said it almost proudly and never broke her eye contact with Brenda.

The tone of the shower changed in a matter of seconds. The damage could not be repaired. Shirley and I could not have been more uncomfortable; none of the women here would ever believe us no matter how much we denied it. Some now looked at us with pity and others looked away in disgust. A few were whispering, "Oh my God, that's terrible!" How could we attend this wedding now, arm in arm with our husbands, knowing these women, whom we had just met, believed we were being beaten at home?

Brenda was out of her mind with anger. What a family of back wood bumpkins she was marrying into and what a lunatic for a mother-in-law she was getting! "No one is ever going to lay a hand on me, Channa!" she stated emphatically and Louise quickly hurried over and placed a supportive hand on her back, nodding in approval.

There was little conversation after that and Shirley and I could not wait to leave. On the way home, we finally got our say.

"Mom, what the hell were you doing?" we asked.

"I'm getting Brenda ready in case your brother hits her. You know your father hits me when he gets angry," she answered, feeling justified by what she had done.

Until then, we had only been slightly aware that there was some heavy-handedness in their marriage. Mom occasionally wore an ace bandage around a leg or an ankle. I remember asking her about it and sometimes she would answer that Dad had gotten angry and thrown a chair at her. As children we didn't like it, but never thought that it was our place to intervene. It was their crazy dance and we left them alone.

"But Mom, why did you include us in that?"

"Because I want her to know it is something that happens to all women so she won't call the police on him." Shirley and I shook our heads.

"But Mom, Brenda isn't going to take any of that." we said. "If Steven ever lays a finger on her, she'll have him in jail so fast his head will spin." We tried to explain, but she was not listening. She was the chicken and we were the eggs.

Finally, the wedding day arrived. It was a beautiful affair. For one night, we all got along with Brenda and her family. She was a Poltzer now, whether we liked it or not.

Steven tried to make a good living for himself and his new bride. But his attempts at making money soured when he joined up with Eric. A property they both owned was taken back by the bank and now it seemed his piece of property was destined to be lost also. Eric had maneuvered his way into the position of handling the books for the newest property. Unknown fees began appearing, property tax bills began being paid late for mysterious reasons, and it wasn't long before Eric and Steven started squabbling. After a good deal of back and forth, another business was sold.

Brenda, who worked in the insurance industry, made considerably more money than Steven did and took every opportunity to throw that in his face.

Their relationship was off to a rocky start. We had tried to warn him, but there was little we could do to help him now.

A COWARD DIES A THOUSAND DEATHS

Mom was now in her late sixties and had developed a bit of arthritis in her hips, but that only mildly slowed her down when it came to babysitting her grandchildren. When Amber was six years old, she spent a weekend with her grandparents. Mom asked Dad to run to the store to get some groceries. When he closed the door behind him, the latch didn't fully shut. Amber opened the door, and was outside quick as a flash. Mom sprinted down the hall, rushing to get Amber, when the heel of her shoe caught on a crack on the front porch and she fell, landing spread-eagle on the lawn. At first, her knee did not hurt much. But once she had recovered Amber and spent some time resting on the couch, her left leg locked up and the pain was excruciating.

Shirley picked up her daughter and Mom downplayed her fall. But by the next morning, Mom could not walk and the pain was unbearable. Dad hurried her to the hospital. It turned out she had torn a ligament, which was inoperable, but physical therapy and pain medication promised to help.

Mom's injury rattled me more than I cared to admit. Although I had gone on to have my own life, I still depended on her strength and authority. This one small injury caused me to look ahead and panic about what life would be like after she died.

After several weeks, Mom's recovery had slowed considerably and we discovered that she was simply continuing to refill her prescription for pain killers on a regular basis. "Dad," Nina said, having never totally relinquished her nursing instincts. "We need to get her off the pills. She has been on them too long." Mom had put on more weight, which made it harder for her to walk. As a family, we finally decided to intervene. We forcibly weaned Mom off her dependency by dispensing her drug in ever-decreasing intervals, but she was changed forever more. She was clingier, more depressed, less active and more frightened about her life and her marriage. She remained convinced that Dad would leave her.

Dad started to call me secretly, imploring me in an almost inaudible voice to help him. "I love your mother, but our life is **terrible**." And he added that additional inflection on the word terrible.

There was nothing worse than hearing my father sounding so defeated, but I felt I could not take sides. How could I? "I'm sorry, Dad, that you're so unhappy, but there's nothing I can do." And it was true. Although I could see perfectly well that their life had deteriorated, I didn't feel it was my place to intervene. Her health was going down quickly. She had trouble walking, refusing to go on drives lasting over an hour. Irrationally terrified that he'd leave her, she demanded that he remain by her side every minute of the day. Cleaning the house had come to a complete stop and she was becoming paranoid about strangers. I felt for him, but stayed out of it.

With no seed money to aid Nina in her fashion endeavors (Mom and Dad had turned her down, insisting she had no need for her own career), she abandoned her dream of going into fashion design and contentedly continued working for the studios. One evening at a Hollywood party, she met a young Yugoslavian man. Soft jazz was playing and Nina was attracted to his oddly familiar accent. He confessed that he had just come from a showing of his artwork at a nearby gallery and proudly handed her some Polaroid photographs he had in his pocket. The two spent the rest of the evening together, expanding their discussion to politics and international issues. Nina liked his intellect and creativity and the two quickly become involved.

Nina was now living in La Jolla with a few roommates, but Mom and Dad still cared for the property. One morning, one of the roommates called Dad to inform him that the wall heater in the house was not working. He drove over to take a look. It was eleven o'clock in the morning, and after repeatedly knocking on the front door, he used his key and let himself in.

As all was quiet, he assumed nobody was home and walked down the long hallway, looking into the room that he and his wife used to call their own. The room was dark, but then he noticed something that stopped him in his tracks. There appeared to be someone in the bed. But it was eleven o'clock and Nina should have been at work. "Nina?" he called over softly. He squinted and saw an unfamiliar face peering at him from beneath the covers.

Nina and Peter had imbibed quite a bit of the bubbly at a gallery the night before, and Peter was still sleeping it off.

"Who are you?" Dad demanded in a stern voice, his eyes almost popping out of his skull.

Peter scrambled to his feet, wearing only his white briefs. He gathered his clothes and attempted to greet the visibly enraged father, hoping to minimize the impact of this uncomfortable moment. But Dad could smell Peter's breath. "You get out of here!" he yelled, pointing a finger outside. Peter abandoned his hopes of a first meeting and ran out the front door.

"Nina, why is there a bum sleeping in your bed while you are busy at work?" Dad questioned after reaching Nina by telephone.

"Dad, what are you doing in the house while I'm not home?" Nina retorted.

"I was here checking up on the heater and found this guy in the bed!"

Nina and Dad now began lecturing and counter-lecturing each other on the importance of propriety when it came to male/female relationships and the issue of when parents should emotionally let go of their adult children. Neither was willing to back off, so eventually Nina angrily hung up.

Within moments, Mom contacted Nina. "We're not letting you stay in the house just so you can support this European nobody!" she ordered.

"I think I'm old enough to handle this myself," Nina answered back. "And I'm not supporting anyone."

Since Dad felt no compunction about entering the house at all hours of the day or night, and refused to guarantee that another such visit would not occur, Nina decided it was time to move out of La Jolla and to some other place with Peter.

The new couple found a duplex apartment and quickly filled it with Peter's art. The apartment spilled over with creativity and it was all this artistry that released Nina's creative side. For years, she had seen fashion ideas, very similar to hers, come and go. But now, after working all this time, she had saved a block of money and no longer needed to ask her parents for financial assistance. Having Peter as her muse, she decided to begin designing clothing. She could do it without anyone's support, and once again, she had come up with an idea.

In the world of music, tight, short t-shirts were all the rage. Nina liked the look, but she was tiny and found that in order to find an acceptable fit she had to look into children's t-shirts. That's where her design idea came in. She purchased plain, white baby t-shirts, colored them and added some white trim, and that was it – simple, yet genius. Giving her creation a catchy name, *Sweet Tees*, she approached one of the hottest boutiques on Melrose, Fred Segal's. Impressed with Nina's sharp and confident approach, the boutique bought her t-shirts on the spot and immediately placed orders for more. Within a few months, she had a major success on her hands.

Nina continued expanding her business and soon began manufacturing her own t-shirts from scratch in a small plant in Pacoima, an industrial district in the San Fernando Valley. Soon she hired sales representation in New York and Sweet Tees went nationwide.

Peter's life was changing as well. His work was gaining great notoriety. He had numerous pieces hanging in galleries and some of his work was being displayed as far away as Italy. Unfortunately though, Nina failed to notice that he was in the early stages of a courtship with cocaine. Until, that is, he started having occasional violent outbursts. At first, she tolerated a shove here and there, as Peter was always immediately apologetic.

One night, though, after another violent episode, she urged him to give up the drugs—to no avail. Shortly after he stormed out of the apartment, Nina contacted me. She had never complained about him before, but now her voice was filled with urgency. "Jaclyn, I need for you to come over right now and help me move everything out of this apartment."

I did not need an explanation; I hopped in my car. Her belongings were already in sloppy piles in the driveway and we loaded everything into my car. Then we went inside to take a final look around the apartment. Peter's latest art demonstrated a clear transition from his earlier work that showed the effect of the drugs. While his early pieces were filled with color and a sense of fun, on the opposing wall hung canvases of dark, black and grey images depicting demons and death. Nina carefully lifted one piece of art off the wall to keep as a token of better times. "I was the catalyst for this one," she explained. And we left.

The two ended up dating and breaking up repeatedly for many years, but in the end, cocaine won and Peter lost, because Nina finally closed the door on him.

Fortunately, Nina's business continued to thrive. She purchased a home in a trendy section of the Laurel Canyon neighborhood that bridged Hollywood to the San Fernando Valley.

Nina hoped Mom and Dad would be proud of her accomplishments, but all Mom could say when she saw the house was, "Who lives up here but hippies?" I suppose we should not have been surprised by their criticism at this point, but we all always hoped that this time—whatever time it was— would be different.

Unlike Nina, Shirley and Eric were beginning to have money problems. Shirley could never get Eric to sit down with her and go over the business numbers with her. She sensed something might be wrong, but Eric always shrugged her concerns off, quickly changing the subject whenever she brought it up.

"There's something going on with our finances," Shirley told me one afternoon.

"What do the books say?" I asked.

"I've never seen the books," she answered.

"What do you mean? How can you not know?" I asked.

"No," she answered quietly. "Eric keeps that in his office and it's always locked."

"Locked?" I said, initially surprised, but then again it was Eric. "I'm sure we can get in there and then you can take a look."

"Even if we go in, I don't know how to read the books," Shirley admitted.

"Well, if you want me to, I can teach you and then you can see where you stand. Or better yet, why don't you just contact your accountant?" I suggested.

Her face turned gloomy. She did not really want to know; it was easier to put her head in the sand. She lived in a beautiful home, had four lovely children, and Eric would figure a way out. She did not speak of the problem again, optimistic that Eric would resolve the money issue. I knew there was nothing I could do for her, but I had a growing sense of unease that I couldn't entirely ignore.

School bussing had begun and I wanted to send Laura and Ian to a better school, one that happened to be in the district Shirley lived in. When I asked if I could use her address, she agreed. It seemed like such a simple request—a mere formality, really—but even this ended up causing trouble. Garth and Ian had misunderstandings at school and Shirley once again blamed me. We moved on, but it came back to haunt us later.

Eric's strategies knew no bounds. Always eager to capitalize on someone else's success, Eric decided that if wood flooring was a good enough business for Gal, he could sell wood also. He rented a tiny storage facility, had a telephone line put in, purchased a container of hardwood flooring and assorted sundries from a competitor of ours and opened for business.

At Global Flooring Supplies we promoted our products in the Yellow Pages, through direct mailings and in newspapers. Phone calls referring to an ad we had placed in one particular paper began drawing a response, but would-be customers were now demanding we match the price a competitor was offering. Who was this company that was undercutting us, we asked ourselves. We were already aware of all the larger distributors in the area, so we scanned the Valley newspaper and located a small ad strategically placed directly below ours. It bore no company name and the phone number was unfamiliar. When we dialed the number, we could not believe what he heard. This was not a stranger's voice, but that of my own brother-in-law!

"What are you doing, Shirley?" I asked, immediately getting her on the phone.

"Who are you to tell me that I can't open a business!" she answered, incensed. "You're not the only person who needs to make a living."

She was right, but it seemed unfair for them to set themselves up in direct competition with us when there were any number of other businesses they could have started. To save our own business, we were forced to contact all our vendors and tell them that unless they stopped selling to Eric, we would stop buying their materials. Eric's flooring sources dried up quickly after that, and he knew that Gal was behind all his problems. Our frustrations with each other continued to mount.

Every time we wanted to believe that relations had returned to normal, some new episode erupted. But, as it turned out, the final blow was yet to come. One day at school, Laura was summoned to the principal's office. She had no idea what this was about as she walked down the hall, but found out soon enough.

"Laura, where do you live?" he asked, holding a handwritten note in his hand.

Her heart pounded. We had prepared for this possibility, repeatedly practicing the answer and even the intonation of her voice. She thought for a moment and recited Shirley's address while she tried to keep her cool.

"Are you sure that that is where you are living now?"

"Yes," she answered, but with her confidence waning.

"Thank you," the principal told Laura and sent her back to the classroom. Time seemed to crawl by as Laura watched the clock on the wall, but at last, the final bell rang and she quickly gathered her belongings and ran outside.

She was visibly upset when I picked her up that day, and immediately told me what had occurred. She reenacted the scene in the principal's office a number of times and we racked our brains, trying to guess who might have instigated this. We tried to stay optimistic and hoped that Laura had done a good enough job so that the school district would believe her.

Three days later, I received an envelope with the official embossed return address of the school board in the upper left corner. I nervously tore it open and it stated what I had feared—that we had been discovered. *At the end of the school year Laura and Ian will no longer be permitted to attend school in this district*, it said. I re-read the next sentence a hundred times, each time hoping it would change. *We have received a letter from Shirley Marlow informing us that Laura no longer lives at this address.*

My own *sister* had sent the letter? My sister? In all Mom's teaching there was always the *outside world,* who you could never trust and *family.* It was unthinkable that Shirley and Eric could have done this. I called Shirley as quickly as my fingers could dial the numbers.

"If you want your kids in our school district so much, then why don't you just buy a house over here instead of using my address?" she sneered.

I knew this was retribution. We would not let them get involved in our business, so they were going to hurt me where it hurt the most, my children. "Why didn't you tell me you weren't going to let me use your address after the semester ended?" I asked, "I would have figured something out. Now they're going to watch me like a hawk!" She remained cold as ice.

This was a turning point for me. Never had a family member turned on me like this. Never had I felt the hatred I did at that moment. This was far more than about the schooling—I knew my kids could get an education anywhere. This was an act of betrayal that revealed the depths of her resentment towards me. Maybe I should not have been surprised, given her behavior in recent years. But the power of denial is strong, and our family's sense of loyalty had always been strong. Clearly, I had failed to take these hints seriously.

"What can I do?" Mom cried when I spoke with her.

"This is Eric's handiwork," Dad said aloud in the background, knowing Eric was usually at the root of all bad things. That might have been so, but Shirley should have acted as a buffer to protect her niece and nephew. This was a new definition of family, and we all learned quickly to adapt. There was family and there was *family*. This group of people happened to share your blood, but that was it. They were not to be trusted with the smallest thing. If your purse was in a room that Eric entered, it had to be hidden. If there was a secret, you were to stay quiet. They were now a new brand of enemy, family yet strangers.

For weeks, I struggled with this. I could not seem to get a handle on the pain. I wanted to turn back the clock. I tried to speak with Shirley, but all we did was yell at each other, spilling out a lengthy laundry list of injustices that dated back to our youth. She harbored such contempt for me, telling me that I had always been condescending towards her and her family, that I thought I always knew best and that she had hated that about me ever since we were young. She said my son had never even attempted to bring Garth into his group of friends and that I had obviously taught him to look down on her son, just as I had done to her. She said I had always wanted her to fail and never wished her to have a house like mine. She went on and on. Nothing I said to placate her made any difference.

I decided to draft a letter to express my side. My typing fingers could barely keep up with everything I wanted to say.

A few days later, after reading my letter, Shirley called. But rather than apologize, she wanted to re-affirm that, although Eric had written the letter to the school board, she would have penned it herself given the opportunity. I seethed. How could I have been so wrong about my sister?

The time came to look for new schools for Laura and Ian. For lack of better options, we enrolled Laura at the local high school, a place that made me very nervous with its gang affiliation signs on the walls and a reputation for violence resulting from a parking lot shooting.

Ian switched to a private middle school that boasted a strong academic policy as well as an excellent sports program. While I was impressed by their curriculum, I gave little thought to the sports program. I didn't think sports could do much for a nice Jewish boy, except get him injured. What I really wanted was for him to learn the basics: reading, writing and mathematics.

With the children all back in school, Mom felt it was time for me to put the incident with Shirley behind me. In her daily five o'clock phone calls, she began applying pressure on me to forgive and forget. "Shirley is your sister and family is the most important thing there is! Just let it pass," she begged, but I just couldn't.

Shortly after school started, the Jewish high holy days arrived. I informed my mother that I would make the Rosh Hashana meal at my house, but would not be inviting Shirley and her family.

My decision split the family and placed my parents in a very awkward position. Mom hated having to take sides. For Dad, it was a no-brainer; he hated Eric and would have come to my home without giving Eric's absence a second thought. But Mom adored Eric and it was much harder on her. I would not relent, so Shirley and her family spent the holiday at home by themselves.

Sitting at the long dining-room table without the entire family in attendance was a mix of joy and sorrow. I was happy that most of the family was together and I did not miss the stress caused by Eric's outrageous discussions. At prior family dinners, he would often entice everyone into volatile arguments. Laura, ever the peacemaker, kept a yellow writing pad beside her at dinner. Whenever Eric introduced a topic she didn't like, Laura would scribble out in large black marker; **NO POLITICS....NO BUSINESS....NO MONEY.... NO SEX!**. Amazingly, everyone laughed and moved on as she boldly held up the sheets whenever we touched on those hot buttons. I couldn't help but notice that the occasion was more solemn without Shirley and her family and, despite my anger, I couldn't help but miss them.

As I had feared, Laura had a difficult time that semester. It was hard for her to break into already long-established cliques.

Eventually, Laura befriended a quiet Persian girl named Rebecca and an Israeli fellow named Noah. Laura also began dating a young man Gal and I couldn't stand. He was an Iranian Muslim. "Does he know you're Jewish?" I asked, not understanding how this could ever work.

"We never talk about religion." She answered. I guess young puppy love is blind to issues of religious contentions.

Ian's school also ended up being a bust. His new school emphasized sports more than I would have liked, going so far as to end classes early on game days, which I thought was ridiculous. I decided that Ian was not getting any kind of education in this school and that he should not return there the following year.

As we fretted over what to do for the kids, a generous offer came in from one of Gal's business acquaintances. "Just use my address," he said simply.

This may not seem like a big deal, but it threw so many of my previously held assumptions into question. Never before had I questioned the truths Mom told me. According to her, all strangers wanted to do was hurt you and tear you down; they would use you, so it was just better to stay away from them. I had gotten so paranoid that I feared going into elevators alone with strange men, but suddenly, here was a person I had never met who was willing to help us out, while my own sister was the one harming me.

We took him up on his offer, going through the necessary paperwork, and then waited for their response.

Happily, a white envelope, embossed with the school district's emblem arrived in our mail box, informing us that Laura and Ian could return to school once again. Although I was relieved that the children could go back to their normal lives, I couldn't let go of this incident and continued to struggle with who to trust.

Meanwhile, Steven, having tried several careers, was still not making enough money to suit Brenda and decided to make a drastic change in his life.

When the phone rang and Steven asked if he could come over, I was thrilled. I loved seeing my brother, especially without Brenda. When he arrived, I noticed that his shoulders were hunched and his head hung low. He looked utterly forlorn and lost. I turned on the kettle and heated up some water for tea as Steven went over to Gal, who was at the table working on some invoices. "Gal, what would you think about helping me open a smaller branch of Global Flooring Supplies?" he asked, his voice low and weak.

"No!" I answered, without missing a beat. "That's not a good idea!" I knew from experience that Gal liked to call all the shots. "You would have to be willing to listen to everything he said," I warned Steven, trying to paint a bleak picture. "You will have no say."

As Steven spilled two heaping teaspoons of sugar into his tea, I could tell he was not hearing me.

"Please don't do this. It'll be such a disaster!" I continued. As I spoke, Gal's eyes brightened. He had always toyed with the idea of Global having multiple locations, but I was feeling uneasy about family partnerships. I had been burned by Shirley and would have preferred not to risk it again.

"I have no other options," Steven admitted. "I need to provide for my family. I'm willing to sign any written agreement and work under any conditions you set. I'm at your mercy." It was an awful moment. "Let us think about it," we finally promised him.

I loved my brother and could only imagine how painful it must have been for him to come to our house, his hand outstretched, begging for a chance. But I also knew my husband. He was a good and kind man and the best provider I had ever seen, but he did not know how to work with a partner. How could this possibly work?

I called Mom and her answer was short and sweet: "Tell him no!" she warned.

"But Mom, how can I do that to Steven?"

"Jaclyn, a coward dies a thousand deaths, a brave man only once," she said. Good words, smart words and probably the best advice she had and would ever give me, but in the end, I did not listen to those pearls of wisdom. Steven was my brother and I felt that if I could construct the arrangement strongly enough, addressing as many problems in advance as I could, it could work. Steven was different from Shirley, and I persuaded myself that he could be trusted. Gal was excited, hopeful that the business would now double in size with Steven's help.

To ensure both my husband and my brother were treated fairly, I scanned the internet for every document I could find to create a just and equitable contract. I spelled out the terms as plainly and with as much fairness to both sides as I could.

Gal agreed to train Steven for a few months. He would have access to all our computer information containing our industry-specific software, vendor and customer information, prices and inventory information. The idea was that Steven would basically be up and running with a built-in customer base as soon as he opened his doors. The catch was that Steven would purchase his material from us at cost and we would be entitled to a percentage of his profit. It seemed like a decent deal for both: Steven got material at our discounted cost, which was far below what he would have had to pay to purchase it himself, while we received discounts for large quantities and Gal would get a percentage of Steven's sales. I hoped everyone would consider this a mutually beneficial arrangement: Steven would finally be making a good living and Gal would begin his dream of expanding Global Flooring Supplies.

Although Steven tried very hard to learn the trade, problems soon began to arise. Steven often vanished for long lunch breaks to visit the property he still owned with Eric. Gal noticed his conspicuous absences and felt wronged.

As Steven's training period neared its end, he found a suitable location for his small satellite shop. Gal and Steven worked hard to build a showroom and a warehouse. Being very computer-savvy, Steven downloaded all our information onto his computer. I helped him obtain all the forms he required, so now he just needed to wait for the inventory, which was paid for by Mom and Dad, to be delivered. We told him that we would of course give him the initial seed inventory *on account*, but that he would need to begin paying that down quickly. To ensure that flooring contractors would be aware of Steven's store as soon as he opened his doors, we placed flyers all around our store, alerting people that they could visit the new location when they were in that neck of the woods.

His sales were as good as could be expected for a new business, slow at first, but picking up daily. But while things were looking up for him in the flooring business, black clouds were appearing on another horizon – the property he shared with Eric was losing tenants. Leasing issues arose and the amount now due on the mortgage was more than either of them had. Steven could not figure out how that had happened; he had watched the books carefully, but the financial cushion they had put in place to cover such lean times had disappeared. He was also shocked to learn that the envelopes containing the property tax payments had mysteriously never been received by the Tax Collector.

"Buy me out," Eric suggested to Steven, but Steven did not have that kind of money and he had no one he could ask for a loan. Foreclosure loomed, and everyone was angry.

CHANGES

Mom never fully recovered from her accident. She visited us less frequently, and started going to the doctor more often. Dad, wanting to know what was wrong with his wife, tried to accompany her into her doctor's office, but she repeatedly refused him entrance. "Stay out here," she told him in the waiting room. When Mom was out of ear shot, he would go up to the receptionist's desk.

"Why can't I go into the room with my wife?" he asked. "Shouldn't I be allowed to know what is going on? I am her husband, after all."

The nurse could sense his frustration, but she could do nothing. "Mr. Poltzer, there is a law of doctor/patient privilege. I'm sorry, but unless you wife says it is alright for you to go in, you'll have to wait in the waiting room." Dad sadly returned to his seat, still wondering and still worried. What was wrong with his Channa?

We all grew more concerned about her health, but when asked, Mom always said she was fine.

Eric's creative bookkeeping had finally caught up with him. The game was up. He owed the state a lot of money, and no one could or would help him out of his bind. He offered to make monthly payments, but the state demanded that the total amount be paid off in one year's time. Shirley and Eric had no way of making that kind of money quickly enough, so they had to sell the beautiful home Shirley loved. However, even this would not satisfy the debt. Their credit would be ruined and a government lien would hang over them for years to come.

Shirley was bitter; her life was a mess. She had always felt a certain sense of entitlement, but nothing was going according to plan. Her husband was a sham. Garth continued to struggle with learning difficulties and had few friends. Her glowing youth and slim figure had changed over time, and she struggled with the fact that she was losing her looks. Shirley, oddly enough, wouldn't direct her blame at Eric, who had never warned her of the financial tsunami headed their way. Instead, she set her sights on Mom.

"What kind of mother allows her daughter to marry a man who can't provide?" she yelled. Mom sat there and listened. She didn't have anything to say, and since the dollar figures involved were so large, Mom could do nothing but join her Shirley in tears.

Ever since Brenda and Steven had become engaged, Brenda had wished the Poltzer family would move very far away. She continued to feel cursed by her bumpkin of a mother-in-law, who said inopportune things at inappropriate times, who ran a messy home and who was a sloppy dresser. She tolerated Gal and me because we had money and were currently providing her husband, and more importantly, herself, with a shot at a comfortable lifestyle, but she was hardly civil to the rest of the siblings.

When Steven and Brenda brought their first child, a baby girl they named Marissa, into the world in the spring of 1992, Brenda took the opportunity to demonstrate to all of us her displeasure at being a Poltzer. Steven's excited phone call informed us that he had become a father and we could not have been more pleased. We all raced to the hospital where we found a radiant Steven, who strutted like a peacock to the infant ward and pointed his new daughter out to us through the glass. We craned our necks to look for the small plastic cradle that housed his little girl, but could not find *Baby Poltzer Girl* listed anywhere. "Where is she?" we asked.

"She's in the second row," he told us, and there lay a little bundle—with a name plate that read *Baby Grossman Girl*. Our exhilaration dissipated, and Mom and Dad were mortified; this was a Poltzer child, whether Brenda liked it or not.
"Brenda had to put her last name on the paperwork for insurance purposes," Steven tried to explain, but it was a pitiful excuse and we all knew the truth.

Meanwhile, Steven's Global Flooring Supplies location was booming. Each month, Steven provided the necessary reports that showed his income and expenses, grudgingly sending us checks for our portion, but there were always arguments, complaints and accusations that Gal was trying to minimize his success. Gal and Steven discussed the numbers and Steven was reminded that this arrangement was in both their interests, and this quieted things down … for a while.

Laura started her senior year back at her old high school, happy to have found her old friends again. Early in the year, the hallway was already abuzz with talk of the senior prom. Laura wanted to go very badly but didn't have a date. Then she came up with an idea – Noah. When she asked him, she couldn't have hoped for a better answer.

He smiled and simply said, "We'll have the best time ever."

Laura and I immediately began shopping. We hit every dress shop we could find. She tried on everything, from black dresses that halter tied to garnet frocks with skinny straps, but the dress that called to her was a beautiful green satin number.

After she and her friends had all their hair and make-up professionally done, they arranged to meet at our house to have their portraits taken. Everyone arrived and the photo shoot began.

Proms are notorious for the sexual activity that goes on, but Laura and Noah weren't attracted to each other—at least not consciously.

Days later, when I processed the photographs I had taken, I pulled Laura aside. "I want you to see something," I told her. In the folder that held all the snapshots was a single image that I felt warranted an enlargement. As Laura's friends stood beside their dates, there was something different about Laura and Noah. While the eyes and body language of the other young women and young men were visibly sterile and lacking in warmth, there was a comfort, an ease – an attraction – between my daughter and this young fellow.

"I don't see anything, Mom," Laura argued.

"Well I do." And there is where we left it.

Ian's return to school was a happy one. He enjoyed all the attention he got from friends who wanted to know where he had been for the past year.

On occasion Ian passed Garth in the hallway and on the school grounds, but the two spoke only minimally. The wedge that had slowly begun to grow between them some time ago was now the size of the Grand Canyon. It was such a pity that these two boys, who had been like twins for most of their young lives, had drifted so far apart.

As Steven's business prospered, he and Brenda became increasingly discontented with the percentage Gal was collecting. They wanted to draw up a new contract. "The payback formulation isn't working. At this rate I can't stay in business," he explained to me. Steven even claimed that Gal was tweaking the numbers to his benefit.

"Steven, you knew what the formula was in the beginning," I replied. "And Gal isn't tweaking anything."

Gal and Steven argued continually, and when it appeared that they were getting nowhere, Gal began insisting that Steven's store be closed. "And tell him to give me back everything we gave him! Let your brother go try and screw someone else out of a contract!" he hollered at me.

Quickly, the phones were abuzz with accusations and threats. Mom's many cries to stop fighting fell on deaf ears. We tried everything to improve the relationship. Steven thought that an unbiased outsider could help and asked his father-in-law to mediate. Gal agreed, sure that any moron would see how Steven was in the wrong. But this didn't help. Arguments continued to rage, and everyone felt that they'd been taken advantage of, including myself. I wanted so badly to remedy this, but no matter what we did—new contracts, new arrangements, new business names—money continued to be owed, resentments festered, and

I grew more disillusioned with my brother with each passing day.

Steven and I both discussed the problem with Mom. As usual, my parents sided against Gal. They were in his home, seated at his table, drinking tea from his cups and they were trashing him. I am ashamed to say I did not do a thing to defend him. The basic Poltzer law was just too firmly implanted into me. I loved Gal, but blood was blood, and siding with my family was just easier.

During that period, it felt as though Gal and I were feuding with everyone. Somehow, despite all our differences, I still loved and adored my family, even missing Shirley and her kids a lot. There was no reason to invite her back into my life, but I did. I continued to believe that my true and loyal sister, the one from long ago, was still in there somewhere. So to end our silent war, I wrote her a letter, expressing my hurt about what I felt had happened. I wrote about how much I wished we could figure out some way of getting back together and asked her if she would meet me at a restaurant to chat. I felt that a public location would help increase our chances of being civil. To my surprise, she called me and we spoke briefly, opting to talk in more detail when we met.

I was nervous. It was a childish wish, but in my heart I hoped I might hear her say she missed me also and was sorry.

That morning, I arrived at the restaurant, took a deep breath and walked through the double doors. I walked up to Shirley, who was already seated and there was an initial moment of discomfort as our eyes met. At first, we kept the conversation light and ordered some coffee. But shortly thereafter, things took a turn. Shirley held nothing back. "I didn't come here to apologize," she began. "You and Gal shouldn't have stopped us from bringing money home to my family."

"Whatever we did, the children were never supposed to be touched!" I told her.

"I stand one hundred percent behind my husband and what you forced us to do," she stated with cold determination. "If I had had the chance, I would have written the letter to the school board myself!" Time had altered nothing. I reached into my purse, threw a twenty on the table and left. I barely made it to the car before starting to cry.

I called Gal from the car, who insisted I cross her out of my life. If only it were that easy! For reasons even I could hardly understand at this point, I just couldn't turn my back on this life-long relationship. Despite everything, she was such a pivotal part of my life. And I couldn't help hope in my heart that she would suddenly wake up and remember we were sisters and take me back.

When I got home, I called Mom. "Jaclyn, just let time pass," Mom begged. "Shirley is meschuge (Yiddish for crazy). "When she cools down you can try again."

I tried looking at the situation from Shirley's perspective. Maybe I did view the world through rose-colored glasses because I was the oldest and always got to wear the dresses first, the one who did not struggle for money and who got pregnant one-two-three. Maybe I did not understand her hardships well enough. I was determined to try again. When I felt enough time had passed, and cursed with a self-destructive need to have my family around me, I contacted Shirley yet again. I had abandoned any dreams of actual becoming close again, but hoped simply that we could learn to co-exist peacefully. But even that proved too difficult. I just had to come to terms with the fact that there would never be any closure.

In 1996, Ian and Garth graduated from high school. The two had never rekindled their former closeness, but on graduation day, they participated together in the commencement march. Everyone in the family was in attendance; even Eric's parents, who had never involved themselves in Shirley's children's lives, made an appearance, although they did not sit anywhere near the Poltzers. The day was hot and we were all seated on tall metal bleachers. There were throngs of people, some with balloons, some with flowers and others with signs congratulating their certain someone. The school band played Pomp and Circumstance and we all strained to see our boys walk down the aisle dressed in the gold and brown school colors. Garth marched first. As he walked along, eyes held up for brief periods of time, I could tell he still had a difficult time making eye contact. It was a trait he had acquired from Eric, except with Eric, it was because he was a slippery character, while with Garth, it was a result of his lack of self-esteem. We all hooted and shouted, hoping he could hear our cheers. Then Ian came bounding down the aisle. Wearing an eggplant-colored suit he had purchased for the occasion beneath his gown, he was smiling as he searched the bleachers for our shouts. We were so loud that he spotted us right away, and gave us a quick wink.

The temperature was in the high nineties. Mom sweltered and fanned herself, trying in vain to get some small amount of relief from the heat, but she sat proudly as her two grandsons' names were called.

Following the seemingly endless speeches, the caps were thrown high into the air and spectators were free to spill onto the field. Families located their young graduates and cameras clicked wildly. Mom didn't walk too well, but with help, she made her way down to the field, where she hugged and kissed her two graduates. Despite all our differences, Shirley and I were civil and it was a good day for the family.

Over the summer, Laura and Noah continued to hang out together as friends, but by fall, they were together as a couple.

Their fledgling romance would quickly be put to the test. Laura was headed to a university in Santa Barbara, about an hour and a half north of Los Angeles, while Noah would be attending a university close to home in Los Angeles.

The two weathered the long-distance romance for two years and I benefited because each time Laura returned home to see him, I got a chance to see her as well. As their bond grew stronger, Noah transferred to Laura's school to be with her and for the next two years, they were inseparable.

Shirley, still faltering financially, approached Nina about employment. Nina's business was thriving, and, having never taken on any partners, she had done well for herself. But what choice did she have when Shirley called? "Nina, I can really use the money and would love to learn the fashion business from you," she confided. Her idea was to work hand in hand with Nina, drinking in all her designing genius, but Nina did not feel it wise to have Shirley that close.

"How about I hire you as my general office person?" she offered Shirley. "Right now I could use someone in that position and I'm sure you can manage it." Shirley would still be exposed to the ins and outs of manufacturing, but from a safe distance.

"I would like to learn how to be a product manager," Shirley reminded Nina.

"I already have a girl who does that and you are more than welcome to watch her do her job on the days when we aren't trying to get things out for a deadline, but then you'll be off the pay clock," Nina explained.

"Why won't I be getting paid when I help her?" Shirley asked.

"Because I need her to concentrate and she doesn't need any help."

It wasn't exactly what Shirley wanted, but she accepted anyway. The two worked together several months. Although it worked out ok in the beginning, things gradually begin to sour. Shirley resented her office job, and Nina was forced to turn a blind eye when she was late with her work.

Finally, the two entered into a new arrangement, in which Shirley would sell the rejects, promising not to sell them as firsts. Shirley assured her she would not.

Shortly thereafter, Nina began to hear bad news from her clothing representative. "Nina, your sister is selling the clothing as firsts and the boutiques are contacting us," Nina's agent informed her.

"Shirley, I can't give you the seconds any longer," Nina informed her.

"But you can to a stranger?" Shirley snarled. Nina did not get angry, she did not yell, she just repeated her statement and Shirley had another turncoat sister to add to her list of useless family members. "You're no better than Jaclyn," she declared. "You are another one who likes to put strangers first before family."

Nina graduated college and was living back at home when Nina approached Laura and offered her a job as her personal assistant. Laura jumped at the chance. Laura adored Nina and the pay was good. The fly in this ointment was Shirley.

"Why are you willing to pay Laura so much more than you were me?" She asked, her voice filled with anger.

"Laura is quick and very computer savvy." Nina explained. "She is not interested in learning the business the way you wanted to. She is handling all those things that make my business run smoothly and you didn't want to do that."

Shirley remained furious at yet another perceived injustice.

Nina busily ran her business, but noticed that while she had a stockpile of money, it was impossible to have a social life at the same time. After careful consideration, she decided that it was time to retire and begin searching for a man. She emptied her warehouse of all the clothing she held in stock, boxed up her sewing machines and locked her factory door. The next morning, she slept in, something she had not been able to do for a long, long time.

Nina was a wonderful study in contradictions. Of all the Poltzer children, she was the weakest swimmer, which was not terribly important as many people live happily without ever learning to swim … except that she loved surfing. And so no one was surprised when Nina sold her house on the hill and purchased a home on the beach in Malibu. The house rested on the sand, so that when the tide came in, the ocean floated beneath her floor. The ocean-facing side of the house was sheer glass, allowing a view of the sunset and the dolphins that routinely swam past and leaped into view. Her wooden porch protruded out over the sand and when the tide was out, she lounged on the beach with her dog, Peoni, by her side. She decorated the house with fine designer pieces and wrapped her king-size bed in the highest possible thread-count sheets with a soft featherbed on top. Nina had arrived.

As was to be expected, when she first showed us her new home, my parents disapproved; in their view, it was too expensive. "Now that you're out of work, how can you possibly make the payments? What if the tide crashes into the house and you drown?" But Nina was used to their lack of support. She loved this house, and nothing they said made the tiniest dent in her happiness there.

One night, Noah called. "Laura, at seven o'clock sharp come out of your house and please don't look out the window," he told her. Noah was a romantic fellow, and we had some idea what was about to happen since we'd all gone ring shopping together some weeks before. Unable to resist gazing out the window, I watched many cars zoom by. A horse trailer passed and parked down the street. There were small children living just a few houses down and many times they'd rent ponies for the party guests to ride.

When the clock struck seven, Laura walked out the front door. There was Noah, dressed in slip-on plastic armor up in the saddle of a Palomino quarter horse. He rode slowly up the driveway toward her as the rest of us spilled out of the house. Jean from the riding stables had arranged it all secretly. Noah swung off the horse and walked up to Laura, went down on one knee, pulled a small black velvet box from his pocket and asked her to be his beautiful bride.

"Yes," she answered, although it was difficult to understand her through her tears. From an ice chest appeared a lovely spread of cheese, crackers and chilled champagne, and the neighbors across the street came out and offered yet more bottles of bubbly for the happy occasion. Then Noah's family arrived and we toasted to our children's happiness and long life together. We were all thrilled.

We were shooting for a 2001 wedding, which would give us enough time to arrange Laura's dream wedding, but first we needed to throw the young couple a proper engagement party. After much discussion, we decided to hold the event in a nearby temple. Laura had selected a café-au-lait colored gown with sequins. Since Mom and Dad's 50th wedding anniversary was around the same time, we had a cake created with their wedding photograph imprinted on it in frosting. I also located their wedding song, "Oh, how we danced" by Al Josen, and prepared to have Mom live out a fantasy. She always wanted to be in the spotlight, so I thought that this would be a perfect occasion to make her wishes come true. I also enjoyed the symmetry of celebrating fifty years of marriage and a marriage-to-be on the same night.

The night of the party finally arrived. I was very excited. My daughter was about to take a major step forward in her life and I was both happy and nervous for her. That night at the party, when the announcement was made that it was my parents' anniversary and the cake was rolled out, it was a highlight of my Mom's life. She marveled at the cake and the picture of her, young and beautiful, with her white satin gown and veil drawn in white butter cream, standing beside Dad, who looked dashing with his mustache and hat. We cued the disc jockey and their song played as they took the dance floor, just as they had fifty years earlier. It took everything she had to dance, but it was a happy moment.

As usual, Shirley managed to mar some of the evening's magic by arriving late and dressing so casually as to be disrespectful, but I was determined to focus on the joyous nature of the evening and have a lovely time in every respect.

Mom's health continued to decline and she remained as secretive as ever. We'd been so focused on trying to understand her health issues that we were surprised when she told us that

191

Dad had gotten ill and had to go to the hospital. "What happened?" we asked.

"Your father ate something bad," she answered, downplaying the event.

We pushed her on the matter and finally learned Dad had gotten sick from eating a bean dish Mom had prepared. The hospital did not keep him long and when he got back home, several of us rushed over to see him and speak with Mom. "Let me see the package of beans, Mom," I said and she pointed to her cabinets.

Mom's cabinets were a disaster. There were out-of-date boxes and containers filled with old dried foods, folded envelopes all filled with spices and toppings long past their expiration date and bugs that lived in and around the food.

When we finally located the beans, we discovered that it was almost ten years beyond its expiration date. We knew this could not continue and I insisted on cleaning it up. Dad was thrilled with the idea, but Mom's nostrils flared. She spoke very quietly. "If you talk about this again, I will change the locks and never let you come over again," she warned. "Don't talk about this any more."

It was clear that she meant it. But we couldn't sit by and do nothing. There was a real possibility that she would accidentally kill my father or herself. So we decided to intervene, everyone that is, except Shirley. She refused, saying Mom needed to tend to her own mess.

That Saturday morning, I let myself in to my parents' house. Mom and Dad seemed to be out, and my other siblings hadn't arrived yet. Resting on top of the television set were family photos in an assortment of frames, and on the wall next to me were yet more pictures of the family. Some showed pairings of children and others were photos of Gal and me and Shirley and Eric. There were pictures of a few of the grandchildren in different stages of growth. So many years had passed and there had been so many changes for the Poltzers.

Shlomo, Nina and Steven soon arrived, and together we waited for our parents' arrival. Mom had told me that she had lots of money hidden throughout the house, so we did not want to alarm her by throwing things away. We would wait until she arrived. We assumed that they'd gone out for breakfast and would be home soon. As I sat there with my siblings, I could almost picture Mom and Dad seated in a booth somewhere. They would order one breakfast meal off the senior citizen menu and tell the waitress that they would be sharing it. Then, when no one was looking, Mom would steal everything from the table she could fit into her purse. The purse was a horrid, black vinyl handbag, filthy from all the food she placed inside. I had tried to upgrade her to one of my old bags, but she would not hear of it. Once we had given her a gift of tiny purse-sized Rubbermaid containers, but she never used them – insisting that that's what God made napkins and plastic bags for.

We heard them pull up. I'm sure they could not have missed spotting all our cars parked out front. When they came in, Mom was initially happy to see us all, but she grew suspicious when she saw our many cleaning supplies on her counter. "What are you all doing here?" she asked.

"We have come to clean your kitchen," I explained.

"We won't throw anything away without your approval," Nina promised, speaking quickly to keep Mom from interrupting.

Mom's eyes narrowed and she began to grind her teeth in anger.

"Channa, what a wonderful thing your children are going to do for you!" Dad made the mistake of singing out.

"Go upstairs!" she ordered him in a low voice, but he did not leave.

"Mom, we'll be very careful not to throw anything away without looking through it thoroughly. We'll open every box in front of you to make sure we don't throw anything important away."

She remained quiet, but she fumed inside. Her little chicks were committing mutiny against the older and wiser chicken, and there seemed to be nothing she could do to stop them.

We were not going to let her disapproval deter us from our mission of mercy. Mom's hoarding was quite clearly a direct result of having suffered near starvation and neediness during the war. A napkin or packet of ketchup would have been a precious thing to have when you were running for your life from the Nazis. Even a serrated plastic knife would have been useful. But that was then and this was now—except not in Mom's world. She couldn't fully move on from that terrifying time.

As we started to empty the cabinets and scrub at the surfaces, Mom remained silent, aghast at our betrayal. Several hours later, the kitchen was spotless and we were done.

"When can you come back and finish doing the rest of the house?" Dad asked as we gathered up our things. "This was such a wonderful thing for you all to do." He complimented us repeatedly as he escorted us to the front door. But Mom, without even rising from the couch simply threatened us.

"If you ever do anything like this again," she said, "I will move and not tell you where we've gone. I am the boss of this house and like it just the way it is." We hated disobeying her, but we knew we'd done the right thing.

One evening, Garth stopped by for a visit. He was eighteen years old now, a shy young man who still had no direction in his life. School had been a bust and he hadn't found anything that called to him as a career. Out of the blue, he asked, "Jaclyn, do you think I could work for Gal?"

I stopped chewing mid-chew. Oh no! I thought to myself. I had gone down this road before. "Why do you want to work for Gal?" I asked.

"Because I want to learn the business, and I think there is a future there for me."

A coward dies a thousand deaths, a brave man only once, played loudly in my brain, but this was my nephew, my Garth.

"Garth," I said, practically begging, "Gal is so difficult to work with and he isn't very nice. Why do you think I do my bookkeeping at home?"

"Jaclyn," he said, almost crying, "I want to get a real job and make some real money."

I sat for a moment and peered out at my garden, wondering why my relatives insisted on trying to mix business and pleasure when it never seemed to turn out well. We spoke for quite a while and I offered up every reason I could think of why this was not a good idea, but no matter how unpleasant a picture I painted, Garth would not budge. He had made up his mind that he wanted to work for Gal and was willing to take any job to start.

I gave Garth's request a great deal of thought, very much tempted to simply tell him no. Mom ordered me to tell him no and Gal was not thrilled with the idea, but I was attached to Garth and felt sorry for him. If I had used my brain instead of my heart, I would have told him it wasn't a good idea, but I followed my heart and gave Garth the answer he wanted and prayed for the best.

Gal and I gave careful thought to where Garth should begin. We thought it would be best to start him at the mill. I had hopes that Garth might learn to operate one of the machines, but Mom swiftly vetoed this idea. She was frightened that he would somehow get his fingers caught in the knives.

So we tried again. The next job we gave him was to help out in the warehouse, pulling inventory.

Garth was very loyal to Gal, and rather than do his job, he took it upon himself to spy on the other employees. When they goofed off, as our workers often did, he tattled—and he tattled a lot. This made him extremely unpopular with the boys in the back. Garth felt he was helping us guard our inventory, one day going so far as to engage in a fist fight with one of our most established sales people.

When I was informed that Garth had been taken by ambulance to a local hospital, I was frightened he was actually injured, but then I began thinking to myself that this was probably something his father had taught him: *if anyone ever hits you, lie down, go to the hospital and we will sue like crazy.* All I needed was a lawsuit from my nephew!

When I arrived, I was relieved to see he was not harmed. The hospital was looking into his claims that his back, neck and shoulders were hurting, and I'm sure if I had not been his aunt, he would have sued, sued, sued.

"What are you planning on doing to the worker that did this?" Shirley asked me, enraged at what had happened. "He's going to be fired, right?" she demanded.

It would probably have been the right course of action, but Gal kept his employees no matter what. Of course, Shirley and Garth were angry, feeling that it confirmed their belief that Gal found more value in strangers than in family. However, Garth returned to work the next day and we offered him a new job as assistant to our delivery driver.

Garth initially enjoyed some aspects of this job, but it was hot and strenuous work. At one delivery location, Garth spotted a swimming pool and had the nerve to ask the homeowner if he could take a dip.

It was not the first time Gal had demanded that Garth had to go, but this time he was adamant.

The next day I had Garth come over. I once again suggested our company might not be the right place for him, but he just shook his head. He did not want to try anything else.

Gal relented once again and we brought Garth back to the warehouse and put him to work filing. But with his dyslexia, even this did not go well. At this point, we were running out of options and we gave him some maintenance work. Shirley called me almost immediately, complaining that he had been reduced to performing menial labor. "I do the sweeping sometimes, and if the bathrooms are really a mess I clean them," I told her. "But I'll try him in the warehouse one more time." Back to the warehouse he went.

As was his custom, Gal walked into the back to see how the boys were doing. As he scanned the shelves, he spotted a sleeping figure. Garth had found a nice quiet location and a soft place to rest—while he was on the clock. Gal did not say a word to him, but that night, he informed me, "No more excuses, he is out of here!" His voice was calm and this was final.

"I will tell him tomorrow, but just let me be the one to talk to him," I said. I hoped to break the news gently. The next day, Gal called Garth into his office, not to fire him, but to discuss work ethics with him. As Garth entered, they were both visibly uncomfortable. Being called into Gal's office must have felt a great deal like being called to the principal's office back at school.

"I saw you sleeping in the warehouse and I am very disappointed in you," Gal lectured. "You'll never do well if you work like this."

Rather than being apologetic, Garth told Gal how lazy the other employees were. He told him that he always kept an eye on the other employees. "Your guys are stealing from you," he asserted, "I am your nephew, your family."

His preaching angered Gal, who felt he had done more than enough for this family. Eric's own mother had never hired him, even though she owned a successful business. To put an end to further arguments, he dismissed Garth from his office and went downstairs.

Gal went to the front counter, where several customers were waiting, but Garth had decided that he was not quite finished yet. There, in front of a showroom full of clients, Garth yelled at Gal. "You are my uncle and I work hard, but you don't care! You don't even care that your workers are stealing from you!"

Customers turned to watch the spectacle. Gal's clientele was beyond sacrosanct and he was not going to put up with Garth for a moment longer. "Get out!" he yelled.

Garth wasted no time and drove directly to my house, expecting that I would remedy the situation, but this time, the answer was no. "But I'm your nephew."

He was livid, accusing me of betraying family and being wildly unfair to him. I held my ground, trying to explain that he would have better luck elsewhere. But the damage was done. My relationship with Garth was destroyed. And then, there was Shirley to deal with. She called later that day to berate me further. Once again, she thought I should prioritize family over my husband. There was much back and forth, all of it futile.

"Shirley, why don't you have him work for you in your store?" I asked, feeling it was a valid question.

"There are little girls trying on stuff and he stares at them and that makes them uncomfortable."

"So I have to give him a job that is stupid and pay him for it?"

"You're rich, you can afford it!"

As she continued, I finally understood that she was still jealous—and still seemed to feel that I owed her in some way. "Jaclyn, you only have money thanks to Gal. You should never have had that life. You don't deserve it." I was furious. I had done my share to help the business over the years. Yes, I benefitted from Gal's hard work, but we deserved everything that we had. If she wanted my life, no one was stopping her from getting it. She continued to whine, listing to me all my good luck over the years: "You got pregnant right away and had a girl and then a boy with no problems. Your husband was a good provider and you have such a cushy life. You don't understand what I'm going through."

"What does it matter what my life is? You have four beautiful children, what about that?"

She brought up all the same old issues, unable to let any of it go. Finally, I slammed the receiver down, unable to take it any longer.

I knew that my sister was like cocaine, and I was like an addict trying to control its effects on me. I did not know how to have a superficial relationship with her, so I decided once and for all to cut myself off from her altogether.

A STAG ON THE HILL

It was the beginning of August and only a month remained before Laura's wedding. It was a wonderful time for me. Nina and my friends threw her a gorgeous bridal shower. It was an English tea and we asked everyone to wear a hat to add a little added panache to the affair. We all had a wonderful time, even Mom, who looked great in the oversized hat Nina lent her. Laura was radiant, I was proud, and the whole event went off without a hitch. I was only sad that Shirley was not there. I decided not to invite her, but felt her absence, just the same.

I watched Laura's face as she opened her many gifts. My little girl was getting married and that blender and crystal bowl that now rested in a pile beside her would soon be resting on a cabinet in a home she would be sharing with her husband. I had such mixed emotions. I was happy for her, yet an ache had begun inside my heart, as I knew from my own experience that once married, she would no longer just be my daughter, but someone else's wife. I remembered my own adjustment, the divided loyalties, the transition from child to head of household, and I hoped with all my heart that it would all go more smoothly for her.

A few days later, Shlomo, who had maintained a fairly pleasant relationship with Shirley, contacted me. "Shirley told me that she wasn't angry about the shower, but she says that if you don't invite her to the wedding, she will never forgive you."

Mom was next. "Amber wants desperately to go to Laura's wedding and she also wants to be a flower girl," pleading with me to change my mind and include them. "There will be so many people there you won't even know they're there." But Mom was wrong; I'd know they were there. I decided to leave the decision up to Laura. This was, after all, her wedding. She agreed to invite them, conceding that she would be busy and that it wouldn't make any real difference.

"I would be happy to have Amber as a flower girl," she told me.

Since we had never done well with phone calls, I drove the short distance to Shirley's house, after informing her in advance by phone, to hash this out in person.

With the assistance of her mother-in-law, Shirley and Eric had purchased a beautiful hillside home. I was uncomfortable as I knocked on the front door. Shirley opened it and we walked silently into the kitchen.

Amber was happy to see me. Then Shirley and I locked eyes, but I had not come to fight; I had come, once again, to make some sort of tentative peace. "Shirley, I have come to speak with you and Garth."

"Well, why don't you speak with Garth first?" Shirley suggested and called to him from the doorway.

He came in, but refused to make eye contact with me, moving around nervously like an anxious cat. "I am very sorry about what happened Garth." I repeated.

"You forced me to clean toilets and gave all the good jobs to strangers." He said. "You never ever stood up for me." It was the same old story. There was nothing more to say. So I turned to Shirley. "We want to invite you and your entire family to Laura's wedding." Then I turned to Amber. "And we'd like you to be one of our flower girls." Amber squealed with delight and ran to her Mom. Shirley seemed to be grateful and as our short meeting ended, we were still uncomfortable. There was so much simmering beneath the surface of our brief conversation, but we said nothing except, "See you there."

When I told Mom, she was relieved and happy. She would be at Laura's wedding with all her "five fingers," as she sometimes called us.

We had located a magnificent strapless gown in a small bridal boutique and had it tailored to fit Laura's tiny frame. She wove her long, red-brown hair into an Italian crystal crown with a floor-length veil that trailed behind her. Her neck bore a three-strand pearl choker with a square diamond clasp, which she had borrowed from her soon-to-be mother-in-law.

It was September 1st, 2001, Laura's wedding day, and every room in my house was filled to overflowing with Gal's entire family, who had flown in from Israel for the occasion.

The wedding was to take place just as the sun set, but a half hour before the formal ceremony, it was time for the Katuba, or Jewish marriage contract, to be signed. The immediate family and closest friends were invited into a meeting room where the rabbi recited a prayer. Then Noah gently lifted the lacy veil that covered Laura's face, a custom that allowed the groom to be sure that he was getting the correct bride. He gave her a tender kiss. Mom and Dad stood proudly beside Laura as they watched Nina, Laura's maid of honor, sign the document as an official witness to this union. Mom could not have been happier – her first grandchild was getting married and she had lived long enough to see it.

After all the religious legalities had been completed, it was time to wait in the stairwell until we were given the go-ahead from the wedding coordinator. I remembered the photograph that I had pointed out to Laura so many years ago. Tears rolled down my face. I was so happy for her. Then, all at once, the music began.

The ceremony took place outside at the beach as the sun was setting. Mom and Dad walked down the flower petal-laden aisle, followed by Gal's parents, the bridesmaids, groomsmen, flower girls and ring boy. The sky was turning violet, and I was told that a lone stag stood on a hillside watching from afar – I wonder what he thought of what he was seeing. Noah's parents escorted their son, who appeared to be bursting with joy. The music changed and the wedding march began to play; it was time for Laura to take center stage. She walked proud and tall, ready to enter the next part of her life.

At the front, Gal and I stopped and both kissed her; then we let her go and she walked forward to Noah. She encircled him seven times, as is a Jewish custom, and the ceremony of joining them began. At one point a prayer shawl was wrapped around them both, binding them as the Rabbi chanted the wedding blessings, and then the two drank from a silver cup filled with sweet wine. Finally, a wrapped glass was set before

Noah and he brought his foot down on it with a crash. "Mazel Tov!" everyone shouted, and Laura and Noah were married.

Noah did not *walk* into the reception – he *floated* in, shaking hands and accepting congratulatory kisses from well-wishers. Everyone took their seats and the music began. For months, Laura and Noah had practiced a choreographed dance production they had prepared for this very moment. As the music played, the newly married couple performed their elegant dance steps across the floor. The grand finale featured a romantic dip, with Noah tenderly planting a sweet kiss on Laura's lips.

Great joy filled the air and the guests jumped to their feet, forming countless circles within circles to do the Hora, a joyful group dance where everyone joined hands and moved to a happy rhythm. Once that was over, it was time for Laura and Noah to take their seats and partake in the Mitzvah dance. The stronger men in the wedding party volunteered to lift them high into the air as they sat on the chairs. Supposedly, this old Jewish tradition simulates a king and queen sitting on their flying thrones. The two bridged their momentary separation by holding a napkin between them. Laura smiled and waved as the music played, confident she would not fall, while Noah held on tight, nervous about hitting the ground.

In an effort to merge the many cultures there, Laura incorporated the Persian Flower Dance, which was wonderful to perform and beautiful to watch. One of Laura's bridesmaids gathered some prepared flower petals and showered them down on Laura as she performed. Her hands wafted and her hips shook and she glowed as she went through the motions. Late that night, those of us still remaining showered Laura and Noah with rose pedals as they got inside their rented white limousine. The night had been glorious and more than I ever could have hoped for.

Then, suddenly, the evening was over. My beloved Laura was no longer a bride but a wife. As I watched her drive off, I thought about how our mother-daughter relationship was bound to change. I hoped I would cut her more slack than had been done for me. I had never really severed those apron strings between myself and my Mom, who wanted us never to leave her. She had always advised against fully emotionally investing myself in the marriage. It had taken me years of counseling to rid myself of these supposed pearls of wisdom and I promised myself that I would not be an intrusive mother-in-law. I would try hard not to voice my opinion about everything and I would not take sides, if at all possible. These were difficult concepts for me to grasp, as I had never learned them at home. But I was determined to try.

In the days that followed days, after focusing so much on my role as a mother at Laura's wedding, I thought a great deal about my role as a daughter, and of how my own mother and I were getting along at the time. Mom could be so disapproving, and was so quick to judge and contradict my own parenting decisions that I finally decided that the only way to protect myself was to restrict certain subjects of discussion with her.

"Are we going to talk about nonsense again?" she would ask when we spoke on the telephone.

"Yes, Mom," I answered, feeling sorry that it had to be this way. We chatted superficially about the weather and Hollywood gossip, as I no longer could deal with her input on to my children or marriage.

Unlike Mom, I applauded my children for their undertakings. When it came to my own accomplishments, however, Mom made it clear that she was unhappy that I had been so successful. When she said it, I could not believe my ears. "I need you to need me," she explained.

"But Mom, I will always need you."

"But I can't help you. Your problems are too big for me." She confessed.

It was such a blow – my own mother was not happy that after all these years, all that work, we had made it. Then and there, I made a personal vow not to do that to my children. I tried very hard to accept the fact that Mom and Dad were broken birds, with a difficult past that continued to haunt them and shape their relationships. Her torturous past would always make her suspicious of the future, and the present was simply a state of anticipation as she waited for everything to go to pieces around her. She was simply not capable of enjoying the moment.

Mom's lack of trust—although understandable in so many ways—had done permanent damage to her relationships. Even Dad was not her blood, and therefore, in some paradoxical way, still a stranger. She adored him, but also feared and mistrusted him, all simultaneously and in equal amounts.

Mom's fears and paranoia had leaked down to me, turning me into a fearful person as well. I rode horses, but laden with anxieties of what injuries I could sustain at any moment. Once, on a ski vacation, I took a ski lesson, and the instructor asked me why I leaned back. "If you are going to ski, you have to commit and lean into it," she told me, but that was how I lived my life, never truly leaning into it, but leaning back and never putting my full heart into it, always fearful of losing it all.

Mom's handiwork could be found on all her "five fingers." While Nina had been a success professionally, she continued feeling like a failure because she had not gotten married. Shlomo, too, searched for the unobtainable perfect match, never wanting his marriage to be anything like Mom and Dad's.

Shirley replicated Mom and Dad's life more than any of us. Jean, the woman who owned the barn where I rode, always told me that if you stare at something, you will ride toward it. Well, Shirley stared at Mom. She and Eric closed out the world and only truly trusted each other. She loved him and hated him, just like Mom and Dad. After she had suffered financial ruination, I asked her if she would marry Eric again if she could do it all over again, and without hesitation, she told me yes. There was no room for friends in their world, unless they could be used for some purpose.

Mom had ensured Shirley's dependence on her by helping her out financially. Shirley never apologized for the need for monetary help, as she felt that this was some kind of reparation for Mom's poor parenting. Mom had always said that if and when the Nazis came back, only Shirley and Eric would survive. Gal was too proud, but Eric would pay off anyone, using anything he had. Mom honored this trait and saw in him a quality that her children lacked.

Steven also retained an unhealthy emotional attachment to Mom, and his selection of a wife illustrated that profoundly. Brenda invoked total control over Steven and was ever watchful of him, but while Mom had equal parts of love and hate for Dad, Brenda had more hate than love for Steven. His continued attachment to Mom proved to be a monumental thorn in Brenda's side, which caused their marriage endless strain.

It was as if Mom had successfully created one giant body—hers—with many heads—ours. Although we spoke separately, we were intimately connected. Injuring one would injure all. It was very difficult to do or think anything without the family voicing opinions, and these opinions were very powerful, affecting all our thoughts and actions. Even as we grew older, we could not separate ourselves.

BAD CELLS LINING UP

In 2002, Nina was about to turn forty. Feeling obligated to celebrate such a milestone with the family, she decided to invite all the Poltzers and a few friends over to her house.

Nina labored feverishly, getting everything ready on the day of her party. Multi-colored dahlias were arranged in a single line on an expandable wooden dining-room table that flanked the window facing the ocean. Beach towels shaded by umbrellas were set up on the sand, inviting us to sit and watch the dolphins play. A soda station was resting on the porch and there was a kayak out and ready. We were all thrilled to leave the heat of the valley for the cool breezes of the sea shore – all except for Mom, who was having a lot of trouble walking. As she was ushered toward a chair by Dad, she grumbled about having to come to yet another function. She had arrived with an obvious chip on her shoulder, but none of us knew why.

Nina began carrying the many plates of foods to the table. Mom stared at the food, but didn't seem to appreciate the beautiful assortment of dishes Nina had worked so hard on. For reasons, we couldn't understand, Mom remained sour no matter how hard we tried to cheer her up.

Ian cranked up the stereo and Laura asked her grandfather to dance with her. He still had the moves and laughed as he shook his booty with his granddaughter. Mom glared at him. She hated being propped on a chair, unable to move. When the song finished, Dad took his place beside Mom, completely out of breath. "So," she began speaking loudly enough for all to hear, "you left me sitting here, all alone, and danced. Did I do that to you when you weren't feeling well?" she continued, reminding him of all his dancing transgressions since they were married. Then she began expounding on all his infractions in general.

"Mom, he was only dancing with Laura," we told her, attempting to run interference.

"Dad was only dancing with his own granddaughter." Nina scolded Mom in a low voice. Mom was silent for a moment, but couldn't help herself. Gal invited Dad to take a walk along the beach with him and Dad agreed, not wanting to fight any more and preferring the quiet of the sand.

Nina was not about to continue allowing Mom to ruin her day. "If you don't behave, I'll call a taxi and send you home."

Mom looked her in the eyes and then lifted her right pant leg. Her leg, from the ankle to the knee, was bloated to twice the normal size, hot to the touch and purple in color.

"What is that!" Nina asked, but not loud enough to alarm any of us. She knew this was not the result of an injury, but an unattended blood clot. "You have to go to the hospital right now!" she insisted. "The minute Dad comes back you are leaving! You can die from something like that!"

Mom had not wanted to share this with her children, but now that she was being attacked and everyone was taking Dad's side, she wanted Nina to see the real source of her crankiness. It now made more sense why she had needed him not to leave her side even for a moment.

The instant Dad returned to the house, Nina ordered him to take Mom directly to the emergency room. She had sufficiently scared Mom, so they were soon on their way.

"Lovely party, Nina. Happy fortieth birthday!" Laura said as she kissed Nina goodbye sometime around midnight. Nina wanted to call Mom and Dad, but it was late and so she decided to wait until morning to call.

"So?" she asked Mom when she got her on the phone the next day. "What happened? What did the doctor say?"

"Well, they took some blood, did some tests and gave me some pills," Mom replied matter-of-factly.

"Probably anticoagulants," Nina stated. "You have to be more careful, Mom."

"I am feeling much better," Mom told her, but Nina was not sure if she was telling the truth or not.

"Can I speak with Dad?" Nina asked, hoping to get a more realistic picture.

Mom grunted and handed the phone over to Dad, but Nina could hear her speaking to him in either Polish or

Hungarian. It was clear Mom was warning him not to say too much.

"What really happened?" Nina asked again.

"Well, we had to wait in the emergency room for hours until she was seen. They took some tests, gave her some medication and according to your Mother, she should be fine," Dad said with concern in his voice.

"Okay, Dad," Nina said, knowing that no one was getting the real story. But for the time being, there was nothing more to be done. We asked Dad to keep us apprised of any developments, but left it at that.

A few weeks later, I arrived on time at my doctor's office and offered up my breasts to the x-ray machinery and technician for my yearly mammogram. The procedure usually involved a certain amount of discomfort, especially since I had rather large breasts. A girlfriend had recently been diagnosed with breast cancer. Although she had not missed any of her mammograms, her cancer had already progressed to a dangerous stage. All around me, it seemed, women I knew were battling this disease and anxiety prone as I already was, I was desperate to avoid it myself.

A few days after my mammogram, I was home with Gal. I picked up the mail and saw a letter from my doctor's office. The letter said that they had tried to reach me and had been unable to. They had seen something in my x-ray that needed further clarification and additional x-rays would need to be taken as soon as possible. I immediately envisioned the worst case scenario—all I could read was that I had cancer. "I can't do it!" I yelled, allowing the letter to float to the floor. "I can't have cancer! I'll die!" I screamed out and Gal came running. I honestly felt that I could never go through what I had watched my friend go through; to me she was made of much stronger stuff than I. I was not going to see my children grow up, dance at my son's wedding or reach old age with Gal. Remaining calm, Gal telephoned the doctor's office and told them we would be in as soon as they had space. Then he took me in his arms.

"Everything will be fine and I'll be by your side every minute. Don't worry, it will be all right," he repeated.

Additional x-rays confirmed that there was a lump in my left breast. It was deep inside, which is why I had not felt anything. A biopsy was scheduled for a few days later.

I knew I could not tell my parents because they would not be able to handle it, but I decided that my children needed to know. They were wonderful, assuring me that all would be well, but that only made me more frightened. There were so many things I wanted still to see and do.

I spoke with my siblings. Nina was my true pillar of strength. I even called Shirley. Her reaction was oddly distant, as she calmly spoke to me as if what I had told her was of no great importance. I decided not to tell Steven because I felt he could not be trusted not to tell Mom.

On the morning I went in for my biopsy, Gal, Ian and some friends came to support me. I sat in the waiting area. When they called my name, I broke down. Ian and Gal held me as I wept. As long as I did not cross the threshold, cancer was just a possibility, but once I went in, I was convinced it would become a reality.

The technician and the doctor could see my panic and held my arms as we went through the ordeal. Apart from the shot, the procedure was not too painful. The doctor chatted nonsensically, asking me about my husband and children, attempting to keep me from thinking about what was transpiring. Then she reappeared into view. "We're done," she said.

For the next few days, Nina and Shlomo called constantly; sending their good wishes and their love, but Shirley remained silent. I had heard of people who completely vanish when someone is diagnosed with a life-threatening illness, but I was disappointed that she was one of them.

When the results finally arrived, they proved inconclusive, so I would need to have the lump completely removed. The letter explained that my cells had lined up in a dangerous manner, and although at present the lump did not appear to be cancerous, it could turn malignant if allowed to remain in place. The news was somewhat positive.

We set a date for the surgery. This time only Gal accompanied me as I walked into the hospital surgical ward. He was good, strong and supportive, but I could not relax. I removed all my clothing and jewelry, put on a hospital gown and put my hair up in one of those horrid little hospital caps. Gal tried very hard to keep me engaged in conversation, but all I could think about was that I was going to be gypped out of a long life. I sensed Gal's trepidation, but he was doing an excellent job of trying not to show it.

An anesthesiologist came in and told me it was time and that he would be giving me something to begin the sleeping process. I kissed Gal goodbye. The next moment, I found myself waking up with Gal there by my side. It was over. The results would not be ready for another 48 excruciating hours.

The weekend dragged on endlessly. People called, trying to keep my hopes up and to wish me well, but I was blank. I needed to hear the doctors say all was well. Although I was surrounded by family and friends, I felt terribly alone.

Monday arrived and I hovered around the house awaiting the phone's ring. When it finally rang, I picked up the receiver and held my breath.

"No cancer, margins clean." The relief was inexpressible. I would get the chance to dance at Ian's wedding and one day hold my grandchildren in my arms.

Days passed and I gently removed the bandage that protected the stitches. Shirley finally called to find out the results. "My margins are clean," I happily told her.

"You know that that once happened to me," she confided. "They scared me like that too." I was stunned—it would have been nice to know that someone else, like my own sister, had gone through this. Why had she never told me? Questions… always more questions.

It is at moments like this that you learn who your true allies are. Gal had once again come through and I had the wonderful opportunity of seeing my children as young adults who were good, kind and loyal to the end. They were with me every inch of the way, but Shirley yet again had shown me that the sister I yearned for had long since vanished.

At Global Flooring Supplies, a new venture was in the planning stages. Steven and Gal might have *said* they would no longer work together, but somehow, suddenly, their past conflicts were forgotten. Recently, they had been working on the idea of designing a floor sander machine that they would manufacture in China. Gal, who had a great deal of experience with the machinery, made some much needed changes to ensure this would be a really fine machine, and Steven came up with a catchy name. They journeyed to China and Gal came home with two working display models. They both agreed that they would not sell the models, but use them exclusively for display purposes and for taking orders. They also agreed to have a set price and not to undercut each other.

The floor covering industry held its annual convention at the beginning of each year in Las Vegas. Thousands of builders, contractors, installers and other industry people were in attendance. Gal planned to rent a space to display Global's wares and gauge the response to the new machine. Much preparation was involved in participating in the show. But even with all the many costs and inconveniences, a trade show was a very good sales tool.

Gal arrived in Las Vegas a day early to assemble the display himself. He worked until the early evening, unloading the boxes and hammering things into position. Early the next morning he grabbed a sweet roll and a cup of coffee and began his day. The show was a busy one and he worked the booth with great pride, standing for hours, speaking with installers and promoting everything Global had to offer. He was anxious to show people the new machine, emphasizing the improvements he himself had been instrumental in designing. "It's a good deal for the money," he repeated as the installers rolled it around and checked under its hood.

Steven also attended the convention but as a visitor. He had made arrangements to meet one of his customers there to show him the new machine. He thought it would be an excellent opportunity to bring the client to Gal's booth so he could get a good look at the sander and have Gal talk his clients into purchasing a machine....from Steven.

The show ended and the displays were dismantled, repacked and shipped home. The show had been a success, and had raised plenty of interest in the machine. Clients offered to purchase the floor model, which Gal and Steven had agreed not to sell. Unfortunately, Steven allowed that same Las Vegas customer to purchase the floor model he had standing on his showroom floor. This was immensely frustrating to Gal. They needed the other model to take more orders to fill a container, and now that burden would rest on Gal's shoulders alone.

Gal and Steven began arguing. Steven began sending customers over to Gal so he could do all the work, showing them the machine. This to created problems, but once the shipment arrived, everyone hoped to put this issue behind them.

June 2004 represented a milestone for me: I was turning fifty. I would have liked to have this day go by without fanfare. But I was in the minority and found myself outvoted as Gal, the kids and Nina demanded I have a big blow-out. Nina generously offered up her beautiful beach house for the event and told me that she would handle all the plans.

They went all out. Sweet little arrangements of roses in tiny bud vases rested in the niche space of Nina's many alcoves, and a chocolate fountain flowed with fruits on skewers in tall glasses beside it. When I walked in, many of my friends had already arrived and I was pleased to see everyone so relaxed. Mom and Dad arrived shortly thereafter, with Mom looking especially cool in her sunflower-yellow shirt and sunglasses.

Ian and Laura got up in front of Nina's widescreen and invited everyone to watch a video they had put together. It is quite something to watch your life packaged all together by others from a selection of photos they feel encapsulates the essence of you. Each image represented a very important part of my life journey. There were images of me when I was five, with very short, almost black hair and giant eyes to match, and then the video progressed through those other landmark moments: first driver's license, my sweet sixteen at the beach, my wedding, pregnancies, my children's bat and bar mitzvahs and all the friends and family shots. As the photos rotated through, I had to admit it: I had had a good life.

When the speeches began, some of the guests recounted tales from my youth, occasions when I had bent the law here and there. Some reminded me of funny things I had said, but had long since forgotten. It's odd how you don't know how you impact people's lives. Then my family members spoke, and it was clear that their words came from the depths of their souls. You always hope that people know how much you love them, and it was clear that they did.

I choked up as I tried to express my appreciation and love for everyone there. It was a perfect moment until my eyes fell upon Mom. She looked downright upset. What could possibly be wrong?

While everyone was partaking in the birthday cake I walked over to Mom. "What's the matter?" I asked her quietly, so no one else could hear.

"Why do you have to throw parties? Just so you can feed everyone?" she asked.

It had all been going so beautifully, but now her words turned everything upside down. I had wanted Mom to be excited for me, but she simply couldn't bring herself to enjoy someone else's happiness. I tried my best not to give her any further thought. But it continued to irk me. Why was my own mother so determined not to be happy for me? I discovered some years later, after much therapy that some parents don't want their children to be happier than they had been. At first I found that hard to believe, but over time, there was simply too much evidence to deny it. Although I'd had a lovely time at the party up to that point, Mom had succeeded in marring the pure joy of the event for me.

POLTZERS CAN'T BE QUIET

The latest family news was that Nina was in love with Boris—again. She had met Boris, a Polish man, a year earlier while vacationing in Montana.

The town of Hamilton, Montana was located in a beautiful valley named Bitterroot, with hundreds of small farms, ranches and orchards. As Nina drove through this lovely region, she could not help but stare at the livestock scattered on the grasslands. When she arrived at her friend Art's ranch house, it was filled with people as promised. All the bedrooms had at least four people staying in them, and for those who wanted some semblance of privacy, there were teepees set up by the river.

Nina was looking forward to being in a small country town. She and her friend Patricia took a drive to the center of town, where they found a gem of a country store that sold antiques and all kinds of clothing. "Look at this!" Nina called out to Patricia as she picked up a short-haired, 70s-styled reddish wig and placed it on her head.

"I love it!" Patricia complimented. "Do they have any more?"

By the time they left the small shop, Patricia and Nina each had purchased a wig and a small assortment of dresses.

The afternoon of the Fourth of July had everyone scurrying about. There was food to prepare and chairs to move outside and place beside the tables where Patricia was planning to serve a late dinner, lit only by a collection of candle-powered hurricane lamps. When they had a chance to take a little break from the preparations, they drank some wine and had their photographs taken in their new wigs.

Meanwhile a pickup truck with some luggage and a dirt bike in the back was heading towards to cabin, kicking up dust. Art turned to see who it was. A tall, slender man stepped out of the car with his twelve-year-old son—Art's best friend Boris and Art's godson, James. He headed straight over to them.

Art introduced them to everyone, including the redheaded Nina.

"What are we doing for fireworks?" Nina asked Patricia, turning away from the new arrivals.

"Boris always gets them," Patricia answered.

"I love fireworks! Can I go too?" Nina asked.

"Alright, but I'll need you to pick up some other stuff, too," Patricia said.

"No problem," Nina told her.

After Boris and his son had had a chance to unpack, they headed back to their truck, and Nina, still sporting her red wig, joined them with a grocery list of items Patricia had given her. The threesome drove over to a makeshift fireworks dispensing station just outside of town. They filled several bags with fireworks of various kinds.

Then they headed into town to pick up the groceries. They darted up and down the narrow aisles, tossing paper napkins and cocktails stirrers into their cart. When they found themselves standing before the produce Nina gently squeezed the tomatoes, searching for the ripest ones.

"You seem especially good at squeezing things," Boris jokingly remarked.

"Better than you know," Nina replied, flirting right back.

At the dairy case, they bickered about which cheese would be best. "I don't mean to boast, but I have spent many a summer in Paris and fancy myself as a bit of a cheese aficionado." She professed. "Would you mind if I made the final selection?"

"Alright, but I get to choose the wine," Boris insisted.

"What a team we make," Nina smiled back. She was hooked.

That evening, their eyes met off and on.

After the fireworks, Nina felt a little perplexed by Boris's attitude towards her. She thought that she had seen something developing between the two of them, but then he had played it so cool all evening.

However, the next morning, he invited her to join him and James for some dirt-bike riding in an empty field. While James was busy pedaling, Nina and Boris were busy connecting, and for the balance of the week, the three of them were attached at the hip. During the heat of the day, they cooled themselves off in the river, then hopped back in the truck and took slow drives, stopping at bridges to toss rocks into the flowing water below.

When they returned home to Malibu, where Boris also had a home, the two began a heated love affair. Early each morning, they both awoke to catch the waves, then sat on the sand and studied how the water curled and receded. Nina often spent time at Boris's house, and on those lucky evenings when James went to a friend's home, Boris would come over to Nina's home where she would prepare a sumptuous dinner, which they finished off with a good bottle of wine.

But sadly for Nina, their romance came to an end when Boris left for the Bahamas for work. She was heartbroken, but when he left, he had given her the impression that he would prefer to just remain friends.

Hearts heal and time passes, and six months later, it was Patricia's birthday and Nina of course was attending the soirée. She was wearing a short, tight black dress and was talking to a handsome, young aspiring film-maker when Boris tapped her on the shoulder. She had not seen him enter the room and was a little surprised that he had made an effort to seek her out at the party. "Nina, how have you been?" he asked, apparently trying to draw her eyes from the other fellow. Although it was presumptuous of him, she was nevertheless pleased that, for the rest of the evening, he never allowed her attention to wander. It appeared that seeing her again had once again ignited his interest in her.

It was now August 2004, and Nina and Boris had been seriously dating again for about half a year. She had become blissfully domestic, getting very involved in overseeing the construction of Boris's new Malibu home. On many mornings, she met with the contractors and answered questions on details like window placement and color selection. She also acted as a very capable hostess at his many dinner parties, cooking everything herself.

"I'm going to Paris on a movie shoot," Boris told Nina one evening. He was under contract, working on a film that was slated to be released the following year. "James is going to spend the summer with his mother, so why don't you come with me?" he suggested.

"I'd love to," Nina answered, and she went on to spend two glorious weeks in Paris with the man she loved.

While Nina was enjoying her romantic adventure abroad late that summer, Shirley embarked on her own first European adventure with her family. Meanwhile, Gal and I felt the need to sleep under the stars. After a little research, we reserved a lovely tree-shaded camping spot in Lonepine with friends. It was a beautiful spot, and Gal and I loved to hike. The day after we arrived, we set off on a long hike. When we returned to the campsite, my friend Karen, who was supposed to have already left, was waiting for me. "Karen, weren't you supposed to be long gone?" I asked.

She gave me a somber look. "The sheriff is looking for you," she said. "There's been an emergency. Cell phones don't work here, but there is a small market nearby where you can make a call."

My heart missed a beat and I felt like I was going to be sick to my stomach. "It's my Mom," I said out loud. "I just know it."

We jumped into her car and raced over to the market.

"Mom," Laura said, answering the phone after a single ring, "Grandma had a stroke. Come home quick!"

"No!" I yelled. I was in shock and all I could think about was that we were five hours away. What if she died and I did not get to see her or speak with her?

Mom must have been sensing for a while that something was wrong. Dad had been telling us that lately she did not want to lie down to sleep, but always insisted on sitting up. Only after much coaxing could he get her to lie down. But on this particular morning, she had gotten up and walked to the bathroom while Dad was asleep. She had the stroke while in the bathroom, on that cold mosaic-patterned ceramic floor. When Dad woke up, his hand reached across to the empty pillow, which was missing its owner. "Channa?" He called out, but got no response. Worried, he got up and walked to the bathroom, where she lay, semi-conscious.

Dad dialed 911. As he waited for help to arrive, he went into a kind of walking shock. Within moments, the paramedics were there. They placed an oxygen mask over her nose and mouth and whisked her away to a nearby emergency room. They told Dad to drive over separately. He called Shlomo, who arrived shortly. Finding Dad distraught and frantic, Shlomo did his best to reassure his father.

Mom had been taken to a nearby hospital. When Dad and Shlomo arrived, neither was permitted to enter her room just yet, as they were still trying to stabilize her. Then the doctor came out and told them that Mom had suffered a stroke. "We don't know the extent of the damage yet, but as soon as we have her settled in, you'll be able to go inside and see her," he told them.

While they waited, Shlomo began contacting the family. Everyone who was in town was now en route to the hospital, but Nina and Shirley were both still in Europe and I was still hiking about in Lonepine.

After an hour or so, the doctor reappeared and told them they could go in to see Mom. Dad took a deep breath and walked in. She lay with tubes connected to her everywhere. Needles were taped on her arms, connected to bags of clear fluids, and the heart monitor beeped rhythmically. Dad walked over to his wife and took her hand, crying openly now. "Channa," he kept repeating, but she would not wake up. He brushed her hair away from her face, but she didn't react. Then Shlomo softly touched her arm.

After what seemed like an interminable drive, we finally pulled into the hospital parking lot, having stopped briefly to pick up Laura on the way. I raced up the stairs. "Mom," Laura warned, "We were here this morning and Grandma isn't able to speak anymore. She also doesn't look very good. There are a lot of machines in the room. So, just be prepared."

As we walked down the hallway towards her room, we passed the open doors of other patients' rooms. This floor must be for the old and dying, I thought to myself, noticing that everyone seemed to be connected to some type of life-sustaining mechanical device. I hoped Mom was not as bad off as these poor people seemed to be.

The first thing I saw was the nurse, who was stationed in a chair watching Mom's room. After waiting a moment, frightened of what I might see, I pulled the curtain aside. I drank the sight of her in with my eyes and approached the bed. "Mom, we're here," I told her, hoping that while she could not speak, she would still know I was there. Her right arm was swollen and bruised and her little fingers were plump and unreal looking, while her eyes stared wildly who knew where. "Mom?" I asked hopefully, but she did not acknowledge me in any way. Feelings of terror overtook me and I had to leave the room; I did not want her to see me cry. This couldn't be real, I thought.

The hour was late and I still needed to go and see Dad, so I kissed her goodbye and told her I would be back in the morning. "That woman is very precious to me," I reminded the nurse. "Please take care of her."

All of a sudden, I was tired, so very tired; seeing Mom in that state and being so frightened had sucked out all my strength, but I still had to go see Dad. It was a short drive to the house, and after knocking on the door, Gal and I let ourselves in. We found him sitting on their family room couch. Shlomo, who was staying the night, was sitting on one of the bar stools, silent.

"Jaclyn?" Dad cried out.

"Hi Dad," I said in a soft voice, and went over and hugged him. "What happened?"

It was hard to understand what he was trying to say, he was crying so hard, but I gathered he blamed himself, "I could have saved her if I had only woken up earlier."

"I don't think that's the case, Dad," I countered in an effort to comfort him.

"When do you think she can come home?" he asked, needing her to be all right.

"I don't know, Dad; hopefully soon."

Gal and I sat with them a while, but there was not much to say.

"I'll come by tomorrow, Dad, and we can go back to the hospital together," I promised him. Shlomo and I looked at each other; we were frightened, both for Dad and for ourselves. No one in the family had ever really given any thought to what our lives would be like with an incapacitated mother. Mom was our rock. For all her faults, she was the one who kept us safely tethered to this world. She was our conscience and our protector.

When I awoke the next morning, I threw on some clothes. I don't remember if I ran a comb through my hair, or even if my clothing was inside out. For once in my life, my appetite had vanished, and I drove to my father's house to accompany him to the hospital. I needed to speak with the doctor and see what was going on. I suddenly felt an urgent need for concrete information.

I held Dad's hand as we drove to the hospital. He was so broken. This giant of a man, who had so terrified me when he chased me around the table with a belt all those years ago, was so diminished. He sat beside me, hunched over, head in hands, desperately afraid of losing the woman about whom he had constantly complained, but whom in reality he could not bear being without, even for a single night.

This time, as we walked down the hallway, it was disturbingly familiar. I again peeked in the rooms filled with the dying elderly and their families seated in bedside chairs. I could see the exhaustion in their eyes. As we came up to her room, at first Dad hesitated, reluctant to face the reality of Mom's condition, but then he mustered his courage and walked in with me and Shlomo. She was still on a respirator and heart monitor. Nothing had changed.

"Channa?" Dad asked her, but there was no response.

Unexpectedly, one of the machines started to beep like crazy and we felt, although no one could confirm it, that Mom knew we were there. Not knowing what to do and fearful some harm might come to her, we left the room and waited for the beeping to slow down. I walked over to the nurse on duty and asked to speak with the doctor.

When Mom's machine grew quieter, we all went back inside. We told her not to get excited, but that we were all there. Dad did not speak; he just held her hand and stared at her. Her chest rose and fell, but we knew it was all because of the machinery. A nurse came in and checked the bag that hung off to one side. Dad began crying and stepped outside; this was too hard for him to bear. I sat beside Mom, trying to speak with her. "I'm here, Mom. Can you hear me?" With her left hand, she had been holding the guard rail tightly and now she let it go and took my hand. I wish I could have been sure that she was doing that as some sort acknowledgement of my presence, but I feared she didn't even know I was there. Nevertheless, I tried to communicate my love to her and that helped ease the pain in my heart.

When the doctor arrived, we practically jumped on him. We were desperate for some kind of reassurance that this was all temporary, that the mother we knew and loved would indeed return to us shortly.

"We are still waiting for the results to see how severe the dámage is."

"Doctor," I interrupted, "my father is concerned that had he awoken sooner that morning he could have called the ambulance sooner and saved her. Is that correct?"

"By all accounts," the doctor said, looking straight at my Dad, "she had only suffered the stroke a very short while before you found her. There was nothing else you could have done."

I hoped that that would ease his mind.

"It looks as though she suffered a stroke on the communication side of her brain," the doctor explained. "She has probably lost the ability to speak, and she might have lost most of her ability on her right side. We don't know whether she will be able to walk too well either. As soon as she stabilizes, we can perform additional tests. We are hoping that happens sometime today."

"A little while ago she took my hand," I told him, hoping he would find it as positive a sign.

"It was just a reflex," he answered, dashing my fantasy that she had known I was there.

His news left us with mixed emotions. No, she was not going to die, thank God, but she might not be able to speak or walk. She would be an invalid, something she had always feared.

After the doctor left, Dad wanted to take a seat in the waiting room. Shlomo and I returned to Mom's room and spoke in hushed tones. While she could not communicate, we feared she might still be able to hear and understand us.

A short while later, a nurse asked us to leave while they cleaned her up. We decided that since Mom would be coming home, we should return to the house with Dad and straighten it up a bit. She would not be in any position to get angry this time, so we cleaned up guilt free. More than anything, it was good to have something to keep us occupied.

Laura, Ian and Steven were at the hospital and kept us abreast of Mom's condition. They told us that she was more stable and was going to be taken off life support. We returned to the hospital.

Nina came directly from the airport to the hospital. From her work as a nurse, she remembered floors like the one on which Mom was staying. When she arrived, Shlomo, Steven and I were outside Mom's room talking. Nina went inside.

"I'm back from Paris Mom," she said quietly. "Can you hear me?"

Mom's eyes were shut, but opened briefly when Nina spoke. They stared into nothingness and then shut again. Nina held her hand and noticed that Mom's grip had some strength to it. It was a positive sign.

The next day, we were informed that Mom would have to switch hospitals now that she had stabilized. We protested, but to no avail. Since nothing could be done to prevent the move, I decided to decorate her new hospital room. Again, I was glad to have something to do as I grabbed an assortment of photographs and took them to have them blown up, planning to cover the walls with images of the family.

When word came that Mom had successfully made the move to the other hospital, everyone hurried over. When we arrived, there was good news; Mom was getting better. I entered the room. "Hey, Mom," I said chipperly, as if she knew I was there and proceeded to tape the blowups onto the walls. "Something to keep you company," I told her, wanting her to know we were always there, even in the middle of the night.

Dad sat in a chair at the foot of Mom's bed. She still was not making any kind of eye contact, but at least she was breathing on her own. We watched Mom in the bed and noticed she had begun doing something new: she was covering and uncovering her legs. It was at that time I saw something I had never noticed before. Her toenails were yellowish and long, the kind of long that made them curl back under. When had this occurred? What kind of children were we that we were unaware our Mom had been taking such terrible care of herself? I felt sick. I had always thought of myself as a good daughter, but how had I allowed this to go unnoticed?

A few of us moved over to the waiting room. I sat there with Ian and Laura and Ian put his arm around me. He gently rubbed my back, showing me the same kind of strength and support as when he had been there for me for the cancer scare. When had he become such a man? "It'll be okay," he told me over and over again.

The waiting room phone began to ring and we all looked at each other, not sure of what we should do or who should answer the phone. Finally, one of the other ladies picked it up. "Is there a Jaclyn here?" she asked.

Who could be calling me here, I wondered, and took the receiver. "Hello?"

It was Shirley calling in from France. "How is she?" she asked. "Should I be coming home?"

"According to the doctors, she is stable and will be here for a while recuperating," I assured her. "I don't think you need to hurry back. When you come home, she'll probably still be here." The conversation was short and sweet.

While we waited, Shlomo, Nina, Steven and I talked about what the next step should be. "I think we should install an elevator that can lift Mom upstairs to her bedroom," Steven offered. We played with the idea of altering the downstairs bathroom to turn it into a wheelchair-accessible shower and bath. They would also need to hire professional help – something Mom would not have liked, but there would be no choice. When evening came, we sadly wished her a good night's rest and left.

Looking back, Nina has had many regrets about the night that followed. A family member should have stayed with Mom, she felt; she should not have been alone during the night hours. Some time during the night, a blood clot moved and Mom suffered a major stroke. The doctors and nurses placed her back on life support and her crazy eyes closed for good this time.

The news was devastating. Nina and Dad were already there when I arrived at the hospital. "I knew moving her wasn't going to be a good idea," I cried. "She was doing so well."

When the doctor appeared, Nina spoke with him. We left Laura and Ian with Dad and Mom. Dad seemed uncomfortable, even a little frightened to be alone with his wife, and the rest of us stepped back into the waiting room. We pulled our seats into a kind of circle and spoke quietly to each other. After talking to the doctor, Nina returned to us and paraphrased what she had learned. "Mom had a massive stoke last night," she said. "It looks as though she has suffered a lot of damage."

"What does that mean?" we asked. Nina had an idea about what "a lot" meant, but we, non-medical folk, needed to have it explained to us.

"It means that she isn't going to be in a wheelchair," Nina explained. "She'll be bedridden, won't be speaking again and probably doesn't know what we're saying to her. They are going to run some tests when she gets more stabilized and then we'll know more."

Our eyes widened and we blinked nervously, holding back the tears. It took us a while to absorb the fact that she was actually now worse, when she had seemed to be getting better. We pulled our chairs closer, needing to be with each other while we took all this information in.

"Is the doctor saying that Mom will never get any better? She will never be able to communicate with us at all?" we asked.

Nina tried to be diplomatic. "It doesn't look that promising. Right now, we have to see if she improves enough to get off the respirator."

Mom's condition remained the same throughout the day. A breathing mask rested on her face and a clear tube was jammed down her throat, the machine taking the breaths she could not.

Later that same day we received more bad news: Mom was developing pneumonia. "Tell Shirley to come home," Nina said with urgency.

We all agreed that Mom would not be left alone anymore and assigned ourselves shifts. Sitting with Mom was a surreal experience – she was there and yet not there. I spoke with her, hoping she heard me, but fearing she did not. She tried to move her breathing mask constantly and I would tell her in the softest, most loving way, not to move it, "You need it to breathe, Mom." But she continued trying to rip it off her face. The room was quiet except for the sound of the machine beeping and the nurses making announcements over the speakers. There were so many things I wanted to tell her, such as how I loved her and what she meant to me, but I could not. Saying those things would make this too real, too close to the end. I was not ready to go there. Instead, we watched the Olympics together and I chatted with her about the team uniforms and what the athletes were doing. When Steven arrived early for his watch, I found it hard to leave. Not wanting to go home, I remained in the waiting area where I was soon joined by Dad and Shlomo, who also arrived early. No one seemed to want to go home.

It might have been the stress or our terror about what we feared was coming next that led us to squabble about the shifts and who would take which one. Everyone had reasons for wanting theirs in the middle of the day, and everyone had reasons why overnight watches were difficult.

"NO MORE FIGHTING!" Laura scolded, having had enough. "Let's just hire nurses twenty-four hours a day. That way, if you can't do your watch, Grandma isn't alone!" And out of the mouths of babes.

Nina contacted a service and nurses were hired for both day and night. It was a comfort to have someone with expertise in the room with us. With someone else there, we did not need to worry about the machinery and what all the clicks and pings meant; we could concentrate on Mom.

The doctor decided to take her off the respirator. Although her breathing was still labored, at least she was breathing on her own. They inserted what they called a trumpet into her nose, a device like a tiny megaphone. Supposedly it helped her breathe, but all it really did was irritate her. We could tell she was getting weaker because she stopped doing that thing with the blanket. She was slowly starting to slip away.

As soon as Shirley arrived, tensions amplified. We had all been getting along well, but she was, as usual, the wild card. Eric started muttering about malpractice and we could see his wheels already spinning. They did not want to be told when they could visit mom; they wanted to come and go as they pleased. This made scheduling slots with Mom difficult – but when dealing with Shirley, what else was new?

Since it was now inevitable that Mom was going to die, I felt it necessary to contact the lawyer she had told me to call when this time came. When I got him on the line, I was frightened about the future and trying hard not to cry, so, without any of the usual niceties, I came directly to the point. "Mr. Steinberg, this is Jaclyn, Channa Poltzer's daughter. My mother is dying and I need to know, so I can prepare my family, if there is anything in the will that is going to be a surprise?" I had this terrible hunch that Mom's will might not be totally straightforward. Checking with the lawyer might have been premature, but I felt it was necessary to prepare us for any potential issues.

"No surprises," he assured me, answering right away, as though he had her file already resting on his desk. "It's a five-way split."

I did not need to know any more than that.

The next day, the hospital social worker wanted to meet with us. "What are your plans when you Mother gets worse?" she asked. Nina grimaced. "We need to have a pre-directive for worst-case scenarios," the social worker continued.

"We'll have to talk about it and get back to you with that," we told her, feeling that she seemed to be jumping the gun. We were here to support Mom to make a comeback, not to get her ready to die. We couldn't face that prospect yet.

"How much of Mom is still in there?" we asked the doctor, hoping the information would help us know what we should do next.

"She's not there any more," he told us. "Add that to the pneumonia and this doesn't look good. I have found when you have a person in this state of health who has suffered this kind of stroke combined with pneumonia, they don't last too long." It was horrible, blunt and to the point.

"You're sure she's not in there at all?" I asked again.

"She is pretty much a vegetable," he said as kindly as he could. "She's having a lot of trouble breathing, so we will probably need to help her and that will mean hooking her back up to a machine."

"Then what?" we asked.

"Then that is the way she will be until she dies and no one knows when that will be." There it was. We would have to be the hand of God and decide. We turned to Dad, but he wanted no part of it. "I can't make this kind of decision!"

"You have to, Dad," we told him.

We asked for a second opinion, but that doctor told us more of the same. "You'll need to make some hard decisions quickly."

"Dad, Mom is basically dead," we explained. "Only her body is alive. She wouldn't want to be kept alive artificially. And if she is in there, even though they say she's not, she can't communicate with us. How do you think she'd like that?"

"So I should refuse to put her back on the machines?" Dad asked, pleading for someone, anyone, to make that decision for him.

"You want to kill her!" Shirley snarled. "How do you know she won't get better? I will never agree to that!" she yelled. Then she and Eric left us and returned to Mom.

The social worker returned yet again. "I really need to have those forms completed or the doctors will not know what to do in case of emergency," she reminded us with urgency, looking straight at Dad.

"I can't!" he cried. "What should I do?" he asked, begging us to help him out of this nightmare.

"You need to sign it, Dad," we told him.

And so he did. Mom would not be placed back on life support.

When we came back into the room, we saw Mom through new eyes. She was dying; there was no denying it now. Her breathing was pronounced and we could hear her struggle for breath. Shirley glared at us from the opposite side of the bed. She hated what we were planning to do.

The nurse took Nina aside to speak with her. "I overheard your sister and her husband telling your mother that you wanted to kill her," she said. Nina's jaw tightened. She whispered to the rest of us what she had been told. Even on her deathbed, Shirley managed to stir up conflict. It made us sick. We decided right there not to leave Shirley and Eric alone with Mom again.

Time both dragged and flew by. Steven went downstairs to take a little break and a short while later I decided to join him. As I stepped into the elevator, I started to cry. A priest walked into the elevator. "If you are having a hard time with something, I am here to help," he said. "I can be a sympathetic ear." He meant well and I thanked him for his thoughtfulness. When the elevator door opened, Steven saw me crying and saw the priest and for a moment held his breath.

"Is everything okay?" he asked.

"Nothing has changed," I assured him.

When we came back upstairs, Nina was speaking with the doctor. "It is time to either put her on the machine or make her more comfortable and let her go," he said. "Which one shall I do?"

"Make her comfortable!" I said, not even thinking. "I don't want her to feel a thing." At this point Shirley walked away.

"I can give her morphine and that will make her comfortable, but she will die without the machines," he explained again.

"Give her lots of morphine and send her out pain free," we told him. Nina and I put our arms around each other and Steven turned away and cried.

Mom's breathing was very shallow now. The doctor returned and added something to her IV. We all looked at each other – we knew what this meant. Mom's only movements were her labored breathing and the morphine even quieted that down. Dad sat in a chair at the foot of her bed and various family members started pacing nervously in and out of the room.

Perhaps I was refusing to accept the reality of the moment, but it seemed to me that whatever was going to happen could not possibly happen that night. "I'm really tired," I told everyone. "I'll be back in the morning." I touched Mom's hand, kissed everyone goodbye and left. I just needed to get away and put this on hold, just for the night. Then I could come back and face it.

It was very late and the parking lot was basically empty. I drove about two blocks and then a voice of sanity yelled at me: "Go back!" I made an illegal U-turn and headed back. I pleaded with Mom in my mind to wait for me. Frightened that I would not be there in time, I ran down the hallway and back into the room. I saw right away that nothing had changed, but I knew that's where I needed to be.

Several hours passed. When the doctor came back into the room, Nina asked him to turn the sound off of Mom's monitoring machinery. The nurse's station would still be able to monitor Mom's status, but we would no longer hear the beeping. He walked over to Mom, turned the morphine drip up and left. "He's hurrying this up for us," Nina whispered in my ear. "Mom is floating on a cloud." No one spoke; we all simply watched her now. A few intense minutes passed, but it was impossible to sustain this vigil without a break. After a while, we opened the door and everyone but Shirley and Nina stepped just outside. After a few minutes, Nina opened the door.

"She's going to pass any minute now; you'd all better come back in." She told us. Within seconds, we were all surrounding Mom, holding her hands, stroking her face. Shlomo bent over her and kissed her forehead. We then began shouting out our love, wanting desperately for her hear us and know we were there with her. Then Mom's chest fell and everyone froze. We held our breaths, hoping it would rise again, but it never did.

Dad dropped to his knees, wailing her name... Hell, we all wailed. The hospital nurse hurried in and shut the door behind her, but it was useless to try and keep Poltzers quiet.

As I held Mom's hand, it still felt so warm. I stared at her hard, wanting to brand her image into my mind. Then I looked over at Shirley, "You have her hands," I said to her, noticing for the first time that she did.

THE POLTZERS MINUS CHANNA

As I stood at Mom's bedside, the reality was hard to grasp. She looked like she was just sleeping, but then, all of a sudden, her body turned cold and her face changed, ever so slightly. The softness to her face was gone, Death had come and taken Mom away. It was time to go. It was a little after two in the morning, August twenty-fifth, Shirley's forty-seventh birthday. Closing the hospital door, knowing I would never see her again, was an indescribable moment. I found myself putting all my feelings and thoughts on hold; my body simply walked. I don't remember a thing about how we all parted or if we said anything to each other. I just remember driving down the street – away, away from that hospital room where my dead mother lay.

After several traffic lights, I pulled over and a dream I had when I was seven years old flooded my mind. I remembered that Mom and I were walking through a tranquil park. Squirrels were scurrying from tree to tree and birds were chirping. A giant Tyrannosaurus Rex lumbered over, knelt down and simply gobbled my mother up. Frantic to get her back, I gathered up some food and traded it for her release. I woke up at that point, terrified, and called out for her. "You can never die, Mom!" I insisted. She reassured me and brushed my tear-soaked hair out of my face.

Her words echoed around in my head. "I'm not going anywhere for a very, very long time." She had told me.

"Give her back!" I cried to myself, there at the side of the road.

She had been so much more to me than a mother; despite how difficult she could be, she was my anchor. Because of her, I never felt alone. I could still hear her voice. I could hear the greeting she always left on my answering machine when I was not home—the way she nagged at me.

When I got home, Gal knew what had happened. He came over and held me, but sorry is such a small word when something like this happens. Finally, I slept.

According to Jewish faith, we were not allowed to leave Mom's body alone, so body sitters were quickly hired. We only had a very few days to bury her, so we had to arrange things quickly. Everyone helped in one way or another. Although Shlomo, Dad, Shirley and I were atheists, Mom felt strongly about God and we felt that she would have wanted a traditional burial. Laura offered up her home for the gathering after the burial and Steven found the rabbi. The details were all in place, so now all we needed to do was prepare ourselves for a very difficult day.

I gave my speech a great deal of thought. I wanted it to encapsulate Mom, but how do you write something that tells people about such a complex person as Channa Poltzer?

Then, the day was upon us. We met with the rabbi before the service so he could speak with us and create a eulogy for a woman he had never met. Dad released a lifetime's worth of stories about his wife. The rabbi sat mesmerized by the tale of Mom's youth in the forest. Dad boasted of how supportive she had been as a young bride and mother to their five children. The rabbi took lots of notes and then told us he knew what he would say.

Each of my siblings had given me photographs that had special meaning for them. We filled up four large poster boards, creating a pictorial tribute to that short brunette woman who always wanted to be a fiery redhead.

The wonderful turnout gladdened my father's heart – he had feared that no one would be there. A sea of friends, mostly mine and my siblings', showed up to pay tribute. I spotted Garth off to the side, using the wall to provide him support. Filled with grief, he was chewing on his shirt, just barely holding himself together. Brenda, showing her usual disdain for the Poltzer family, did not bring her son Kevin to the service. We were seated up front in the small chapel when the rabbi began his service. He looked out at the crowd and began recounting Mom's exploits in the war. He then talked about how she had stood by her husband, children and grandchildren.

This day was going to go on, whether we liked it or not. Mom would be buried, whether we liked it or not. She was dead, whether we liked it or not. "Is there anyone here who would like to share some thoughts?" The Rabbi asked. We all stood up, needing to say our goodbyes out loud to Mom before she was put into the ground. It was a moment of tremendous sibling support as we held each other's arms and helped each other walk up the stairs to a curtained area reserved for family.

Shlomo spoke first. He spoke loudly, clearly and with a hint of anger. He began by describing what our mother had been like. He next spoke of her journey through the Holocaust and then of her marriage and the creation of a family. Finally he turned, directly facing Mom's casket which rested on a stand, and spoke to her, "Why didn't you take better care of yourself?" he said as he clenched his fist, gazed upwards and said her name in a kind of chant. His voice was quivering, but he remained strong.

I hated public speaking, but this was different; this was speaking to my mother one last time. My legs were pounding, so Laura and Ian each grabbed one of my arms and guided me to the microphone. I unfolded my speech and began to read:

As most of you know, my mother was a unique individual. She showered her husband, children and grandchildren with unconditional, unending, all accepting love, but she was also so very frightened by life in general. She always reminded me of a broken bird.

She was incredibly proud of her Partisan participation, but I think that that also was a cause of her profound fear and distrust of the world in general. But she was capable of tremendous compassion. I remember my parents being at the mall when Mom came upon a crying child. Being a mom of five she knew that frightened look and asked the child if he was lost. Through tear-filled eyes, the child said, "yes." A man came upon the scene and said that he would take the child to the manager. My mom, being the mom she was, took the child's hand and said, "NO! WE will both take the child to the manager. Not until that child was safely delivered to the manager did Mom let go of the child's hand.

Within the safety zone of her family she was safe and free to voice her very loud opinions with every ounce of zeal she had. She could say all those odd, out-of-place sentences and words with full acceptance and love. And love her we do. Nowhere is there a mother such as this.

In her unexpected parting from us, it gives me some comfort to know that the five of us are all together, united in our tremendous love and admiration of a tiny Holocaust survivor who couldn't bear to throw anything away and liked to hide money in her bra.

I can't even begin to imagine my life without her. How many times have I passed along some pearl of wisdom from the Channa Book of Life..

The one single thing I will miss most about my mom is her voice, but her voice is now in my head for now and always.

She is my strength, my rock, my Momila.

Mom, I love you, always have and always will.

I cried, not really caring if the kind souls sitting in the benches understood me, but I needed to say this. When I took my seat, sandwiched between my children and siblings, I felt safe.

Shirley had written a poem of sorts. She was, I think, saying she was sorry to Mom. She was sorry for the fights they had had and told her, in that poem, how much she had appreciated the fact that Mom always accepted her.

Steven was next. "Mom was an artisan and each of her five children was crafted with gifts from god." He proudly proclaimed. Then he applauded the attention and support she had given us.

Nina's speech was an empowering one on behalf of Mom. She covered the adversities Mom had overcome and spoke about her strengths and goodness. She told a story about how Mom had once reprimanded her for something she did, except Mom secretly liked Nina's little dishonesty and had faked it for public eyes to see, winking at Nina so she would know it was alright with her.

Gal got up and spoke of my Mom as a fighter. He seemed genuinely proud of her soldier-like spirit, even though the two had not always had the easiest relationship.

Laura, who had been crying throughout most of our speeches, composed herself and spoke about the grandmother who had allowed her to clean her chandelier with Windex, whether it needed it or not; a grandmother who had allowed her to enter the *magic* closet.

Ian held his feelings in and stood tall as he spoke of his grandmother, a woman who spoiled him rotten and who had been taken from him much too soon.

When Adam, Shirley's third-born, stood up, he carried in his hand a plastic trash bag. We could not figure out what it was for, but he explained. "Grandma Channa and I used to make potato pancakes together, so I decided to give her the ingredients so she could have them forever," he said.

"After the service, we all drove to the burial site. The drive was brief and wound up a road with green pads of grass on both sides. Name plates checkered the sod every two feet or so. Some had flowers, potted plants and wind chimes next to them. City views embraced us on one side and tall mountains on the other. Beautifully pruned pepper and evergreen trees grew throughout the cemetery, providing shade to those lucky sites that rested beneath them. Mom's site was ready for us and a number of folding chairs had been set up next to it for family members. I always hated the idea of placing someone into and under the ground; it made me remember a childhood song about worms crawling in and crawling out.

All the men in our family except Dad escorted the casket to the site. People milled around, talking quietly, until the rabbi asked for silence and the Kiddush was recited. Dad walked over to the wooden box that held the body of the woman with whom he had spent most of his life, dropped to his knees and draped himself over the casket.

Then the casket was lowered down into the ground. As is Jewish custom, everyone threw handfuls of dirt onto the casket. A long line formed behind us and I walked away, unable to face this ritual. But a friend came over and led me back to the grave. "You need to do this," she said. I knelt down and took a handful of the rich, warm, brown earth and held it.

"Please, Mom," I cried, not really knowing what I was pleading for. I then allowed the dirt to spill through my fingers.

Finally, Adam came over and gently emptied the contents of his bag: a can opener, a box of matzo meal and a few russet potatoes.

It was over. The book on Mom's life had shut.

Everyone drove to Laura's home and the usually quiet street filled with cars. A friend brought the soundtrack of *Fiddler on the Roof* to play in the background because my parents always loved that music, thinking it mirrored the story of their three daughters. We set up the posters with Mom's photos and we took comfort in how closely people studied them. Dad sat on the couch and spoke and cried; there were many kind people to whom he could pour out his heart.

Several hours later, the final guest left, and only the family remained. We were all at a loss as to what to do next, unsure how to go on with our lives. And we hadn't really faced the matter of what Dad would do. But for now, our first task was to just get through these first days, without our anchor. I think we were all a little stunned by what an impact our far-from-perfect Mom had had on each of us. She was so injurious to our mental health, diminishing our self-confidence and tearing down anything good we did. And yet, she was still somehow central to everything. She influenced everything we did. Every time we thought about doing something, we would hear her voice. Yes, it was often a voice of doom and gloom, but it was our Mom's voice. From now on, we would be totally responsible for our own lives. Yes, we could continue blaming her for our faulty upbringing, but the rest of our lives were up to us; we could do what we said we always wanted to do, and Mom was no longer here to stop us. Hard as it is to believe, it was comforting to have someone else on whom you could blame all your failings and fears.

Mom had also held us all together. When we did not want to see each other—which was often—she had pulled us back together. Now what glue would bind us? And then there was the fact that she was the buffer between us and death, for as long as she lived, we were not next in line. The world seemed quieter now, and I did not like it. I missed my five o'clock phone calls to her already.

Sitting Shiva was the customary Jewish week-long period of grieving, which involved reciting special prayers and abiding by certain rituals, such as not eating our own prepared foods, avoiding showers and covering all the mirrors in the house. Following the custom would have been out of character for the Poltzers. But because we were proud of our Jewish heritage and appreciated the traditions of our people, we conducted our own version of sitting Shiva. We ate dinner those first few nights all together at Mom and Dad's house. The poster boards from the funeral displaying Mom's photographs were propped up nearby and we told stories about Mom and family life. The tales were sad, yet funny, and Dad cried, but we all needed to be together.

It was such a shame that it had taken Mom's death to bring us all to the same table. Dad softened a bit and even extended a hand of truce to Eric. No one argued; we were all together in our pain and sadness and it felt more bearable with everyone nearby. Even though Shirley and I had had hard times in the past and now felt that I had done the wrong thing in disconnecting Mom too soon, those meals were nevertheless harmonious affairs. Temporarily at least, we shared our sadness and mourned together.

While our lives changed a great deal, Dad's world imploded. He had always complained about how unhappy he had been right up to the end of their life together, but she ran his whole life. Even in her immobile state, when the mere act of standing up and walking was difficult for her, she had still controlled everything. We traded off staying in the house with him. By day, we kept his mind occupied with house cleaning (actually, we were not simply cleaning; we were in search of the hidden cash that Mom always told us was stashed throughout the house). We also wanted to find any important papers. Mom's affairs were now Dad's affairs, and he knew nothing. By night, we listened to the sounds of our father's weeping filtering through the walls. There were no words to console him, but we wondered whether he was weeping because he missed her so or because he felt guilty for being angry at her.

Always happy to be busy, I launched a thorough, no-holds-barred house cleaning. We set a large trash can in the center of the family room and began working methodically through everything, starting with the breakfast table in front of us. On the table sat a bowl containing an assortment of items, including a tin cough-drop box that lay between some napkins and pens. I was just about to toss it but took a quick peek inside. There I found a small wad of cash, rolled up and secured by a rubber band. I chuckled, and handed it to Dad. He sat on the couch, shaking his head. I checked in the pockets of a sleeping gown that was draped over the breakfast room chair and found a few hundred dollars safety pinned inside. Mom had never left the terror of the Holocaust. She had always prepared for the worst. We found things everywhere, tracking down hundreds of keys— to what, we did not know. We even found a pair of safe deposit box keys in the false back of a picture frame. Who was she so afraid would find them?

We still had not opened the locked closet in the master bedroom because we had not found the key. Eric came over with an electric screwdriver and simply removed the inexpensive lock that had prevented Dad's entrance all these years. The tiny room was a dazzling example of Mom's contradictions. While she was a total and complete failure as a housekeeper, she kept incredibly organized tax and banking records. Tax returns, dating back to the 1980s, were carefully placed in plastic wrap with their corresponding bank statements and cancelled check stubs attached.

A small free-standing cabinet rested against one wall, and this contained her beloved coin collection. In another drawer we found an accordion file lying on its side. I pulled it out and checked through the different sleeves. In it were lists Mom had written, lots of lists, and the numbers on one of them were three and four digits long. It appeared to be a list of bank accounts and probably safe deposit boxes. There were also old photo albums, the kind with paper corners holding the fringe-edged black and white photographs in place. I grabbed all of them along with every hanging family portrait I could find and put them in my car for safekeeping. I planned to give them all back when I felt Dad would not discard them in his cleaning frenzy.

On the first Friday after the funeral, Steven asked if we could all attend his synagogue's service so we could have Mom's name read aloud as one of the recently deceased, a Jewish custom. While it was of no particular significance to us, we agreed because it seemed to mean a lot to Steven and we wanted to be supportive.

We each arrived at the temple around the same time. As we walked from the parking lot together, Eric pulled Shlomo aside. "I have been doing some thinking and I don't think your father should be managing La Jolla any more. I'm going to request he stop as soon as possible." An assortment of tenants had been living in the old La Jolla house and Dad happily and loyally drove over to check on it regularly. Often Mom sat in the car while he walked around the property making sure all was well. Now, with Mom dead, Eric and Shirley began to see green, and they wanted to get their hands on it. Eric's suggestion stopped Shlomo in his tracks and he winced, realizing that time had already run out on family unity. He knew that today's visit to the synagogue would probably be the last time all the Poltzers would pull together.

It took a while for me to fully realize all the things Mom's death would ultimately mean. While on horseback, I confessed to a friend that I was broken-hearted over the fact that any grandchildren I would have would never meet Mom. They would never hear her stories or taste her potato soup. My girlfriend gave it some thought and then came up with a fantastic idea. "Make sure not to throw away any of your Mom's clothes and then you can have them made into a lovely quilt for your grandchildren one day."

I loved the idea. Mom would be able to spread out her arms over them symbolically. I selected some of Mom's favorite pieces, things I had seen her in a million times, and brought them home for a serious washing. As I held Mom's things, I could not help bringing the armful of shirts and dresses to my face. Even though they no longer smelled like her, they were still Mom.

Amid all the grieving, Eric and Shirley just could not leave well enough alone. They seemed to have Mom's death confused with Christmas and were anxious to see what they got. So they began pushing to have probate opened and the will read. I had already been assured by Mom's attorney, Moshe Steinberg, that the estate would be a five-way split, but Shirley knew she was Mom's favorite and was hopeful she might be getting a little extra something.

Nina called Shirley to ask her to hold off, but to no avail. Eric, an experienced pest, barraged Moshe with endless phone calls and threats.

Unprepared for such an attack, the lawyer opened probate by mailing each of us a letter, along with a copy of Mom's most recent will, dated 1983.

Reading a will is like reading a note from the dead. It started off simply enough, listing Nathan as her husband and identifying each of us as her five children. The executor was to pay off all her debts and give Dad all the furniture and the car. But then the will took an odd turn. Mom had not returned to Dad the family home on La Jolla or the home they had lived in on Lancer Street, which he had written over to her years earlier. As a result of her irrational fear that Dad would run away, she had insisted he sign the two properties over to her as a kind of guarantee that he would not leave her. Although for all intents and purposes they still owned those properties together, Mom's will did not return them to Dad. Instead, she gave him only a life estate in the house on Lancer Street, the home he was currently living in. A life estate would grant him all the benefits of ownership, but in reality, he would not be the owner. Mom further decreed that if that house were to be sold, the money would not go to Dad, but to her five children. I read on, stunned by what I came to next.

I leave my house to Steven Poltzer.

The sentence was vague at best and written in an odd manner, but we knew that she meant La Jolla when she said "my house."

What the hell was this? I had thought there weren't supposed to be any surprises. I would call this a big surprise!

The moment I finished re-reading the paragraph, my phone rang; Dad had also received an envelope and was quite upset. "I get nothing?" he asked.

"It doesn't look good, Dad, but don't get excited," I told him. "There has to be another will; we just have to find it."

The phones kept ringing until near midnight. Nina, Shlomo and I spoke, asking each other and ourselves how Mom could have done this.

Shirley had also received the letter and called me. Although the will shattered all beliefs she had that she had always been the favorite, she did not appear worried. "There is a deed giving us the house equally," she explained confidently.

Deed ...Schmeed! We would tear the house apart and find the other will, the will that would correct this gross error. It had to be somewhere. Shlomo and Nina searched through the house, while Dad and I began visiting all the banks on which we had found paperwork.

Going to banks with a visibly upset and impatient father was not easy and banking red tape did not help matters. There were forms to complete and procedures to follow when one spouse had died and the remaining spouse wanted to transfer the joint money into his own name, or to access a safe deposit box. Having to go through this process was demeaning for Dad; he had been Mom's loyal life-mate and this should not have been this difficult. And then, after submitting to the entire procedure, we were often told that Mom had closed this account long ago. Dad fumed, but we continued.

Mom was a fervent believer in not keeping all her eggs in any one basket, so she banked at many different locations. But since she also did not want to walk very far, her banks were at least near each other.

Finally, we were down to only five more safe deposit boxes to check and we entered the first bank optimistic that we would find something. We carried an unassuming straw beach bag Mom and Dad had gotten while they were on vacation in Mexico many years ago. After presenting the required death certificate and our identifications to the teller, we retrieved the box and went into the private room that banks have reserved for such moments. We set the dark grey, oblong metal container on the desk and opened the lid. Inside it was a folded sheet of paper, which turned out to be a will, but unfortunately it pre-dated the one we already had. We were disappointed, but there were four more boxes remaining, four more reasons to keep our hopes up.

The next two boxes were empty, just bare boxes on which Mom had continued paying rent for years. Where had the contents gone? What had she done with all that cash? I had my ideas. Shirley always had her hand out. And Steven, how did he afford his submarine sandwich place, which he ended up having to sell? How else did he pay for any of the properties he owned, which he ended up losing? I was pretty sure those two safe deposit boxes had been filled with cash at one time, until Steven milked Mom and Dad dry.

Box number four proved to be a bust also. We had no choice but to hope that the will we sought was folded neatly in the fifth box, but gaining entrance to it would require a court order. Mom had never added Dad's name to the box and we had found no key, so it would need to be drilled open. We convinced ourselves that the will had to be there – why else all the secrecy? Now an executor, not Dad, would have to open the box. It was horribly insulting for Dad and we were not all in agreement that we even wanted Mom's attorney as our executor. He did not seem able to fend off Eric's demands and we wanted someone who could remain impartial. And so, entrance to the safe deposit box would remain blocked a while longer, until we could all agree on an executor.

Meanwhile Dad's need to clean out the house had become insatiable. Whether it was because he could not bear to see her belongings because he missed her so, or because he was so angry at what she had done to him, he wanted everything of hers out. He threw things away with a vengeance, tossing without carefully inspecting the mounds of paperwork. We tried retrieving things from the trash cans, but no one knew how many things we never got to see. The furniture was next; pieces were gathered and moved to the garage for disposal.

Dad decided to sell everything at a weekend garage sale. Sprawled in some sort of organized bedlam were the remains of my parents' life together. Mom's shoes were all lined up in a row. Her trusted pressure cooker, which she always refused to teach me to use for fear I would blow myself up, sat with some platters and other kitchen things. Small items, such as her plastic beaded necklaces and cassette tapes were placed on a rickety card table and sold quickly, to our surprise. But much of it didn't sell. It was old, tattered, too worn out to be of any use to anyone. All weekend, we stood there with Dad watching the pile of stuff. Finally, it was carted off to Goodwill. As I walked through the cleaned, streamlined house, I noticed how quickly it was losing the feel of Mom.

The stress Dad felt as a result of the estate issues began affecting his health; he would not eat unless someone was with him, but it was difficult for us to be there during the day because we all had other commitments. I managed to stop by each noontime, but I could do little to alter his mood. All of us— except Shirley—took shifts with him whenever we could. When I spoke with Shirley, it was clear that she was hurting, but just as an injured dog bites, Shirley was in biting form. "I think Dad left her on the floor for a while before he called the paramedics because he wanted her to die," she said.

"That's nonsense, Shirley!" I answered. "Dad loved Mom, no matter how much he complained. He's having a terrible time without her."

"Really? I understand that he couldn't wait to empty the house of anything of Mom's. Did anyone ever check with the hospital to see how long she was on the floor?"

"No, Shirley, no one did. It wasn't necessary," I answered, annoyed by the accusation.

"And now," Shirley began again, "he must be thrilled that Steven is getting the house." Her words had a jealous and sarcastic edge.

"No, he isn't," I said. "Dad says he's spoken with Steven and that Steven assured him he would sign the paperwork to give it to us all equally."

"Well, I hope so," she answered bitterly.

"Shirley, if Dad comes to the reading of the will, and Steven is willing to sign the paperwork for a five-way split, you'll sign it, won't you?" I asked, knowing she always had an angle working.

"Sure, I will," she promised.

"So I can tell Dad that if Steven is ready and willing, we'll all sign the paperwork that day?" I wanted to make sure we had no confusion about this issue.

"Yes," she said again.

When a phone rings and the voice on the other end is Eric, you instinctively know there is trouble afoot. "All the spouses aren't coming, correct?" he asked me in regards to the upcoming reading of the will. I had spoken with Shirley a few days earlier and I thought that I had already addressed this issue. "This is a Poltzer issue. Spouses are not invited and that also means *you*," I said straightforwardly.

"Gal and Brenda aren't going?" he asked, yet again.

"No, Eric, they aren't!" It was simple enough; only the five children and Dad were to be there.

A week and a half later, the big day arrived, with all the anxieties that accompany such a sad occasion. No one relished this day, but we were hopeful that it would all go smoothly and bring closure to this mess. Shlomo, Dad and I drove to the attorney's office together. "Steven's in a tight spot," Shlomo said, feeling badly for his younger brother, and we all nodded in agreement.

We came upon Steven on our way up to the attorney's office. He was friendly enough, although I could tell he was a bit tense. He could either keep La Jolla but alienate his family, or split it five ways and anger his wife. It was a no-win situation for him, but he had made a promise to Dad. I only hoped Shirley would sign the paperwork without creating any problems. Nina soon arrived and a few moments later, Moshe came out. He began to shake everyone's hand, but I refused, still angry that he had lied to me about there being no surprises. *It's a five-way split,* still rang in my ears.

He led us into a large conference room where we all took our seats. Shirley was last to arrive, and, not surprisingly, brought Eric with her.

"Eric can't come in!" we said in unison to Shirley as they both entered the room. Eric did not say a word; he simply turned around and took a seat in the waiting area.

"But he's already here, why can't he just come in?" she asked.

"No." we repeated in unison.

"But that is such nonsense," she spat, her face reddening and her nostrils flaring. She actually looked like Mom for a moment. But we held our ground, despite Shirley's ridiculous pouting.

After rattling off the compulsory condolences, Moshe opened up a folder labeled *Channa Poltzer*. On the outside of the folder, I could see a handwritten note that said, "Do not send mail to home address." Mom had obviously gone to great lengths to ensure that Dad never learned what she was doing to him or us. He read aloud the numerous pages containing logistical and legal instructions from Mom. He repeated the bit about giving Dad a life estate so that he could continue to live in their home. Dad bowed his head. Then Moshe recited that one ghastly sentence that we still couldn't believe: *I leave my house to Steven Poltzer.*

"Moshe, didn't you tell me that it was a five-way split," I reminded him, so angry I could barely contain myself. He hemmed and hawed, refusing to acknowledge or deny anything and then continued reading from the will.

All eyes then turned to Steven, and we began discussing the five-way split. "I need to go outside and speak with Eric," Shirley told us and quickly left. It was irritating that she couldn't seem to do anything without him. After all, this was a family issue. If she could just sit tight, we could fix this injustice.

After a few minutes, she marched back in, carrying an envelope in her hand and not bothering to close the door behind her. "Can Eric come in now?" she asked again, but it was not really a question. "This is ridiculous. He should be here, he has some information."

"No," we repeated.

Although she was annoyed, she moved on. She had something that she could not hold back. "Moshe, did you check the ownership of the La Jolla property all the way back?"

He quickly glanced at his paperwork. "Yes, I did," he mumbled.

"Really? Then how do you explain this?" And with that, she slammed down a copy of a Grant Deed recorded on August 19, 1971. "How do you explain this deed giving all of us an equal five-way split?" She felt victorious because she and Eric had uncovered something the rest of us had not. She clearly enjoyed putting her siblings in their place—well beneath her. We were all taken aback, grabbing copies from the stack she had prepared.

Channa Poltzer hereby grants to Shlomo Poltzer, Jaclyn Poltzer, Shirley Poltzer, Steven Poltzer and Nina Poltzer in equal shares as tenants in common ...

Steven was silent. He had enjoyed his role as Dad's dutiful and generous son. He wanted everyone to recognize his kindness and generosity, but now his triumph was eclipsed. Both Shirley and Steven were playing a perverse game of chess using the family as pawns, but we were not interested in any of their games. "All right, Shirley brought in something that pretty much makes the signing of the five-way split seem unnecessary, but let's just have Moshe write up an agreement that the estate is going to go five ways anyway, then we won't have any of these issues hanging over us," Nina said in an effort to move things along. But Shirley was not done yet.

"Shirley, you promised you'd sign the paperwork and wouldn't cause trouble," I reminded her, but it fell on deaf ears. She flipped through her paperwork and stared at Steven. "What about the $72,000 loan you took out against Lancer Street? It's still due and you need to pay it back!" Steven had taken out that loan to avoid bankruptcy when the property he owned with Shirley and Eric was taken back by the bank. With this banking slight-of-hand, he avoided had bankruptcy, but Shirley and Eric had not been that lucky, and now they wanted revenge. Everyone sighed in frustration, why did she have to be like this?

Nina yanked on Shirley's shirt sleeve. "Fuck the loan. Let's get the La Jolla property resolved first."

Shirley paid no attention and turned her rage toward Dad, "And I don't think you should be managing La Jolla any more."

Dad and the rest of us were dumfounded, and the meeting quickly disintegrated into a raging argument. Shirley was unstoppable. She was willing to sacrifice everything to get back at Steven.

Having been exposed, Steven got up and headed for the door. He decided to go home and seriously reconsider whether he wanted anything more to do with this greedy family. He had come to save the day, but from now on, he would think more about saving himself. We knew in our hearts that once Steven went home to Brenda, she would be in charge.

Thanks to Shirley, nothing was accomplished. Feeling such disgust toward her that we could barely contain ourselves, we gathered up our things and headed to our cars. We were so close, but close wasn't good enough.

The period that followed became a silent waiting game. We were stuck in limbo and needed to nudge Steven into keeping his promise. Nina was the go between with Steven and Shlomo tried very hard to find a way to keep the family intact by speaking with Shirley. But the battle lines were drawn and everyone had dug their heels in.

We turned to Dad for assistance, hoping he could speak with Steven and persuade him to resurrect his offer, but Dad couldn't or wouldn't, stating that he had tried but with no success. It Steven would only split the property, it would have moved us all to a better place, but he remained silent. Yes, there was the deed that had now made its appearance, but why go through all the legal highs and lows when Steven was in the unique position to resolve this dispute instantly and equitably.

TOVAH

Dad's health continued to worsen and we worried about him constantly. Two months had passed since Mom's death and he was twenty-five pounds lighter. His clothes hung loosely on his now skeletal body. His belt, the same type of leather strap he once slid from his pant loops to swing at me so forcefully, was now pulled to its final hole.

But life must go on, and we decided to slowly wean him of our nightly sleepovers. Dad needed some professional help exorcising his many feelings, both good and bad, about Mom.

Nina and I contacted a local organization and learned of a support group comprised of Holocaust survivors. "Dad, we think it would be a good idea for you to go to the Jewish Senior Citizens support group for the recently widowed," we both suggested. "Would you consider giving it a try?"

"Not yet," he told us, not feeling quite ready to take that step. We understood and put that idea on hold, knowing we'd need to try again, soon.

Once someone has become a widower, women appear, like vultures, out of nowhere. One widow named Helen had begun pursuing Dad even before Mom died, calling every couple of years to check in. Once, she had gotten Mom herself on the phone, who had instructed her never to call again. But once she heard that Mom had died, she was back. Mom had been dead a little less than three months when Dad's phone rang. "Hello, Nathan," Helen said in her eastern European accent. "I'm so sorry to hear about the loss of your wife. I'm sure you are suffering so." She said all the appropriate words, but they lacked any sincerity. "I don't mean to be disrespectful, but the last time I called," and she hesitated, "your wife was very rude to me." She was brave now that Mom was gone.

"I'm very sorry," Dad began, "but Channa could be that way sometimes," he continued, acting like the gentleman Mom always hated him for being. Personally, I think he should have stood up for his wife, but in his mind, she was gone now and there was no need.

When Dad mentioned the phone call to Nina and me the next day, we instantly recognized that bird of prey. "Don't worry," Dad tried to assure us. "Helen is just being polite. There is nothing more to her phone call than that." But Helen called again soon after, and this time she told Dad that she just *happened* to be coming to Los Angeles with her daughter and wanted to stop by. Dad offered to take them both out to dinner.

Nina and I were concerned; we knew that Dad could not stand to be alone. "He'll end up marrying the first woman he's aimed at," we both agreed, and it was not going to be *that* woman, not someone Mom had loathed. We were not opposed to the idea of his getting remarried, but we wanted the woman to be someone without any history attached to the Poltzers, someone neutral, preferably someone we had never met before.

"Dad," we told him, "Helen has her eyes set on you."

He smiled and shook his head like a young school boy. "No, she is simply coming out with her daughter to straighten out some issues with her late husband's estate."

"Dad," we countered, "you are tall, handsome and in great shape. You are a hot commodity and she wants you."

"You're giving me a big head," he smiled back.

But we weren't kidding. Finally, we told him we'd never come over again if he married her. It was harsh, but he needed to be shaken out of his naïveté. He seemed to have heard us.

As promised, Helen came out and he gallantly took her and her daughter out to dinner. Much to her chagrin, nothing came of her flirting.

Dad finally relented and agreed to consider the grieving widows' and widowers' sessions offered at the Jewish center. We offered to accompany him, but he insisted on going alone.

On the first Tuesday of the month, Dad walked into the meeting place. Feeling a little hesitant, he peered through the open door where a small sign indicated **Bereavement Support Group** in bold letters. A therapist sat on one side of the room. The other participants were already seated in a circle, their faces all bearing a similar sad, frightened look. Dad took a deep breath, entered, and took a seat in the circle.

The therapist welcomed everyone and began speaking about the feelings that come when you lose your mate. Prior to attending the session, Dad had confessed to us that he was frightened he would end up crying in front of a group of strangers, but it turns out that everyone in the session was crying. Being new, Dad spoke first. He spoke about her death and his feelings of guilt for not hearing her fall. Spilling out his thoughts to sympathetic ears felt good; he was not boring them, and they knew all too well what he meant. Dad decided it was worthwhile and that he would return.

Soon enough, Dad actually started looking forward to his meetings; there he could cry for himself and for others.

There was another reason Dad looked forward to these sessions; he had taken an interest in a recently widowed woman who sat quietly to his left. Her name was Tovah and her husband had died one week before Mom. Although she had had a long time to prepare for her husband's passing, she missed him deeply. She was a pious woman, observing the Shabbat at sunset each Friday, and was very involved with the temple. She had a family of religious children, some of whom lived in Jerusalem and were currently involved in rabbinical training. She was not the kind of woman we thought our father would be drawn to, but he surprised us all. Tovah was the polar opposite of Mom.

When Dad first told us about her, we cautioned him to take it slowly. It had only been four months since Mom had died, and Tovah was the first woman he had even thought about. "Dad, you're a healthy and handsome man, take your time, you'll have your pick of many eligible women."

"No," he answered, "she's the one. She is very pretty and very nice."

I was shocked and saddened at how quickly and easily Mom was being replaced. I understood he needed to be married but it still hurt.

Dad's love life was not the only one that was improving; Shlomo had recently met a lovely divorcee named Linda on a Jewish Internet dating site. After a successful first date, they had started seeing each other regularly. She was very vivacious, just the kind of woman Shlomo had always wanted and needed. We were all happy for him.

Knowing of Dad's infatuation with Tovah and understanding that he would probably end up marrying her, we thought it best to tell Shirley. Maybe if she heard it from us, rather than from a father with whom she was currently having issues, it would be easier for her to understand. In between speaking with her about her anger at Mom's death and the entire estate mess, I touched on the inevitability of Dad's remarriage. As expected, Shirley went wild. "He's already dating?" she bellowed. "He doesn't need to get married," she stated emphatically. "He's supposed to remain alone and be loyal to his wife for the rest of his life."

"But Mom's dead," I answered.

"Just barely," Shirley snapped back. "If Dad gets married, don't you think our husbands will know it's perfectly fine to remarry when we die?"

"And you don't think they will remarry?" I asked. "I'm sure Gal will get married right away. He can't be alone and you're not under some fantasy that Eric isn't going to get married, are you?"

"I hope not," she told me.

"Well, you can hope all you want," I answered, "but they'll be married in no time."

"So where's the payoff for being a good loyal wife?"

"There is none. Certain men just need to be married, and Dad, Eric and Gal are that type," I answered.

Meanwhile, just as Dad's and Shlomo's lives were looking up, Nina was hitting a rough spot. Earlier that year, the housing market had shot up and Nina decided that since she was with Boris, it would be a great time to sell her much beloved beach house. The beach house sold quickly and she happily moved all her things and her dog Peoni over to Boris's house.

But living with Boris was not working out as planned. For one thing, her attention was badly divided between her man, her father, and the family's estate hell. Boris also was proving unsupportive as Nina strained under the pressure of everything that was going on around her. She adored him and tried everything she could to make it work, but the writing was on the wall. So finally, she left him.

One week when I was over at Dad's, he asked me to meet Tovah. Now that Dad felt it was time to begin introducing her to our family, I realized just how serious they had become. I could not imagine what meeting Dad's next potential wife would be like. Mom was still such a vivid memory. I called Nina and told her how uncomfortable I felt about Dad's request and how disloyal I felt towards Mom. "Dad can't make it without someone," she reminded me. "Do you want to sit with him morning, noon and night for ever more? We should thank Tovah for coming into Dad's life and making him happy." She was right, but I still had a hard time coming to terms with it. Nevertheless, I accepted Dad's invitation.

Dad had selected a nearby Mediterranean restaurant. I wondered what Tovah would be like. Would she be from the old country like Mom? Would she speak with that funny English-Yiddish accent we had grown up hearing? Would she look like her? Dad sat facing the door and waved me over. As I approached the table, I studied her. She was not heavy, nor was she slender, but she was well groomed. She was dressed in muted, solid colors, so unlike Mom, who had always loved bright patterns and the color red.

We said hello and politely shook hands. We spoke awkwardly for a few minutes, and as she talked, I noticed that her English was perfect, with only a hint of an accent.

"Do you speak Yiddish?" I asked.

"No, I never learned it," she replied.

She had allowed her hair to go naturally gray, something Mom's vanity would never have allowed, and she wore glasses, another thing Mom refused to wear. I had my answer: She was absolutely nothing like Mom.

Dad sensed our discomfort and tried to help. Then he rested his hand on hers and my heart broke. That hand rightfully should only rest on Mom's hand. Then Dad mumbled a compliment about Tovah and kissed her on the cheek. It was a terrible moment for me. The old saying "life moves on" is so insufficient for an instant such as this. I wanted my Dad to be happy, but it was all much too soon. I could still hear her voice calling me for our daily phone calls. And all of a sudden, I had to introduce the Tovah's voice into my life. When we finished our lunch, I told her it was nice to meet her. I was not lying – she was pleasant, but she just was not Mom.

Dad's affection for Tovah intensified and he made a concerted effort to have everyone meet and embrace her. One Sunday afternoon, she invited everyone to her home for lunch. When we walked into the house, we could not help but notice that the house was immaculate. Portraits of her family hung all around. Tovah was a pleasant hostess and a good cook and Dad beamed. He was very much at home in her house, which made us all very uncomfortable. Why was he so proud of a woman he had known for such a brief time?

Shortly thereafter, he told us all of his intentions: "I'm planning on marrying Tovah," he told us. "We're going to wait one year, per Jewish law."

We were surprised at their haste, but told him we'd be there.

Tovah did not say a word, but Dad quickly refused our offer. "We have both decided that it would be best if both sides of the family were not at the service," he explained. We sat quietly, absorbing the information. "We've chosen August 25th for the wedding date."

My eyes opened wide and I pulled him aside. "Dad," I whispered, "that is the anniversary date of Mom's death. You need to move it." I was surprised he had not remembered that.

He and Tovah discussed it and he called me later to tell me of their new date, August 26th. I had hoped they would schedule the nuptials a week or two later, but could do nothing. I had to come to grips with the fact that Dad was angry at Mom, and in some way, he was getting back at her. But the selection of that date was hard on all of us.

EMAILS, PHONE MESSAGES AND FAXES

During this same time, Gal was in the process of ordering more hardwood flooring from China when Steven called and asked if he could add some sanding machines to the container, and pay the difference. Despite Gal and Steven's many disagreements, my brother's request seemed relatively benign, so Gal agreed.

When the shipment arrived, the bill was higher than expected due to additional customs fees for the sanding machines. When Gal asked Steven to reimburse him for the additional fees, Steven was full of accusations and refused to pay. This, together with the family's estate crisis, ignited Gal's frustration. Rightly or wrongly, he decided that now was the time to take a stand. Though the sum was small, Gal wanted justice.

"Steven, if you don't pay up, I won't release the machines!" he vowed. The next thing I knew, my phone rang, and Steven was on the other end of the line. Once again, he wanted to pit me against my husband, but this time, I did not respond as he expected.

"Steven, the difference is only a few hundred dollars, so why don't you just pay him the difference and call it a day?" I suggested. "If this is so unacceptable, what about we just send them back to China and you can arrange the shipping for yourself. I'm sorry, Steven, but there's nothing I can do." It was finally time for me to take my own stand and straighten out my loyalties. Gal may not be my blood, he was my life mate and he would come first from this day forward.

Shlomo, Nina and I discussed the estate question and what would happen next on a daily basis. Since Shirley was so volatile we had to leave her out of the loop and Steven was a large question mark. No banking entity was interested in being the executor of such a small estate, which meant that Moshe Steinberg would remain our official executor.

Eric should have been content that he found an executor he could easily control, but he was often his own worst enemy. Unable to control himself, he began to dig into Moshe

Steinberg's past. It turns out that Moshe Steinberg had been disbarred for several years for defrauding an insurance company. To make matters worse, it was during this period of disbarment that he had drawn up Mom's will.

Shlomo, Steven, Nina and I talked about it at length and decided we wanted Moshe Steinberg gone. "I'll have my attorney draw up a letter informing Moshe we don't want him to stay on," Steven announced. We assumed that since Eric had supplied us with the information that he and Shirley also wanted Moshe out, but we were wrong. This was just another part of the chess game Shirley and Eric liked to play. They decided to be the good cop to our bad cop and contacted Moshe, assuring him that they wanted him to remain our executor. This would hopefully earn them brownie points with him, because according to a stipulation in Mom's will, the four of us could not get rid of him unless all five children agreed.

Yup, Shirley and Eric got us all again, but now our guard was up. They clearly just wanted to be contrary.

So when Shlomo, Nina and I received a phone call from Steven with an offer, we considered it seriously. "How about you guys agree to let me have one hundred percent of the estate and then I'll sign back your portions to you, but I'll keep Shirley's part as a leverage to make her behave," he offered.

Although Shirley was being difficult, we hated the idea of Steven holding back her portion. As we discussed the offer further, Steven continued skirting the crucial issue of how much he would give back to us. We feared he was not planning on a five-way split, and when we asked him, he just answered that it depended. This was all much too vague for us, so we refused his offer.

Speaking to Steven now proved as frustrating and unreliable as speaking with Shirley or Eric. "It appears we have another turncoat in our midst," Shlomo sadly stated.

Our phone calls back and forth continued to prove fruitless, so in an attempt to keep all the inheritance to himself, while not losing his family, Steven decided to write an email that would explain his side of the story.

From: Steven
To: Shlomo, Jaclyn, Nina

Try as I might I have been unable to express my side of the story to you all. I therefore have decided to clear my conscience here.

Mom had five children—five children whom she loved equally, but did not treat the same. Some of us were urged on to be brave while others where told not to take too many risks. She loved us all the same, but recognized that her five children had five different needs. Yet, she always wanted us to be equally successful.

*When Mom wrote her will two of you were already married, conducting business, buying homes and starting families. I, too, wanted to begin amassing some wealth and approached Gal and asked him if I could be partners with him in his next endeavor. Gal told me no as he was already in business with his own brother and saw no place for me. I was disappointed, but realized I had my own brother with whom I could go into business. However, that fantasy was soon dashed when Shlomo told me **NO!** I do not understand why he wouldn't go into business with me. After all, many other families go into business together. I got the feeling he didn't trust me and I don't know what I ever did to deserve that apprehension.*

Eric, on the other hand, being the man he was, never wanted to go into business alone and was more than happy to join up with me. And so, in my desire to start a business of my own, I was repeatedly lured into unholy alliances with him.

Whenever Eric and I entered into a real estate or business arrangement together, it proved to be a monumental mistake. Without any authorization from me he withdrew money from our joint business account and failed to pay the property taxes. Once when it was time to rent out the properties Eric found us a tenant but kept a substantial portion of the first's month's rent as his commission.

Because of all his shenanigans we ended up losing one of our properties to foreclosure, which meant that I would be exposed financially because of the way the title was vested. I decided at that time to protect the Lancer Street property from being seized by creating a false obligation payable to Mom in the amount of $72,000. My plan was to show my creditors that Lancer Street was heavily leveraged, thus protecting that property.

In regards to Shlomo, I have never refuted that he was entitled to his full share and wanted very much to give him his money, but knowing Eric the way I do, I didn't feel he would be any match for Eric's constant barrages and requests for money.

I understand that you all might feel that I am only speaking about Mom's love rather than fairness because I am the recipient of a larger portion of the property, but money truly doesn't represent Mom's love for us. Rather, her love is there in our memories. In reality, Jaclyn and Nina already have large homes, expensive cars and ample money in the bank, and while everyone wants more money, some of us don't simply want it, but need it. I have two children and would like to be able to send them to fine schools and take them on lovely vacations.

All my life I have tried to keep peace in the family, even in the face of being treated very badly, but this time I know in my heart that Mom wanted it to be this way and that she would not want me to bow to pressure, even from my own brothers and sisters.
Simply put - I refuse to buy your love.
Steven

I read his email a number of times. At first, I felt a little sad for him, but then, as I digested all he had written, I remembered how incredibly talented he was at bending the truth. This mess was not about wealth and who did or did not have it; this was about fairness and justice and equitable family relations.

His explanation about the $72,000 loan made sense—EXCEPT that he was clouding the title to a piece of property other than his own home. Why place a lien on a house no one would ever associate with belonging to him? If he realistically was trying to protect himself against having his assets seized, he should have protected his largest asset, his own home. No, his reasoning made no sense; it only confused the issue.

Shlomo read his email and, feeling a little wounded at Steven's accusations that he had always refused to join him in business, quickly shot back a response.

To: Steven, Jaclyn, Nina
From: Shlomo

Being the eldest my memories are long and I can remember back to a time when we lived on DeKalb Avenue and Mom lit the Fright night candles.
I do agree with you that Mom's five children are all very different depending upon where they were in the birth order, and so each has their own perspective. And after

259

reading your email I find your writing is very compelling, but if we read what Shirley, Nina and Jaclyn had to say, their words would also paint a pretty interesting picture. I feel that the real truth is a compilation of everyone's side.

I am a little surprised to learn that you were disappointed with me when I refused to go into business with you. I grew up hearing Mom talk about money issues, like the loan to Isaac and Dad's experiences with Morris, and I watched as family members had nothing but problems with each other when it came to issues of money. Very early in my life, I promised myself that I would never go into business with anyone in my family. I never meant to put the spotlight on only you.

In regards to fairness I want to tell you a story: When we were all little, Mom sent me to McDonald's to bring home hamburgers for the family. At the time hamburgers were twelve for a dollar and we had five children and two parents to feed. Now by your description Dad and I should have gotten the bulk of hamburgers as we were the oldest and hungriest; but NO, each child received one burger and even though I drove there, I never got a disproportionate amount of food.

On weekends I'd come over to visit Mom and do my laundry. On those times when Dad wasn't home, she'd talk and I'd listen. She usually didn't have nice things to say about Dad and kept implying that if and when the time came she would pay Dad back for all the bad things he had ever done to her. When I dared try to defend him, Mom would ask me, "Who is the chicken and who is the egg here?" Then we'd argue some more and she'd call me her enemy. When Mom died and we learned she had left Dad penniless I thought that since it wasn't Shirley who received the bulk of the inheritance, the rest of us would do the just thing and give Dad back that which she had taken from him. I would not have expected Shirley to do the right thing, but you proved to be just as selfish. I had always heard stories about you and now I feel justified in my decision never to go into business with you.

There should have been money in the safe deposit boxes for Dad to live out his life with, but you and Shirley made sure that there wouldn't be any and now you and Shirley continue to be the most vocal about whatever is left. Enough!

Everything should go back to Dad!
Shlomo

Nina read Shlomo's response and felt it was her turn to weigh in.

To: Steven, Shlomo, Jaclyn
From: Nina

I'm so angry I am having trouble gathering my thoughts and writing this. In reading your email it appears that your angst is mainly directed at wrongs Eric perpetuated against you and you need to remember that this isn't an Eric issue. My objective here is to prevent our Dad from being destitute.

You shouldn't be angry at Shlomo; he is a humanitarian and wouldn't have wanted to go into a business with any of the family.

Whatever your issues with Jaclyn and Gal are, she has always been a good and loyal sister to you and doesn't deserve your anger.

Maybe way back when, before you were married, Mom wanted to help you out more, but that was then. In the meantime Mom often said that she'd like to change her will, but that she could never risk Dad learning what he had coming his way. She knew that if he had learned what she was planning he would have left her. Let's just think about how Mom would have changed her will had Dad died first. You and I both know it would have been a five-way split.

Splitting the money evenly would have been a noble thing for you to do to help soothe the Poltzers' aching souls. I can accept not getting my rightful portion, but can't you see the pain this is causing Jaclyn and Shlomo. And your contention that Eric would somehow trick Shlomo out of his money is ludicrous.

We are not asking you to buy our love, just for some peace of mind and a chance to get on with our lives.

Nina

As far back as I can remember, I had taken on the role of Mom when Mom had been unwilling to parent. I had never wanted that job, but I felt it was my duty to try to do something. I hoped that I could sway Steven into doing what was right. Deciding email was not the answer, I gave him a call.

"Steven, can't you see that this is killing us!" I told him.

"Jaclyn, you and Gal have lots of money. I don't understand why this should hurt you so much," he replied.

"Who are you to tell me that I can't have what I am entitled to? It would have been different if you had given me the opportunity to make my own decision, but you decided for me and that is wrong."

"Jaclyn, I'm sorry you feel that way, but after everything Gal has done to me I am not going to give you back your portion. Gal is the real reason for all these problems and you are only going after me because of him. He is too greedy and you are doing nothing to stop him. The way the business arrangement was I couldn't hope to succeed and now he is trying to screw me with the freight cost." I seethed at his accusations.

"Steven, his dealings with you should have nothing to do with you and me, and as for the business agreement, I personally wrote up that agreement, not Gal. And I did it as fairly as I possibly could. Regarding the machines, I told you to pay the three hundred dollars which would have avoided all of this and now that same three hundred dollars will cost us both thousands in legal costs!"

"Then just tell Gal to tell me where the machines are!" he insisted.

"And what about the five-way split?" I reminded him.

"Forget about that and let's just go after Steinberg's malpractice insurance," Steven suggested.

"Steven, just let us all have what we are all entitled to!"

"Mom wanted it this way!" he stated. "This is what she wrote."

"She wrote it before you married Brenda! You and I both know Mom hated her and wouldn't have wanted *her* to have everything she had saved up all her life."

"The way to make yourself whole is to join me and go after the malpractice insurance," he repeated, ignoring my comments about Brenda.

This conversation was going nowhere. I had only grown more frustrated, angry and hurt. As soon as I hung up the telephone and as quickly as my fingers could type, I sent out an email to Steven.

> **To: Steven, Shlomo, Nina**
> **From: Jaclyn**
>
> *After speaking with you and listening to your explanations that because of Gal's actions I am not deserving of my full portion of the money, I wanted to tell you to KEEP THE MONEY, I DON'T WANT IT. The explanation*

that I don't deserve it because of something that is going on between the two of you is bogus and a weak excuse for being as selfish as you are. You and I share the same blood, which is something that I always remembered when we dealt with you, but obviously you have forgotten that fact.

I told you years ago when you sat at my table drinking tea that Gal wasn't an easy partner. I begged you, I pleaded, but you NEEDED a business and were willing to do ANYTHING to get it.

Then, when you sucked every piece of information and advice from us, took all the names and information off the computer, which you continue to use to this very day; when you then simply told us that the repayment system wasn't working for you and that you weren't going to pay us, if you had been anyone on this earth other than my brother, Gal and I would have had you in court so fast your head would spin. BUT, you and I share blood and I would never do that to a brother of mine.

Yes, you did introduce us to the idea of doing business with China, and that has been a big boost to our business, but then again without Gal's help and handholding, do you really think you'd be in business now, making any money any all? If you are suffering in your business as you say you are, it isn't Gal's fault; if it were, then I guess it would also be Dad's fault that Eric didn't do well in his business.

The idea that that measly amount of money you paid us represents payment in full for all the information you TOOK from us is a joke. Do you have any idea how much time Gal and I invested in adding all that information into that system you currently use? The seed money for our business was not loaned or given to us by a parent; we earned it as we did the house and the cars and everything else for which you seem to begrudge me. I never begrudged you, but rooted for your success. It's a shame you couldn't or wouldn't do that for me.

Now in the wake of Mom's fuckup, your siblings are in terrible pain and you continue to perpetuate this upon us. Each of us is deserving of that equal part of our family memory that the family house represents, but Mom sadly entrusted that to you.

Keep my ten percent; it is soiled by the man you have become.

Jaclyn

The five of us continued arguing via email and phone. Accusations flew in all directions and were aimed at everyone. "What about the cash that was supposed to be in those safe deposit boxes? How can Dad be expected to live with no income coming from his property and no money in the bank? Where is all the cash?" Nina, Shlomo and I asked repeatedly.

"What do you mean?" Shirley asked, feeling unjustly accused.

"Mom always told us that her safe deposit boxes were filled with money," I replied, "and now they're all empty. We know you and Steven got a lot of it, but we had no idea you got all of it!"

"And you never got any money from Mom?" she shot back.

"No one got as much as you two did," I answered her.

"I have an idea," Eric interjected. "What if everyone puts up two hundred dollars and we all take lie detector tests. We'll ask everyone if they got money from Mom and whoever isn't lying or got the least from Mom gets to keep the money."

"This isn't a game show!" I answered. "Besides, the only people who took money and need to prove themselves innocent are you and Steven." I realized it was an unkind thing to say, but it was also the truth.

"Who the hell do you think you are?" Shirley yelled. With that she hung up the phone and began typing, but the only one to receive this email was Shlomo.

To: Shlomo
From: Shirley

I am so sick of listening to Jaclyn preach about how I behave. I have never told Jaclyn off without provocation. She is now telling me that I got $500,000 from Mom and Dad. This is not true; the real number is around $60,000 and that is over a thirty-year span. When I asked Jaclyn how much she got from Mom she never answered me, but instead bragged that she made just too much money to have a need to borrow any. "If that is true," I asked her, "then why did Mom and Dad have to help you with your rent when you were first married?" Even though she would never admit to it, I am sure that Mom and Dad helped her out financially with the down-payment for their first house, but she would never tell you that. And what about the $10,000 Mom paid Jaclyn when Gal and Steven were fighting about the wood business? Mom paid that so Jaclyn would allow Steven to come to dinner for the holidays. I also know for a fact that Mom gave Laura $10,000 for a down-payment on their new home and who knows what Mom gave them for a wedding gift.

Jaclyn talks a good game about how much she cares for Dad and she talks about how much money she has. Well, she is only worried that he will run out of money and need her to help him pay for things. I remember when Eric and I talked to her about insurance for Dad we couldn't get her to agree with me about it. Well, it's time to put your money where your mouth is and give Dad your portion, but no, she won't do that.

Any time I challenge her she tells me that I am just jealous of her. Well, she pays a big price for that great life style she brags so much about. She will forever have to wonder if Gal married her for the green card or not, and then there is the issue of his fidelity. She feels guilty and beholden to him for everything, which is why when Gal messes up a deal she fights so ferociously in court getting him his money back.

She also wants to blame me for Garth hating her, but whatever happened between the two of them is her own fault alone. I don't try and influence my children ever. Garth is angry with her because she gave him duties like washing toilets and then took money from Mom for having him work for her and pocketing it. Jaclyn wanted to only pay him $5.00 an hour, but Mom rushed in and gave her an additional $2.00 per hour. Garth didn't know that it was Mom who was making up the difference, but when he found out that Jaclyn wanted to pocket it, he lost all respect for her. I think the real reason they fired Garth was that she just didn't want him to learn the business.

When Garth and Ian went to school together, Garth really needed his cousin to be there for him, but Jaclyn obviously raised Ian to be like her and he turned his back on Garth. All these things changed Garth forever.

Jaclyn needs to stop being so secretive and take responsibility for what she has done in her life. The way she and Gal handled Steven was disgusting. They sent in strangers to open up a business near him in the hopes of driving him out of business. At least when I want to tell you I am angry I tell it to your face and don't sneak around your back.

When Eric and I found out that it was Jaclyn and Gal that had our wood flooring ad pulled I told her that I wasn't going to allow her to use my address any longer. I gave her two weeks' notice and then I followed up on my promise. I am sure that if it was she providing the address for Steven's kids she would have done the same thing.

I have always maintained that we should all take a lie detector test and see who is lying, but she has always refused.

Shirley

As emotionally troublesome as Steven's email was, Shirley's was a killer. I did not know who was sicker: Shirley for believing in a past that bore so little resemblance to the truth or myself, for knowing all of this about her and still yearning for her so.

Shirley's intentional twisting of the facts made my head spin. I had made every effort to be open and honest with my siblings, taking their sides many times when I probably should have defended my own husband. Many of her accusations were devastating, but the worst was her comments about Laura, who never did anything but adore her grandmother. I had tried so many times to fix things with Shirley, but this time, I was truly and definitively crushed.

One more email found its way to my mail box. It seemed that Steven still wanted my cake and he wanted to eat it, too.

To: Jaclyn, Shlomo, Nina
From: Steven

I need to clarify some things. Jaclyn, I don't blame you for Gal's actions. I am all too aware that you and I share blood and I am not using this issue with Gal to refuse you your money.

When I first entered into the contracts with you and Gal I never had any intention of defrauding you, but I truly feel I was taken advantage of.

The deal was that I pay eight percent of the gross sales to Gal. You do the books and you know that I would be lucky if I cleared ten percent, so eight percent is too high a price to pay. This isn't opinion, but a fact. And I did all this for an annual income of $18,000.

I paid him everything that I owed him and changed my company's name, but he still contacted the vendors and told them not to sell to me. This made operating my business nearly impossible, but I couldn't give you back your computer system because I was already hurting badly.

I truly appreciate the start you gave me and have tried to act fairly with you. I have never wanted to fight with you or Gal and in fact would have liked to continue doing some kind of business with you.

Mom warned me to be careful of Gal and Brenda often told me not to be so free with my information about China when it came to Gal because he wasn't that forthcoming with me, but you are my sister and I wanted this to work.

You and Gal have been successful and that is a wonderful thing, but Mom wanted that

for me also. I didn't trick her out of La Jolla—
she gave it to me of her own free will.

By her action Mom wanted this for me
and if she wanted this for me, why don't you?
The portion of money you would get from the
house wouldn't really change your life, but it
will mine.

Memories are the most important thing
that Mom left behind, not her money.

It's easy to say what I should have done,
but if this had happened to you, please be
assured the decisions would have been a difficult
one. I love my sisters and brothers and never
meant them any harm. I want them in my life and
want them to understand that I need this money
for my family. I want you to think hard about
this before you continue being angry with me.
    Steven

More accusations, littered with more lies. I even checked with Gal to see if there was any truth to the numbers Steven was throwing around, but Gal explained to me in detail how these numbers simply weren't accurate.

Steven truly seemed to believe that he was speaking for Mom. But none of us, including him, could have known what was on her mind. We only knew that that will was written before Brenda came along and before Steven got into the flooring business, and that he had no right to tell me that I should not ask for a piece of the family home in which I had grown up.

He is right that Mom was more than her money. but La Jolla represented so many things. It was the house where we grew up and its walls knew our history well. La Jolla and Lancer Street were the only pieces of Mom we had left.

It was early morning, and I was just beginning my morning tasks of feeding the dog and heating up the water for coffee when the doorbell rang. My head turned and my eyebrows rose in surprise. I peered out the window. There, standing in front of my door, was a young man holding a set of papers. I guessed that a stranger at our door at six in the morning holding paperwork could only be a process server.

"Don't open the door!" Gal told me softly. Steven had initiated a lawsuit over the machines. Unable to serve us at home, Steven simply had the papers served to Gal at work.

"And this is the brother you have been protecting all these years!" Gal hollered at me over the phone as he drove home from work. "You should have let me sue him when he stole all our information!"

I listened to him vent, but there was little I could do other than apologize for putting him through all of this.

When I got home, I listened to the phone messages.

"Are you having a wonderful day…because I am!" Brenda's voice smugly sang. I felt sick. She was taking a truly wicked kind of pleasure in all this. How mistaken I had been about family and loyalties. When I turned on the computer and checked my email, I found yet another communication from her in which she threatened to tell Dad if I didn't turn the machines over to them.

I sat there, dumbfounded, not believing that Steven was allowing Brenda to do this. I printed out a hard copy, grabbed my pen and added a few words to Steven. I punched his work fax number and sent it off.

I am really unable to tell the difference between you and Shirley.

Steven never responded.

271

BACK TO UZHGOROD

When Mom first died, before all the estate problems arose, Dad had asked us to join him on a journey back to his home town, Uzhgorod. It was located near the easternmost tip of the Carpathian Mountain Range in what was then Czechoslovakia, but now Ukraine. He wanted to see it again and wanted very much to have his grown children accompany him to document it. Mom had always refused to go back, having no desire to return to the land that had treated her so badly. On numerous occasions when I asked her why she was so adamant about not returning, she always replied that *they* would find her if she returned. "Mom," I explained, "the Nazis aren't looking for you any more." But she could not get past her fear. Now that she was gone, some of us were prepared to make the journey with Dad.

Shlomo, Steven and I were on board immediately, but when we asked Nina, she said no. "The trip will be too emotionally complicated," she explained. "Mom won't be there, but Steven will, and I just don't want to go." Shirley decided, and Dad agreed, that it would be better if she did not come along either.

"We don't understand how you can go if Steven is going also," Nina, Gal and even my own children repeatedly asked me. "How can you stand to be around someone who is basically trying to screw you?"

Shlomo and I gave it a lot of thought and came up with a plan to call a "time out" of sorts while we were all together. "This trip is too important to Dad, more important than our squabbling over a house," we explained.

I truly felt that Shlomo, Steven and I could rise above the inheritance issue for these two weeks. I would make sure that the subject just didn't come up. Shlomo was finding it a little more difficult, but somehow I was able to place my concerns in a bubble and put that bubble in my pocket.

We met up in Kiev, in Ukraine as I was coming from Israel after spending a week with Gal's family. The Kiev airport was small, so, despite the language barrier, I managed to gather my belongings and find Shlomo and Dad quite easily. Steven would join us the next day. Shlomo was seated on a wooden bench beside some luggage and Dad was pacing, obviously upset. While going through the security screening, an airline employee had asked him to put his blue jean jacket through the x-ray machinery. He had carefully folded it and placed it onto the conveyor, but by the time he and Shlomo came through security the jacket was missing and no one seemed to know where it had gone.

We had been told by our travel agent that we would need to take a short train ride from the airport in Kiev to Uzhgorod. But when Dad asked around, we were dismayed to discover that it would take over seven hours. We had no other options so we headed to the station.

The train we boarded appeared ancient and could easily have been one my father had actually ridden when he was young. We took our places on the uncomfortable wooden seats, surrounded by people who looked like actors in a rural period drama. Dad was still upset about the jacket incident, but his mood lifted when he struck up an acquaintance with a middle-aged couple seated in our section. It had been decades since he had spoken the language of his youth, but he had a real knack for languages and it came streaming out. Seeing him seated in that ancient train talking to fellow Ukrainians made me smile.

He asked the couple what it was like to live in the Ukraine now that Communism had come to an end. Surprisingly, Dad had long been a fervent admirer of Communism. Despite having lived in America most of his life, he considered it far superior to capitalism. He'd kept fairly quiet about it in front of Mom, who loved the country that had provided her with a safe haven. But now, there was no one to stop him from singing its praises.

Shlomo, exhausted from the flight and succumbing to jet lag, leaned his head back and attempted to sleep, while Dad, now filled with energy, talked on. I dozed off as well.

The train made countless brief stops at the many, many small towns. About every fifteen minutes, the interior lights came on and the conductor called out the name of yet another town. No one seemed to get aboard, but many people got off. When our train ride finally came to an end around two in the morning, Dad shook the hands of his new friends and they slipped each other their addresses on small pieces of paper. We collected our things and stepped out into the night air.

The Ukrainian government had obviously decided that there were far more important cities with which to concern themselves than Uzhgorod. What once was a quaint small town now showed obvious signs of neglect. Dad suggested that we walk over to the hotel. "It's probably not too far and I want to stretch my legs a little after the long train ride." (In actuality, it meant: I don't want to spend the money on a taxi). A man at the train station pointed us in the right direction.

As we rolled our wheeled suitcases along the decrepit street at this late hour, we encountered few cars. Street lights were few, the sidewalk was in extremely poor condition, and we could swear we noticed strange characters lurking in doorways. Shlomo's suitcase lost one of the metal rods that ran through it. Normally, he would have tossed it away, but this time he kept hold of it as a possible weapon. We walked on, searching for the name of the hotel the travel agent had given us. We did not have high hopes for it, but we were tired and ready to settle in just about anywhere.

Finally, we saw lights announcing the Zakarpatye Hotel. It appeared to be the largest hotel in the area, but that was not saying very much. Its façade was not beautiful or landscaped, and there were no bellhops to assist us. As we entered and I looked around, I felt like I was in some kind of governmental institution Against the plate glass window sat tattered and uncomfortable-looking sofas acting as some sort of reception area.

Behind the desk stood a taciturn-looking woman; we had obviously interrupted her late-night television show on her small black and white television set. She didn't bother to lower the volume, but rose up and located our reservations. She took copies of our passports and handed us a set of keys, uttering hardly a word.

The closet-sized elevator could only accommodate two people, so we went up in shifts. The hallway leading to our room was reminiscent of an old rusty battleship, with red corrosion on the edges of surfaces and paint peeling away from in places. Our room was musty, with four small beds and a television on a rolling table. I wondered when the room had last been occupied. I opened the windows to allow some fresh air in, but inadvertently also let in a wave of mosquitoes. However, it was very late and we were exhausted. We decided to call it a night and went to bed.

Several hours later, the sounds of the city awoke us. After a quick breakfast in the lobby, we ventured out to do a little sightseeing while we waited for Steven, who was scheduled to arrive later that afternoon. Now that it was daylight, taxis were available in front of the hotel. Dad walked over to one driver and asked if he knew where the Jewish cemetery was. Dad had lost a brother before World War II, and since there was only one Jewish cemetery in the city, he knew he must have been buried there. Most of the Jewish population had long since left Uzhgorod, but this driver knew another driver who knew someone who most likely knew where the cemetery was, and if we were willing to wait, he would make the necessary phone calls.

Dad remained near the lobby awaiting the new driver's arrival while Shlomo and I took a little walk around. Across the street from our hotel stood a Catholic church surrounded by a chain link fence. The church, which seemed to be mid point in its renovation, had a Russian flavor to it with tall turrets capped with blue tops; the largest of the towers was a shiny silver with a cross standing tall and proud against the indigo blue sky. Along the street, shaggy, dirty, mongrel dogs roamed freely.

Before long our driver arrived. A small slender man with white hair, he wore a baseball cap and appeared to be in his late seventies. He spoke no English, but few people in Uzghorod did. Dressed up for the occasion with a dark-colored jacket and a striped tie, he politely opened our doors and we all got in. He was not a driver by trade, just an elderly Jewish man who could use some extra cash. Dad explained why we were all there and the little man turned back and smiled at Shlomo and me.

While Mom was alive, we had learned very little about my Dad's past, but now, with her gone, Dad was free to tell us his stories and now, in his home town, I could create a visual image to match his recollections. Outside on the steps looking out onto the town, I couldn't help but wonder what this place was like all those years ago before the hell of war enveloped it.

The driver pulled away from the hotel. After passing a few intersections, we entered a residential area and eventually came upon a wrought-iron fence. Decayed and resting askew off its hinges, it had a rusted Shield of David or Jewish star welded into it. Tall weeds were gradually taking over the fence.

"Are you sure your brother is here Dad?" I asked.

"This is the only Jewish cemetery in town," he answered. "I know he is here, but I don't know where."

On a bench near the entrance sat a wrinkle-faced woman, her hair pulled back and held in place by a kerchief that covered her head. She had a small pile of old soda bottles filled with water beside her, but they were not for drinking; they were for washing your hands when you were done visiting the dead. It's an old Jewish custom to wash the death away before you left a cemetery. The woman was the self-authorized, unpaid keeper of the place and stared at us as we walked in. Who were we and what did we want, her eyes asked us.

Dad explained who we were and then inquired if by chance she might know where his brother's grave was. She shook her head. Locating Dad's brother would be no easy feat amid the tall, dense grass. Many of the headstones lay on their sides or were broken, and the narrow walkway, which should have kept visitors off the graves, was missing in parts and had completely disintegrated in other sections.
We tried hard to be respectful, but were forced to step over graves and even directly over toppled head stones. We stayed to our right as we walked up and down the many rows, scanning those headstones that were still legible, searching for the one that would mean so much to Dad. Some of the headstones had faces

etched into them with names and dates. We noticed that many stones had the mark of the Kohanim or Kohan clan etched into them. This symbol signified that the person buried here was a direct male descendant of Moses' brother, Aaron. When the temple in Jerusalem still stood the Kohanim performed special prayers, and so men proudly had their heritage and clan affiliation displayed. The driver grew antsy and motioned for us to head back to the car. Dad saw the impatient look on the man's face and felt discouraged. "Come on, everyone!" he called out. "Just forget about it." He started back toward the car. I walked with him and the driver toward the exit, but Shlomo was not yet ready to give up. He veered off to the left and kept searching.

Just as we reached the exit, Shlomo called out: "Dad, I think I found it!"

Shlomo ripped the weeds out, allowing the light to fall upon the stone's carved name: ***Polczer Isador***. Isador, as Dad told us, had been out riding his bike near the bridge in town along the cobblestone street when he hit a bump, tumbled off his bike and was run over by a bus. If there was any positive way to think about this at all, it was that he had been spared the ovens of Auschwitz and had an actual final resting place that could be found these many years later.

His gravestone leaned backwards and a little to the left. On top of the granite slab, the mark of the Kohan tribe, signifying that Dad and his brothers had Kohanim blood coursing through their veins, and some Hebrew writing were chiseled in. Dad gently rested his right hand on the stone and began to cry. So much had happened over his lifetime, and Dad had never had a single family member of his own with whom to share his experiences. It was an emotional moment, and both Shlomo's and my eyes filled with tears. I was glad that it had been Shlomo who had found the grave for Dad; it would be something special a son had been able to do for his father.

When we returned to the hotel, we were drained, both from jet lag and from our emotional time at the cemetery. We all settled down for a nap.

When a knock came on the door, it was Steven. It was an odd sensation; I was happy to see him, yet simultaneously, I was still angry at him. Shlomo, who was also uncomfortable, stayed cool towards him, but Dad beamed; now that Steven had arrived, we could really begin our trip. This clearly meant so much to Dad, and I was glad I had made the effort to come.

Steven showed Dad the video camera he had brought for the occasion and the two discussed the details of filming a Nathan Poltzer autobiographic novelette. It would include narration by Dad and even reenactments. I guess you could say Shlomo and I were going to be the extras for the documentary.

With our little group fully assembled, we decided to begin walking through Dad's life right away. First on the list was the Uzhgorod city square. As we approached it, the streets, buildings and familiar intersections began awakening Dad's long-dormant memories. He saw a shop that used to be the hardware store where he had once worked.

He hurried across the street, not even watching for oncoming traffic, and we followed him inside. It was now a children's shop filled with baby strollers and piled high with infant paraphernalia. Dad walked up and down the aisle. "I used to work here many years ago," he told the young salesgirl, even though she showed little interest in that fact. "This used to be a hardware shop." She smiled politely and I suspect she was probably glad when we left.

We continued walking until we came to the base of a bridge that connected one side of Uzhgorod to the other. The Uzh River flowed swiftly beneath it, dark and blue. The banks sloped steeply and were covered by grass with a smattering of wildflowers in bloom. Off in the distance we saw the silhouette of a young man fishing. The sun was low in the sky and we were all bathed in a golden light.

After taking in the scene for a few moments we made our way across the bridge. An adobe and beige opera house constructed in a mixture of Byzantine and Moorish design stood over to the right. In my father's youth, it had been the local synagogue, the same one where his father had spent so much of his time. "When I was young, there was a large Jewish star made out of stained glass." Dad explained. Long ago, the oversized

Mogan David had been replaced by ornate brick work and all proof that it had ever been a Jewish house of God was gone.

We passed the synagogue-turned-opera-house and came upon a stairway. "This," Dad told us, "led to my childhood school." After climbing the stairs, we discovered it was still in operation. We walked through the heavy double doors and into the school lobby. It was painted school-house green and had student art pinned up on the bulletin board. Dad placed his hands on the metal railing and started up the stairs.

"No Dad, I don't think they'd like that," we told him. "Let's just leave." His eyes looked upwards – he wanted to visit his old classroom and sit at his old desk – but Shlomo pushed open the front doors and Dad turned and followed him.

The following morning, we set off in search of Dad's childhood home. It was a bit of a walk from the hotel, and along the way, Dad continually asked passing strangers for directions. Some warned us that that part of town was now inhabited by gypsies and to watch our wallets. We eventually entered an area that was separated from the city proper by a gully. This was the unpaved, downtrodden section of town, and by the looks of it, it had not seen any improvements since Dad was taken away. There were no street signs or landmarks and Dad was not even sure of the street name where his family home was located.

We wandered along the roadway; onlookers stared at us from their front yards. A couple of young men slowly peddled their bicycles past us. We decided to split up to increase our chances of finding the house. Dad provided us with a description of it and the house number as best he remembered, and we spread out, two and two. Since the streets and houses were built very close together, we were still in close enough proximity to each other and could call out to each other if we found it.

As we looked at the homes and the numbers, we noticed that all the houses appeared to have the same numbers from street to street, but none matched the description of Dad's home. Then, a voice called out from over and around a block. "We found it!" Steven yelled loudly. He and Dad had seen the old A-frame house with the number eighteen on a small white plaque above the door.

Shlomo and I hurried over. From the dirt road, the house looked ramshackle. A grapevine was growing alongside a metal gate, and metal screening surrounded the house, obstructing the view of much of the yard. By the gate stood a gypsy. He had a dark complexion and dark, steel-gray hair. Dad walked over to him. "This was my home when I was a small boy," he told the gypsy. "Me and my three children have come to see where I grew up."

What must the man have thought? Steven's video camera was running and my camera clicked madly. Dad hinted that he would like to go inside and the man agreed to let us take a look at his old home. He pushed open the gate and a dog began barking. The front yard, which used to have a bit of lawn, now had been replaced by a second, attached home that was obviously being rented to some other gypsy family.

"I used to draw water out of this pump," Dad told us, pointing to an iron hand crank in the yard. The barking continued, coming from a small watch dog, chained to a wooden dog house.

"We used to grow all our vegetables in the garden back there," Dad pointed.

The gypsy opened the door and explained who we were to his surprised family. They did not rise or even speak to us, and honestly, they did not look too happy about our intrusion. What most struck me was the size of the house. It was so small! How could an entire family live here? It was stranger still to think that my Dad was once a young boy here and that he and his many brothers and sisters slept and ate here. The walls were dirty and the low ceiling made me feel claustrophobic. We walked out of the kitchen-living room through a small doorway into the bedroom.

"I used to sleep here with all my brothers and sisters," Dad told us. It was not the proudest of moments for him, but he needed to show his family his past. The room was extremely dark, as the sole window had been cemented over to accommodate the adjoining house. A single bed rested against the wall. How had it been possible for Dad to live in that room with so many people?

Dad spoke and Steven filmed. "This was the way I grew up and you get used to what you have," Dad explained. He continued, saying that his father had not been around very much, spending much of his time at the synagogue, so the children had had to go out and make money however and wherever they could.

It was time to leave. Dad slipped the gypsy a few bucks, told him thanks and we were on our way.

Steven was mesmerized by Dad's stories; he could not seem to get enough, asking an endless stream of questions while we walked back to our hotel. As we turned a corner, Dad slowed his step and fell silent for a moment, staring at the fenced shell of a brick factory. "That is the place where I first stayed when they rounded all of us up, before they took us to the camps," he stated as the sun shone into his eyes, causing him to squint. It was in bad shape; its metal girders stood tall, but were heavily rusted and some of the walls had fallen down.

We walked over to get a closer look. We looked around, searching for a loose board so we could get inside, but found none. Steven decided to crank up his camera anyway. "Okay Dad, we're rolling." Steven instructed him. Dad pointed at the one-time factory, re-telling the story of that fateful day. Then, all of a sudden, two men approached us. "You have to stop filming!" they informed us.

"Why?" we asked.

"Because you are on private property," they replied.

We all grumbled a bit and then crossed the road. When we turned towards the building from across the street and Steven resumed filming, the two men came over. "You can't film here either," they insisted.

"Is this private property also?" we asked.

"This is the building I was put into when the Jews were collected up during the war," Dad informed the men, not with anger, but with sorrow.

"You are incorrect; nothing like that ever happened here," one of the men countered.

"I was here and I know what happened!" Dad told them.

"Well, you cannot film here!"

Here it was staring us in the face – our first experience with the denial of what happened to the Jews during the Holocaust. We were stunned by their flat-out lies. "And who are you to tell us that?" I said, behaving like the American I was, determined to express my rights.

"We are the Secret Service," one of them answered.

Now I have never met or seen a secret service person in my life, but something deep inside me told me that the Secret Service did not care about us or this old run-down brickyard.

"Show me your passport!" he ordered, sounding a lot like the Gestapo I had seen on television.

"No! Where are *your* papers?" I asked, incensed. I was livid that we were being pushed around like this.

Shlomo looked like he was ready to explode. It was beyond insulting that they had the audacity to suggest Dad's memory of being interned hadn't really taken place. Our bodies tensed for a fight. Unprepared for our challenge and lacking any authority, they just walked away. Dad was agitated. Had nothing changed during all these years?

We milled around the small grassy area, staring across at the brick yard, trying to envision what it must have been like. We were still trying to register the fact that these people could not or would not acknowledge the atrocities they had committed. Then, a few footsteps from where we had been standing, Shlomo found a memorial. It was made of dark gray granite and was about waist-high. Most people probably walked right past it, missing its symbolism completely, but it confirmed that this spot was indeed where Jews had been collected up and held for the Nazis.

Steven turned the video camera back on and Dad continued telling his story. He told us about that horrible day, about the fear and confusion he and his family felt as they were imprisoned in that brick factory for weeks, with no provisions and no explanation of what was happening. I had of course heard about this place from Dad, but standing in front of it brought the reality of his experience home to me. I was shocked anew that this could have ever happened. It was so small, how could the numbers of people that Dad told me were in there for weeks survive? I kept wondering if I would have been able to make it if it had been me, and I seriously doubted it.

By the end of the day, we had seen everything we were going to see in Dad's home town. It was now time for the next leg of our trip: Germany. We opted to hire a driver rather than take the train.

On our way back to Kiev, we got to see the lovely countryside in daylight. The land looked well maintained, though stuck in a bygone day. Homes were small with wooden or thatched roofs, white window frames and colorful doors. Black and white storks stood one-legged perched in nests on a small number of chimneys. The land was fertile and green and dotted with the occasional horse and sienna-colored milk cows grazing. Many farms had vegetable gardens in neat rows, some curving to accommodate the earth's natural irregularities. My favorite sights were the picturesque old-fashioned haystacks. Women appeared to be doing a fair amount of the work in the fields and I spotted a heavy-set lady clad in a lavender short-sleeved dress with a tan kerchief holding up her hair as she worked the land.

Interspersed between the farms were clusters of homes. Dad smiled as he commented on how people grew their own grapevines for the sole purpose of making their own wine. Even though his father had on occasion drunk a little too much, he had fond memories of grapevines and wine making. "Stop the car!" he suddenly told the driver as he spotted an elderly Ukrainian woman seated in front of her home. Her face was furrowed, her hair short and her bright blue blouse was cheerful as she sat there in front of her chain link fence. Dad spoke with her for a few moments and then told us she had invited us to see her wine-making still. We followed her down a narrow walkway to her home. The basement wine room was dark and dank with many dust-laced cobwebs.

The woman proudly showed us her two prized wooden barrels and offered us some of her home-stilled wine. She pulled out an empty glass soda bottle and from the barrel spigot poured some of the reddish-purple liquid into it. We cordially, although hesitantly, accepted, feeling obliged to taste the liquid in which she took such pride. I worried for a moment about whether those wine barrels were ever cleaned, but we raised the bottle to our lips and gave it a go. Vinegar was all I tasted, but we were polite as we sipped. Soon we were on our way again.

It was a pleasure to see Dad so happy. He was thrilled at how well his trip to Uzhgorod had gone and optimistic that he would continue having good fortune in Germany.

We had planned to spend two days in Munich before continuing on to Macht Schwaben, but I could already feel my agitation building. Here was a country filled with people whose family members had probably done ghastly things to my own relatives and no matter how hard I tried, I could not seem to get past that.

Our first afternoon in Germany, we strolled over to the heart of the city; Marienplatz. It's a lovely open-air plaza with tall Bavarian, Gothic-styled, multistoried shops carrying cuckoo clocks and beer steins in every shape and price range. We marveled at the famous clock tower, the Glockenspiel, whose tallest tower seemed to touch the lightly clouded sky. A giant clock was mounted in the uppermost area of the tallest tower and its hands were gold-colored. Midway down from the clock face, a dual platform stage featured full-sized colorful figurines that jousted and turned, dancing to forty-three bells playing out folk tunes three times daily.

We decided to take a city tour. When we saw a sign that read, "Hidden World of Adolf Hitler Tour," we knew that this three-hour walk was the one for us.

Our Irish-born tour guide explained what we would be seeing and boasted that he spoke not only English, but German, French and Italian. "Let's begin!" he announced and we and the other tourists gathered up our possessions and followed him.

We began our tour by visiting the Hofbrauhaus, a favorite German watering hole. The guide explained that it was where Adolf Hitler made his first speeches, rallying his fellow Germans to rise up against their neighbors.

Next he led us to the building that had once housed Hitler's Munich office, the Braune Haus. "Please keep your voices down," he instructed us, "this building is still in use." He then pointed to an inconsequential-looking door on the second floor that was visible from the downstairs. "That was Adolf Hitler's office," he explained.

As we climbed the wide staircase and my hand glided along the railing, I wondered if Hitler had ever placed his hands here. We quietly walked up to the top of the stairs, looked around and slowly walked back down.

We then walked on to the Feldherrnhalle, where Hitler had once been arrested and sentenced to a brief prison term. As I stood there, I pondered how my family's history would have been different if Hitler had abandoned his aspirations for world domination once he had been freed from jail. Mom and Dad could have had normal childhoods. They would have grown up in their home countries, married and had children. Their lives would have been completely different. The area in front of the Feldherrnhalle, called the Odeonsplatz, had served as a parade field for the SS and Hitler had often stood on the steps, motivating his soldiers to obliterate those in his way. I looked out at the square and imagined I could faintly hear the sound of German militia responding to their leader.

As we finished our tour, I could not help but find it fascinating that the Germans lived in such a state of denial. None of the places we visited contained any reference of any kind to Hitler. It appeared that since he had lost the war, the Germans had chosen to simply obliterate him from history. I certainly didn't want Adolf Hitler to be honored in any way, but to refuse to acknowledge his existence is to ignore history. I would have liked to see these places marked in some way, to remind the world of this monster and his actions.

After two days in Munich, it was time to head to the town that really held Dad's history – Macht Schwaben, which was located an hour's train ride from Munich.

As it traveled along the tracks, Dad began recognizing the countryside. He saw memorable names, Dachau and then Macht Schwaben. "This is it!" he told us excitedly. It was difficult to understand how this could not be entirely full of bad memories, but after the war he had lived there for a little over two years. It did not so much represent the war to him as the beginning of a normal life after it. Now Dad wanted to show it to his children.

We stepped off the train into Macht Schwaben, a sweet little town with groomed gardens in front of freshly painted homes. Although many years had passed, Dad's memory was keen. He immediately headed for the apartment where he had lived right after the war. He was a little concerned that the buildings might have been renumbered, but then he saw that familiar manila-colored building. A woman was out in front sweeping the stairway. He spoke with her, explaining who he was and why he was there. She looked up but never smiled. This time, there was no kind invitation to enter, as there had once been long, long ago. Dad pointed to a window on the second floor which had a flower box jutting outwards towards the street although there were no flowers growing in it. "That was my apartment," he told us. The woman kept sweeping, but kept listening to us with one ear.

From there, we continued on to a busy street. Dad remembered that street, but did not know any of the shops that were now open for business. When we came upon a dry cleaning establishment, Dad went inside to speak with the owner. Shlomo, Steven and I rested on the outside stoop, trying to envision what the street must have looked like with jeeps filled with men in army-green uniforms and swastikas on their lapels. We tried to picture what it must have been like coming out of a camp into the German population after you had survived the horror and lost everyone and everything.

"It's such a small world," Dad said happily as he came back out of the shop. "They know the family I told you about and are going to contact them by phone!" He failed to mention that this was the family of his old German girlfriend, Lizalotte. What a coincidence that we should walk into a dry cleaners whose owner knew someone whom Dad had known almost sixty years ago. After a few minutes, the owner came out and told Dad that she had made a call. Someone was on their way over to see him right away. It seemed they all remembered Nathan and wanted to see him also.

Dad was beside himself; he had wonderful memories of this family and his old flame. He laughed at how well everything was coming together. We did not have to wait long before a blue four-door BMW pulled up. It was driven by Heinz, Lizalotte's younger brother. He had grown into a pudgy middle-aged man and had come to see the Jew with whom his sister had long ago been so enamored. Their eyes met and they smiled. Dad introduced each of us and Heinz motioned for us to get into the car. The two of them chatted as Heinz drove. This trip to Macht Schwaben was now taking on a life of its own, and Dad could not have been more pleased.

After a few minutes, we pulled into the driveway of a lovely split-level home, its white stucco blanketed by ivy. Before we could even knock, the front door opened and there stood the fair-haired and blue-eyed Lizalotte. Without any awkwardness, she and Dad hugged warmly; each was happy to see the other. We were all ushered through the house and into the yard, where a table was set for a quickly assembled, but lovely luncheon. Lizalotte introduced her daughter, a younger version of herself, and Dad introduced us to her. While the young daughter spoke a fair amount of English, Lizalotte did not, so the parents carried on a conversation in German and we *kids* spoke in English. We had little to chat about, so she excused herself and went back into the house. Dad and Lizalotte continued talking while we ate. "Dad is certainly having a lot of luck on this trip," Shlomo whispered to me.

"What do you think the odds were of his finding Lizalotte after all these years?" I answered him.

Steven watched Dad and listened attentively, asking questions on those few occasions when Dad translated for us.

Shlomo and I grew sleepy as the warm afternoon sun shone down on us. I got up to amble around the garden and hoped that Dad would notice that some of us were not enjoying this all German-speaking reunion as much as he was. Maybe I was acting like a spoiled brat, but I didn't want to spend time with this German family and especially this woman. Yes, Dad had told us repeatedly that she was good and kind, but she was German and I couldn't get past that pivotal fact. I felt their meeting was somehow disloyal to Mom's memory and the suffering she and Dad had both experienced in the war, and it felt wrong to see him derive so much pleasure from it.

Lizalotte had been widowed for several years and it was clear that she was still in love with Dad. I was glad he had his heart securely set on Tovah, for I would not have liked him to marry Lizalotte, no matter how kind she might have been to him after the war. I knew I wouldn't be able to overcome my hatred of this country and its people.

Amid their recollections of the past, the subject of where we were staying came up. "Well," Dad smiled, "we haven't made any reservations yet." We had all assumed we would simply find an inexpensive spot somewhere, but Lizalotte took the reins and told Dad that she would make all our housing arrangements. She quickly went inside and contacted a friend who owned a little hotel across the street from the train stop. She came out smiling, and Dad graciously accepted.

We all climbed into the car again, but this time space was a little tighter because Lizalotte, comfortably seated next to Dad, was coming with us to introduce us to her friends at the hotel. After a brief car ride, we pulled into a parking spot. We all smiled because the hotel could not have been nicer; it was nothing like the half-star hotel in Uzhgorod that our frugal Dad had insisted we stay in. This four-star, garden-flanked hotel had clean rooms and lovely soft beds with high thread-count linens.

I got my own room, whose window opened to a beautiful garden. The sweet smell of flowers drifted in, rather than those wretched mosquitoes. I was grateful that Lizalotte had made these arrangements because Dad would never have allowed us to stay in such a lovely place. We headed across the street to catch the train back to Munich, where we would retrieve our luggage, and then return to Macht Schwaben that same night.

When we checked back into the hotel, we were surprised to find that Lizalotte had left a message for Dad. In her note she explained that she would be busy for the next two days, but would love to see him again as soon as she had some time off. She also wanted him to make sure to save an evening for dinner … and bring his children too. Dad smiled – he still had it!

The next morning, Dad and Steven figured out a time line of sorts for the video. Our first location would be where Dad made his daring escape. We boarded the train and passed through a few towns before Dad saw the spot. Dad hurried off the train, and the three of us followed with our camera equipment.

It was a delightful little area with one or two cars parked on the street and houses off in the distance. Dad walked purposefully along the railroad tracks. Steven, bubbling with excitement, lifted the camera to his eye and began interviewing Dad. "So what does it feel like to be back?" Steven asked.

"I am happy to be able to come back here and show my children the places of my youth," Dad spoke, turning to the camera every few strides. Then he stopped when a dark red train passed in the opposite direction. He came upon a steep grade that separated the tracks from a beautiful field of mustard. "This is it!" he said. "This is where we came out of the train, but instead of climbing into the trucks we hid in that waterway. And there," he pointed, "that is the farm house we first ran to where they threatened us with rifles and we had to leave. Then we ran into that forest over there." Through the tall golden grass, way off in the distance stood a long white barn with a red roof. "The grass was this high back then, which is why they didn't see us when we ran away," Dad explained.

"Let's do a reenactment of your escape!" Steven suggested as he secured the camcorder to his tripod. "I'll pretend that I'm your accomplice and Shlomo can run the video." Shlomo began moving towards the camera.

"No!" Dad said loudly as he stepped forward, virtually blocking Shlomo from getting to the camera, deciding for some reason that Shlomo was not competent enough to handle it. "Why don't you run the camera, Steven?"

"Dad," I snapped, "Shlomo can run the video!" It was a hurtful remark for him to have made, especially since it had always been Shlomo, not Steven, who had cared so diligently for both Mom and Dad. Steven did not say a word. This was not a complex camera to operate, but he was not about to disagree with Dad. After much loud discussion over the fact that Shlomo was more than capable of performing this simple task, Dad acquiesced. The hurt was evident in Shlomo's eyes, but there was no time to say anything. I had never really noticed it before, but now I saw clearly Dad's blatant partiality towards Steven. For the first time, as I saw them walk together in matched stride, I became acutely aware that the two seemed to be of a single mind. I wondered why I had never realized it before.

Shlomo shook it off, positioned himself behind the camera and Steven and Dad began to perform their reenactment.

Dad was not grandiose, but you could hear his pride as he described defying this unstoppable foe. He knelt down near the weeds to show how low he had crouched and he pointed and told us how after a short while, they had been captured again. We all smiled because we knew, of course, that Dad had ultimately made it out. He framed it as a grand adventure—he was not going to simply capitulate and die as the Nazis had wanted—and his pride enabled us to enjoy the harrowing details of his escape.

The next day, we headed to Dachau. We all knew it was going to be the most upsetting part of the trip, but that it was important if we were to gain a better understanding of our Dad's experience. While we waited for our train to arrive, a German man approached us. "What are you doing here with all that camera equipment?" he asked in English through his strong German accent.

"Our father has brought us here to visit the death camp he was interned at," we replied.

"There are no death camps here," the man said unemotionally.

My blood began to boil. It was happening again! "My father was in that death camp!" I stated.

Dad hurried over and pulled his folded camp documents from his pocket. "I was in Dachau," he stated firmly. "Here are my papers!" He extended them towards the man, but this German fellow had no intention of looking at them. In fact, he physically recoiled from the papers. Then he turned away and refused to speak to us.

I was livid. "You know, Germany is a lovely country, but they need to suck out all these horrible people!" I said, loudly enough for him to hear.

Dad was now embarrassed by me. "Not all the Germans are bad, Jaclyn; many are good," he tried to explain. "It wasn't the people, it was the situation they were put into."

I was annoyed at how easily he excused them. How could he forgive them when I could not? Dad and I don't share many political views, and one of the most glaring differences was his insistence on accepting and forgiving the German people. Maybe if he was little angrier at them, I could lighten up, but each time he spoke well of them, I hardened my own stance against them.

We boarded the train and arrived less than an hour later. Three taxi cabs waited across from the train stop at Dachau. We walked up to the first one and Dad spoke through the car window. "We'd like to go to the death camp," he said simply.

"There's no death camp here," the driver stated matter-of-factly and turned the volume up on his car radio, taking another drag off his cigarette.

"What is it with these people?" I said loudly.

This time, even Dad grew troubled. "Then what are these papers?" he asked the driver as he shook them at him.

Shlomo was on the verge of slugging the driver in the mouth, but it would have done little good. I studied the older pedestrians who strolled past us and wondered if any of them had been Nazis. I couldn't help myself. We were so overly sensitive at this point that everyone looked like a Jew killer. I was worried that we'd encounter this attitude for the remainder of our trip.

Another cab driver approached us. "They won't admit to it," he told us in a charming Italian accent. "But I can take you to the camp if you'd like." We gladly accepted.

Our driver's wife worked for an organization that catalogued paperwork from the Holocaust. He looked at Dad's documents. "If you can give me a day or two, I can have my wife get you a copy of her organization's findings about Dachau," he suggested. Dad nodded, very appreciative of this man's efforts on his behalf. He drove us to the camp entrance. "I hope you find whatever it is that you are looking for," he told us.

The walkway near the curb showed little evidence that such a gruesome place lurked just a short walk away. Pleasant and clean, the area outside the camp resembled any museum entrance. As we got closer, we found a monument that acknowledged that this was indeed a camp, but upon further study, we noticed its message was incomplete. It mentioned only that this was a place where Jews, gypsies, gays and political dissidents had been kept and put to hard labor, but not that they were murdered systematically, their bodies burned to ashes with only their shoes, hair and gold teeth left behind in large collection bins as evidence that they had ever been there. The entrance had been sanitized so that visitors could feel better about the experience. To me, it seemed like just another effort to cover up the stark truth of what had transpired here, and once again, I felt defensive and frustrated.

We walked beneath the main office's archway to a tall, black, ornate iron gate. *Arbeit Macht Frei,* "Work Makes Freedom," had been forged in iron. But we all knew the brutal reality: Work staves off death for a short while. Simply touching the gate shot pain through our hands. How many poor souls had walked through that gate and never walked back out? I couldn't imagine what it must have felt like for my father, to open that gate after all these years and walk back into that camp. We entered without uttering a word. What could we say? It was clear from the look on his face that the memories had raced back and that he once again inhabited his own private nightmare. Much as we wanted to support him and to understand, we all knew that we never could fully grasp the reality of what he had gone through.   My first impression of the camp was how clean it was, almost park like. The pathway was covered with gravel, and the outlying perimeter of the camp was covered in a carpet of freshly mowed grass. In the center of the grounds stood a lone barrack, the others having all been torn down. This structure stood as a reminder of what the housing was like. But my father shook his head. "This wasn't what it looked like at all," he said. The only indications that other barracks had ever stood on the grounds were large cement blocks with numbers chiseled into them. There was no explanation of what the numbers represented, but Dad knew. He walked across the gravel with his head down and his hands behind his back and then stopped at number seven and stood quietly.

"This was where my barrack was," he explained with desperately sad eyes. Part of him had never wanted to return, but he also needed to come; he needed to show us this place. He also needed to show himself and the world that the forces that had destroyed his family and threatened his very life had not won, and that he had lived on. Ultimately, he had triumphed, and we were there as living proof.

We walked the full circumference of where his barrack once stood, Shlomo a few steps behind the rest of us. All around the grounds, encircling the concrete slabs, was fencing with spiral razor wire bunched up in multiple rotations at the tops and bases. Every twenty feet or so, a solitary sentry structure stood, each one identical to the next, containing a single door, a single four-paned window and a viewing platform. I could see in my mind some Nazi smugly sitting there, all well fed and cozy with his gun pointed at the walking skeletons below.

We made our way to the lone exhibition barrack, which stood dead center on the grounds. The wooden door had a plain metal pull handle that clicked the door open when pressed. There was a single step up and suddenly we were inside, walking on plain wooden plank floors that creaked with each step. The small entrance area was spotless, with windows that cranked open to the courtyard. Opposite these windows was a wall filled with lockers.

"There were no lockers!" Dad blurted out, disgusted. "They took everything from us; we didn't have anything to put in lockers!"

The walls were clean and even appeared freshly painted. A small area off to the left featured five brown toilets lined up against the wall, Again, Dad shook his head. "These weren't here either; there were just holes in the floor boards!"

But the biggest farce were the sleeping accommodations, which were clean, seemingly newly constructed wooden bunk beds. Where were the original beds? The ones stained with urine and blood stains which had dripped down the boards, carved with messages for the new arrivals? Where were the bunks that broke under the weight of two or three men trying to sleep in a bed wide enough for one? No, this was not a realistic representation of Dad's death camp, but an advertisement for a summer camp for children.

When a young German guide walked through the barrack, reciting her script about this "work camp" to a group of English-speaking tourists, Dad could not contain his anguish. "Why are you lying to these people?" he asked loudly.

"Excuse me," she answered back with a German accent.

He held out his papers for her to see. "I was here in barrack number seven. I am a **survivor** of this camp, and what you are showing and telling these people is a **lie!**"

Shockingly, she walked off without a word, taking most of the tourists with her. But some visitors remained behind and spoke with Dad, asking him questions about what it was really like to be there, how he had escaped and what his life had been like to this date. Some had Jewish stars hanging from their necks. They seemed to be close to my age and were there to see what their family members had had to endure. Their stories were similar to Dad's. Two tourists asked if they could have their photographs taken with him. Dad stood proudly with his papers in his hand as his photo was taken over and over again. Steven pulled the video camera to his eye and captured every moment.

Dad was not happy about the way the camp was portrayed to the public, but he felt vindicated that day, if only by a small number of people. As I watched my father, then looked at those bunks and out the windows to the common areas, my eyes welled up. Man is so cruel, I thought. I hated that my father had to suffer so, and the reality hit home as I stood right where it had happened.

There was one other building we had yet to see, the one with a chimney.

"I'm going to stay here," Dad told us as he sat down in the shade of a tall eucalyptus tree. "I don't want to see it."

We understood. A part of me did not want to see it either, but I needed to. I needed to see this horrible place where the individuals who had been so important to my Dad had been so unimportant to others.

The crematorium was initially hidden from view, sitting beyond another collection of gates and further shielded by tall trees. From the exterior, it looked like a charming little structure with dark, red-brownish bricks and a lovely chimney that reached to the heavens off to one side. The building's purpose was still concealed as we entered. The entry room was the area where the prisoners were supposed to undress so they could take their *showers*. It seemed pocket-sized for the number of people it had had to accommodate, with no real place to put their things; but then again, they did not have much. I followed a group that was being escorted by a guide into the next section, the shower room, which we all knew was not a shower room at all. Mock shower heads protruded from the walls, hiding the gas piping behind them. The room was so clean. Where were the scratch marks on the walls from the dying who had tried to claw themselves upright again? No, these walls were plastered, pretty as you please. I tried not to listen to the guide's blathering. They didn't truly represent what had happened here, but I stood for a while looking at the walls, trying to envision what it must have felt like.

We left the gas chambers for the oven room. Two brick pizza ovens with iron doors sat on the cement slab floor. Again, it was cleaner than clean, with no hint of the innocent ones that had been burned to ashes. It made me sick. "These ovens were used for cremation purposes only," the guide recited unemotionally. "It was the method used to dispose of persons who died while in this work camp."

"Death camp!" I said, correcting her dim-witted statement. "If this was only a work camp, then what were the gas chambers in the other room for?" I added, knowing I would get no honest reply here. The guide ignored my correction and continued delivering her memorized speech. I was increasingly livid as I looked around—this sanitized version of this camp was an insult to the survivors, as well as the dead.

The only place that truly reflected what this "work camp" had really been like was the officers' quarters, which had been converted into a museum. Here, large black-and-white posters told the real story. I still could not understand why they had not retained the camp the way it really was. The images here finally contradicted the "evidence" we had been shown so far, but their impact was very much weakened. Although the photos told a heartbreaking story, their message was diminished by the fact that the site itself presented such a different version of the events that had transpired here. An accident.... I did not think so.

We found Dad still seated beneath that same eucalyptus tree. "Let's go, Dad," we told him, and we all left.

We were quiet during the train ride back to our hotel. Dad leaned against the window, gazing out at the scenery, but I do not think he was seeing anything. I wondered what he was thinking about. Was he remembering his family and what they looked like the last time he saw them? Or was he reliving those terrible emotions he must have felt as he lay in those cots beside the dead and dying? Perhaps he was even questioning why and how he was lucky enough to make it out. What could I say to him after an afternoon spent in a place like that? We didn't speak about Dachau again. Dad had done what he felt he needed to do. I'm not convinced he would ever find the closure he sought.

In the evening, Heinz called and spoke with Dad. He wanted to offer himself and his car for the following morning and Dad appreciated the gesture. After such a difficult afternoon, it was nice to think that the morning promised a better day.

Heinz arrived early the next morning. After an exchange of pleasantries with him, Dad and Steven decided we should try to locate the barn where Dad had taken refuge. Dad described it as best he could and a light went on in Heinz's head. "I think I know which barn you are talking about," he said. We were all dumbfounded that he could recognize that barn from such a scant description.

We drove out of town and through a farming area, and then turned into a wide dirt driveway. After a few moments, a house came into view. It was white with green trim and its companion, a detached barn, stood in close proximity. Dad grinned as he stepped out of the car; he and Heinz knocked on the front door. A deep throaty bark came from the door moments before it opened and a sturdy German woman came out with her Rottweiler. The three of them spoke while Shlomo, Steven and I stared at the barn door. So this was the place, and that was the door – the same door Dad had entered to hide from the Nazis who tried to hunt him down – and that stout woman had once been the child of the Staubach family who had permitted Dad and his friends to stay in the rafters of the barn years ago.

Dad laughed and shook his head. "This is the place, and she says she even remembers me!" She gave us the go-ahead and we opened the barn door. We found the interior of the barn just as Dad had described it, with tall rafters and Dad's old loft up high and over to the right. Dad retold the story of that night. His hand was outstretched with his fingers pointing upwards towards his sleeping loft, his voice echoing into the emptiness. Meanwhile, I looked around and absorbed the history of this place. I peered up towards the loft where Dad had used only hay to keep himself warm and wondered how cold it might have gotten here on those nights.

When we stepped out of the barn and pushed the door closed, the woman asked Dad in German if he had been there that night with some others.

"Yes!" Dad answered. "She remembers," he said, turning to us. He thanked her profusely and we all got back into the car and drove off. It was lunch time now and Dad asked Heinz to take us somewhere to eat. "It'll be my treat," Dad offered happily.

We stopped at one of the many restaurants that had fermenting vats of beer displayed behind plate glass windows. The day was warm, so we sat outside under an umbrella. Steven eyed the beer selection and ordered a tall cool one, as did Dad and Heinz.

"Just water, please," Shlomo told the young beer maiden.

"Come on, Shlomo," Dad challenged, "All the men are having beer." He slapped Steven on the back in an act of camaraderie.

"No, I don't want any," Shlomo answered.

While Dad and Heinz chatted, Shlomo, Steven and I could not get over the barn, the loft or the lady with the big black dog. We had been fortunate to find almost everything we had hoped to see.

"I'll need to start getting back," Heinz informed us as he looked down at his watch. Dad handed the waitress some money and Heinz drove us back to our hotel. "Nathan, remember Lizalotte wants all of you to join her for dinner tonight," he reminded him.

"Of course," Dad answered with a smile.

There was yet another message waiting for us at the front desk of our hotel, but this time it was from the nice Italian driver we had met at Dachau. *Please call me when you return,* it read. Dad obliged and told us that the driver would be over right away.

"My wife has made these copies for you," the Italian man told Dad. "It's quite a few pages and I'm sorry, but it is written in German."

"That's all right," Dad told him as he took the heavy beige envelope from his hands. Steven pulled out the contents and flipped through the paperwork. Even though we did not know what it said, it appeared to be very thorough and included many photographs of people and documents. Although the paperwork did not include any listing of Dad's name or his photograph, it contained a great deal of information about the camp. It somehow was a relief to him that all that he had suffered had been recorded for posterity.

"Thank you so much," Dad said.

"You're welcome," the driver replied kindly.

"Do you happen to know where Muldorf is?" Steven asked.

"The airplane hangar?" the driver questioned.

"Yes," Steven replied, a little surprised that he knew about it. "No one seems to know where it is."

"That's because it is tucked away in the forest, but I know I can find it," the driver said. We climbed into his cab and drove out to a heavily forested area. He pulled off the main road, heading down an unmarked, unpaved, un-cleared road. Nothing so far foretold that there was anything historical coming up, but then, in the middle of nowhere, a small, highly discreet sign indicated that we were approaching Muldorf, the location of the World War II secret airplane hangar. The driver stopped the car as we could drive no further and we began traveling on foot. We were undaunted as we dodged low branches and shrubbery that cut our legs with pointed barbs.

When I first saw Muldorf, it did not look like an airplane hangar, but appeared to be an open-ended cave, with a large boulder resting near the entrance. All evidence that a work camp had ever been there had been long since removed and the forest had grown over any parts that might have been left behind. On that boulder a Jewish star was spray-painted in blue. This was the memorial? We climbed up on the roof of the cave. I walked over to the edge to look down and realized that this was probably the spot where Dad had allowed his lice to fall like snow flakes onto the Nazi below. I smiled, but then remembered that Dad had been forced to lug countless heavy sacks on his back for days and days. It was difficult to envision it, but then I had seen many things that were hard to envision. There was so much to absorb about Dad now that we were seeing his actual past.

Lizalotte had left instructions at the hotel desk that she would be by to pick us all up around seven. It had been a long day and I was simply not up for a long, social dinner with people I hardly knew. "Dad, would it be alright with you if after dinner I politely made my apologies and walked back to the hotel?" I asked him, knowing that my absence would most surely not bother anyone.

"No!" he told me sternly. "Why do you have to embarrass me?"

"Dad, I'm not trying to embarrass you, I'm just going to explain to them that it was a long day and that I have a headache. They'll understand. I'll say it very nicely."

"Then don't come at all!" he told me abruptly.

I was taken aback by Dad and this surprising revelation about his priorities. I was emotionally raw after the day. I had gone back in history and visited a difficult place, and I ached for my father and for a now dead mother. I wanted all of us to be together, but I felt Dad was ignoring my own needs to maintain a good face in front of Lizalotte. After all I had done for him on this trip, I felt as though I wasn't that important and that hurt....a lot. There wasn't much to say after that, so I returned to my room.

When there was a knock on the door, I felt relieved, assuming that Dad had changed his mind and was not going to leave me here by myself. However, when I opened the door, I was surprised to see Steven standing there.

"Dad wants me to ask you to talk with Shlomo about his eating."

"Shlomo's eating?"

"He eats kind of loudly. Can you maybe tell him to chew a little more quietly? We don't want Dad to be embarrassed," Steven explained.

"Are you out of your mind?" I yelled. "No, I'm not going to tell Shlomo anything!" And I flung the door shut. I was beginning to understand why Dad would stand up for Steven in his bid to get all the inheritance money. It was becoming increasingly clear to me that Steven was just a younger version of himself.

It was almost seven o'clock when Shlomo knocked on my door to tell me they were leaving. I wished him a good evening and watched them walk down the hall. Dad had not asked me to reconsider, and I was hurt at his lack of caring.

Alone and agitated, I treated myself to an ice cream at an ice cream shop around the corner from the hotel for dinner. I returned to my room and took a long, hot bath and thought about the trip and my parents. I now more fully understood why Mom had shielded us from Dad; he could be a wonderful man, but also cruel. He needed to be liked and was willing to use his children to gain the approval of others. I was more aware than ever that Mom and Dad had worked best as a unit; one without the other could be a hurtful, harmful thing. I missed Mom a lot, but after seeing this country, I understood better why she was a loon. Jewish lives had been considered so worthless, so expendable. Mom had had to carry the horrible cruelty she had witnessed with her always.

I heard about the evening at breakfast the following morning. Lizalotte had been a lovely hostess and was a fine cook. Dad had explained to her that I was absent because I was not feeling well and I had not been missed. Lizalotte and Dad were going to spend our last day catching up on the old times, so Shlomo, Steven and I decided to go visit castles. We particularly wanted to see Neuschwanstein, whose claim to fame was that it was the model for the Disneyland castle.

It would be only the three of us, and although we had made it an unspoken point not to discuss the family, the strain was palpable. Getting there took us two hours by train, but proved to be a worthwhile diversion. The fairytale stronghold stood proudly on a hill surrounded by a thick, dark forest. A walk across a long expansion bridge offered a breathtaking view of an azure blue lake and the many castle spires that glistened in the afternoon sun. After hiking in, we took the castle tour and it was glorious on the inside as it was on the outside.

Dad and Lizalotte said their final farewell and Dad promised he would write, still failing to mention he was getting married in a few weeks. I think Lizalotte truly felt Dad would return to Germany soon. It was a little misleading, but I guess it was easier on Dad to leave her hoping than break her heart with the truth.

As we sat in the lobby of the hotel, Steven walked over and sat down beside me. "Jaclyn, isn't there something that you can do about Gal so we can put this machine problem behind us?" he asked, not confrontationally, but in a friendly tone.

"Steven, I'm not going to intervene. I asked you, I begged you to please just pay the bill and this would all be finished. Now look what has happened," I explained.

"But Gal is being so nasty."

"You know, Steven, I am not the only one with a spouse that can be nasty." And I hesitated, "I didn't want to tell you this, but a while ago, when you sent the process servers to my house at six in the morning, that same day, Brenda called and left a lovely message for me on my answering machine." Steven moved around in his seat uncomfortably. "She asked me on the recording if I was having a *wonderful day*, because she was. So you see, we both have difficult spouses." He went silent; we were back at our original impasse, so we spoke of it no more.

Finally, it was time to return home. Just as Mom's death had revealed some truths about our lives, so had this trip. Dad was not who I had thought he was during those first few months when he had first become widowed. I had worried so much about him then, feeling so badly about his loss. Now I saw that he was capable of meeting his own needs just fine.

TIME TO END THIS MESS

With the trip to Uzhgorod behind us, it was time to seek some sort of resolution to our family predicament. Shlomo, Nina and I sought out an attorney for some clarification. We wanted an impartial third party to read the documents and tell us who was right. Since we wanted Steven to know we were not taking an aggressive stance, we invited him to join us for our appointment. "We don't want to fight; we only want justice," we told him.

The three of us made it to the appointment, but Steven was a no show. "Can we just have a judge look at all the paperwork and render a decision without a trial or going to court?" we asked the elder firm member.

"Of course," he replied. "I will prepare a summary judgment which will state your position that since the deed was written open-ended, all the property should be included in the deed, thus emptying the estate and leaving nothing to be willed over. This falls under the statute of *After Acquired Title,* and after looking at your things, in my opinion you have a good case."

"So we won't need to go to court or anything? The judge will simply read our paperwork and render a decision?" we asked one more time, making sure we fully understood.

"No court, no trial, just a judge's decision," he assured us.

We were relieved. *After Acquired Title* might just be the solution to our problem. But things did not go as smoothly as we'd hoped. The older attorney handed the case over to his son, and things slid downhill from there. The son was not nearly the attorney his father was. He was busy, very busy; too busy to answer our calls or respond to us in any way. It would be a while until the paperwork would be filed in court.

Steven felt we were gearing up for a fight, so he hired his own attorney to protect his grab for La Jolla. We became aware of her involvement when all of us received letters introducing her as Steven's representation. We were a little taken aback that Steven was taking this position, but then again, we had all known for some time now that he wasn't the brother we had once thought he was.

Meanwhile, the dispute between Gal and Steven remained unresolved. He sent Gal a check for the amount they had originally agreed on, along with a written promise that he would never do business with him again. But he also filed a restraining order preventing Gal from sending the machines back to China. This further infuriated Gal and because he was so stubborn he refused to take the check or tell Steven which container held the machines. The container now languished at the shipping dock, and with hundreds of identical containers at the dock, Steven was stuck. So he got Dad involved, who called to nag at me about Gal. I told him he was only getting one side of the story and tried to keep him out of it.

Shirley, who had been unusually silent as these various conflicts evolved, was growing still angrier at Dad for his lack of participation in resolving the estate matter. He had remained conspicuously quiet while Steven talked about getting one hundred percent of the family home. Shirley, feeling tremendous animosity toward her father, sent the executor a letter stating that since Dad no longer owned any part of La Jolla, he should no longer be permitted to manage the property. This was the same property Dad had worked for while he stood in that frigid meat locker, leaving home at four in the morning, day after day for years, until he graduated and worked morning, noon and nights at the liquor store – the same property he paid for and watched like a parent watches a child. Managing the property gave him a sense of pride and a reason to wake up each morning. Unfortunately, according to the law, if one person involved in such a legally ambiguous situation claimed he was unfit for the job, then the executor had no option but to terminate Dad's role.

Dad was devastated; first Mom had screwed him out of his rightful inheritance, and now one of his children was following up. If he didn't manage the property, he would not be able to collect the rent, and he needed that money for his living expenses. We were furious with Moshe, but he held fast; the law was the law.

As a result of Shirley's actions, Moshe hired a management company to oversee the property. Dad would not receive a penny. Instead, the management company would collect the rent checks. Since half the estate was still undesignated, half of the money would go into an estate savings account until it was declared who owned that half. The balance of the money would be distributed to the five children equally.

According to Dad, the management company was doing a lousy job. The garden wasn't being maintained to Dad's standards and the renters weren't happy, Dad had cared for that house since 1962 and now it was being handled by a company of strangers, and these strangers were allowing it to fall into disrepair, all because of Shirley and Eric.

This action against Dad was the final blow. We no longer considered Shirley to be part of the family, but she did not seem to care. She continued to feel justified in her action.

In an effort to spare Dad from feeling the fool Mom had made of him, everyone, except Shirley, decided to sign our portions of the collected rent checks over to him. This action seemed to give Dad some peace, but he was still upset that he had to have his children sign over checks that should have been written only to him. We wanted to spare him the discomfort of coming to us, hand outstretched, asking for money that should have been his all along.

It had also become clear that even if our attorney was successful in getting a judge to stand with our contentions about the estate, Steven and Shirley were not about to give up their positions so easily. The prospect of a law suit loomed.

Strategies for entering into court actions usually revolve around attorneys' expertise in locating and exploiting legal loop holes, and Steven decided to pull out all the stops. He and his attorney, Stacy, searched and searched until they found what they hoped was such an ambiguity. Steven was going to ask the court to have the deed Mom wrote in 1971 thrown out based on the fact that none of us had known about its existence. Knowledge of being a property owner is one of the main criteria in validating a deed. When Mom had written that deed, everyone had been a minor, except Shlomo. Mom had obviously been given some bad advice about this being a legitimate method of giving her young children property while maintaining control of it legally.

Opening that final safe deposit box was now more imperative than ever. It had been ten months and the court had given Moshe Steinberg the go-ahead to have the box drilled open. Dad, Shlomo and Moshe were all there while they waited for the locksmith to do his work. The drill whirled and curled shards of metal fell to the floor. Finally, he opened the small locking mechanism.

Moshe carefully carried the slender box to the counter. He put it down and pulled open the top: Empty. No will, no paperwork, no money. Our hopes for a quiet resolution vanished.

Dad was virtually penniless. Mom had taken the houses from him and left him with almost no money. It was unimaginable. Shirley and Steven had milked Dad and Mom dry, yet these two were the ones fighting the hardest and the meanest for every last drop of everything that remained. I was angry with Mom for doing all this, but I was still angrier at my two siblings. How could they justify their actions? Mom had done the family a great wrong, but it could have been easily rectified. Why, why, why hadn't she worried about doing this to her children? Why didn't she care enough to risk writing something that would correct her will? I knew these were futile questions and that I would never get any satisfactory answers, but as this process dragged on, I asked them again and again.

Shlomo summed it up for us: "Well," he said, "Mom thought of us as her five fingers, but it appears she gave Steven the thumbs up and the four of us the middle finger."

The one-year anniversary of Mom's death was rapidly approaching. Any excuses or postponements in the ordering of her headstone were no longer available. Since no one else seemed to be addressing that issue, I took it upon myself to make the arrangements. I contacted everyone, requesting their input. The selection of which photograph would be the winner of that prized position was easy: it was a beautiful portrait of Mom, one

I knew she always loved. We would have room to list her name, birth and death dates, the fact that she was a wife, mother and grandmother and two more personal lines. Shlomo came up with the first sentiment – *She will never be forgotten* – which he felt expressed Mom's profound presence in our lives and the life of her husband. Steven came up with the final one: *She was a one of a kind.* Even with all she had done to us, we had risen above it and created a lovely monument to represent our Mom when we got together on the day of unveiling.

Gal decided that since Steven saw nothing wrong with suing family members, it was time to call Steven to task for stealing our business information and refusing to make it right. I supported Gal in this case, as Steven had developed a swollen head, mistaking my loyalty to him as weakness. Gal and I had treated him well out of kindness, not weakness. But that time was over. Papers were drawn up and filed in the county courthouse and Steven's attorney was served. Our lawsuit sought monetary justice from my brother. He had not kept his word and it was time he made good on his promises.

Things became quite contentious between Steven, Gal and me. Phone calls, letters, emails all flew constantly. There were depositions and subpoenas for paperwork and so on it went. Dad accused Gal and me of being vindictive, but not wanting to fight with my father, I quickly changed the subject whenever it came up. The lawyers had a field day, racking up bills while the family stood by. Court dates were set and postponed constantly, and new manila envelopes with legal documents arrived regularly for our review.

August arrived, and it was time for the family to come and unveil Mom's headstone. I arrived at the cemetery early to make sure everything was ready. There, lying upon her remains as a kind of permanent cloak rested a dark-gray, polished granite grave marker with her face laser-cut onto it. Somehow, looking down at her, I forgot for a moment about the mess she had created, the hurt in my heart, and my fractured family and remembered the Mom I had known and loved. I thought about how she looked sitting on her couch and how we chatted about my camping trip that last phone call before she died. She looked angelic and gentle with her head resting upon her crossed hands. Her fingers were adorned in some kind of dark nail polish. Her hair had a gentle wave to it. The text looked beautiful and appropriate.

Alone for the moment, I looked around this place we had selected for her; it was tranquil as the sun shone brightly on this hot summer day. I walked around a bit, reading the names off the other stones.

Soon the rest of the family began to arrive. I was gratified to see that everyone had been able to put their hurts, disappointments and angers with each other and Mom aside long enough to gather and tell Mom just how much we loved and missed her. Shlomo and his girlfriend, Nina, and Dad arrived together. They walked over and took a seat on the chairs. On those chairs rested a few yarmulkes for the men to place on their heads and mourners' booklets containing prayers and suggested readings. Nina arrived carrying a beautiful bouquet of flowers, as did Steven and his family. Gal and the kids arrived next, and after waiting a brief while longer, we resigned ourselves to the fact that Shirley probably was not coming.

We opened the books and began reciting the mourners' Kiddush for a mother, then for a grandmother, and then the blessing for a wife. Everyone spoke as clearly as we could through the tears, and some read writings, notes and even poetry of a more personal nature. Then the papers were folded and lovingly left atop her gravestone. We ran our fingers across the recessed etching of her name. Nina and Steven placed flowers by the gravesite and some of us set small stones on the granite slab, which would remain there long after the flowers died, reminding Mom we had been there. Everyone stayed for a short while, not speaking to each other; then one by one, we all left.

Twenty-four hours later, it was Dad's wedding day and as per Dad and Tovah's request, none of us attended. "Don't you feel strange that we're not at the wedding?" Shlomo, Nina and I asked each other on the telephone. "Dad is an atheist and yet he's marrying a woman who is devoutly religious." Tovah was planning on moving in to Mom and Dad's home. Soon, the old family home would become a kosher home. It would feel odd visiting there, seeing not just the things we had grown up, but Tovah's as well. The furniture would be blended and family portraits would now rest in collections on separate walls.

"Do you want to stay with Dad morning, noon and night?" Nina reminded me, thinking pragmatically. "We should be glad that Dad has met someone." And she was right, but it was still difficult to think about Dad standing there under a Chupah. I still needed more time to feel comfortable with this new relationship.

Steven was determined to be given a fair opportunity to speak with us (except Shirley), hoping that we could come to an agreement that could begin to heal the family's wounds. He suggested we try family counseling and we agreed to give it a try. We all thought it best not to involve Shirley at this stage.

The therapist's office was arranged to inspire a mood of tranquility. Nina, Shlomo and I sat on the couch while Steven and the therapist selected chairs opposite us. The therapist was soft spoken and began leading the session in a productive direction, asking us each to explain what we felt was preventing our family from reconciling its differences.

The three of us spoke first. Then it was Steven's turn. As we listened to him, we recognized his same old story. As he registered the anger on our faces, he got angrier himself. Then he paused and we took that opportunity to cut in. "I don't appreciate being blamed for Gal's wrongdoings!" I yelled. "Especially, since you are no saint!"

"How dare you mention my money, Steven!" Nina lectured. "I have never been anything but kind and supportive of you."

Shlomo could barely wait for his opportunity to speak. "I never went into business with any of my siblings!" he said, "and

I didn't decide that just to hurt you, but because I have watched a lifetime of bad dealings."

The counselor turned and directed her questions towards Steven. "How do you expect them not to get angry at you when you are asking for one hundred percent of the family home? You can't have it both ways." Steven turned beet red. He started ranting, staring straight at me.

"You know Gal is at the root of this mess!" he said. "I now understand why Shirley threw your children out of school. If I had had the opportunity I would have also!"

"I can't believe you are saying that!" Nina exclaimed. "There is never any reason to go after someone's children!" Nina continued, furious on my behalf.

The counselor, seeing that things were rapidly spiraling out of control, redirected the discussion. She tried to bring up other issues and problems, but everyone had dug in their heels.

"What would it take to give this family some peace?" she asked.

"A five-way split!" we answered emphatically.

"I can't do that," Steven said honestly. I imagine Brenda had already earmarked that money, and coming home without a fair amount of it would cost him his family and children.

From that point on, between the shouting and crying, percentages where tossed about. Steven kept repeating that we could all be made whole if we joined him in his malpractice suit against Moshe Steinberg. But we did not want to trade one lawsuit for another; going to court was too emotionally draining. And it was not our fight.

We had come to the end of our session and saw no reason to schedule another. After that, I decided that the time had come to sever my relationship with him altogether. I couldn't face the pain of dealing with him anymore. He was no longer family to me.

When another large manila envelope arrived in my mail box, I knew it could not be good news. The court had decided that we could not move ahead with our plans for a trial until we had attended family mediation. "Not again," we said to ourselves. We had just finished family counseling, and knew that mediation had little chance of success, but we had no choice. The date was set and we were ordered to appear.

Being in Steven's presence had now grown painful. We rolled up our sleeves and drove over to Moshe Steinberg's office, the designated location of our mediation.

When I arrived at the office, I found that Shirley had already arrived, and this time, without Eric. Dad had also arrived and was pacing nervously. Steven and his attorney, Stacy, had arrived earlier, but remained in a corner, separate from the rest of us. While we were waiting, Nina, Shlomo and I were chatting, and the subject of Steven's loan came up. Dad interrupted, "He never got any money!" We ignored him, since we knew that he had no idea what Mom had done with any of her money or their estate.

But someone did hear him and paid close attention. A moment later, Stacy slithered over to him. "Would you be willing to sign a testimony stating that you know for sure that Steven never got any money?" she asked.

"I sure will!" Dad said, and she hurried him away into a private office where he signed the paperwork, never considering that he might be wrong and that he was inadvertently taking money out of his other four children's hands.

Everyone was on edge. We wanted to make this mediation productive and hoped we could resolve a few issues, but the mediator had his own agenda. First he met with Moshe Steinberg and the attorney Moshe had hired to represent him. Their meeting lasted an hour or so until they finally returned and told us that they wanted to discuss some inconsequential financial issues first, such as how payments for property taxes would be made and how small maintenance bills should be paid. Only after those issues were resolved would they tackle the major problem, La Jolla. "We don't want to talk about that!" we explained, wanting to stay focused on the matter at hand.

"I'm sorry," the mediator began, "but that is not how mediation is done. We need to have these primary legal issues resolved first." A mutiny quickly erupted and we told the mediator and the attorneys to get out.

It seemed that only our rage against an opposing force could bring the Poltzers together at this point. All the strangers left the room and the rest of us spent the better part of the day trying to come up with a solution, but to no avail. Once again, nothing had been resolved.

A few weeks later, Steven sent us the following proposed settlement: Steven would receive forty-three percent; Nina, Shlomo and I would get twelve percent; Dad, six percent; and Shirley, fifteen percent. There would be no further discussion pertaining to the loan, so that issue would be dismissed. The offer hinged on one thing: it was contingent upon my agreeing to *walk away* from Gal's and my law suit against Steven, stating that we would pay his legal bills and tell him where his sanding machines were.

Gal went through the roof. "We're not paying his $30,000 in legal fees! I'm not going to pay him one penny, and don't you even dare ask me!" he added as he stormed off.

But Steven still was not done. When the phone rang, I heard his voice on the line. "Jaclyn, just so you should know, there is an error on that offer. Your portion is less five percent," he rattled off and hung up. I was dumfounded.

"This is the brother you always protected!" Gal rubbed in, but he was right – this was the brother I had prevented Gal from going after when I should have allowed it. Again, under the veil of a settlement for family peace, Steven was asking me to side with him to the detriment of my husband. Gal was right about taking a stand, although I wished he had not chosen this moment to seek justice. I had to refuse Steven and stand with my husband. I realized that it was not fair to Nina or Shlomo, but I felt that I had been put in an unfair position.

Shlomo and Nina were disappointed and probably even a little angry with me, as the case could have been resolved there and then. But, they forgave me quickly and we stood together as I told Steven no.

It was about this time that Shlomo, Nina and I changed attorneys. Nina studied case law on the Internet and located a new lawyer that specialized in *After Acquired Title*. He was positive that he could get us our five-way split. "Just leave it to me and I'll prepare you a sure winner summary judgment," he assured us. We were optimistic again. Nothing would feel better than getting what we deserved and not having to say thank-you to Steven for it.

The lawsuit between Steven and Gal continued. The judge stated that we needed to try mediation. We hated these forced meetings, but again, we had little choice.

As soon as we entered the room, the bickering began.

"Jaclyn, do you know how much this is hurting Dad?" Steven said, trying to engage me not as a combatant, but as a caring and concerned son and brother.

"Who cares about your father!" Brenda suddenly blurted out. I hoped Steven had heard her and grasped what kind of woman he was throwing away his family for.

Somehow, a deal was finally brokered that Steven and Gal both agreed to accept: Steven would give Gal a certified check for the cost of the freight and Gal would finally divulge the identity of the container. They would each absorb their own attorney fees and agree to drop any other lawsuits. So no one won, except the attorneys. The original $300 bill had ended up costing each side $30,000 in legal fees.

Unfortunately, putting pen to paper was not a feeling of relief, but of severe bitterness; Steven and Brenda hated compromising and so did we. As Gal and I walked out of the room, Steven called out nastily, "Have a nice life!"

"Drop dead," I answered back.

The estate drama continued to escalate. In June 2006, Nina, Shlomo and I were served with notices that we were going to be deposed. It should not have surprised us, but it did. Two years had passed and we were so tired of it all, waiting for the day when justice would come and this would be over. So much of our life had been eaten up by this mess and yet, it continued like a recurring nightmare.

I was the first to be deposed. Stacy, wanting the home advantage, chose her office as the location of the deposition. Our attorney was waiting for me when I arrived.

Stacy, with a welcoming smirk invited us inside. As I settled into her office, I felt like the fly to her spider. The stenographer was to my left. Steven and Stacy were seated directly opposite me. My attorney pulled up a chair beside me and the door shut.

"I don't want to have Steven here," I stated.

"It is his legal right as the party requesting the deposition to stay," I was instructed, and Steven smugly remained in his seat.

Stacy's strategy in deposition taking was easily evident; her questioning always directed me back to some answer she was looking for. As the person being deposed, it was my job to try and stay unemotional; I did not want to blurt out something that might fortify their case.

"Yes. No," I repeated, being as uninformative as I could. I could feel her fishing for corroboration that I knew nothing about the deed. Unfortunately, I had to admit that I had had no knowledge of it, thus playing right into her hands.

"Does the fact that your brother and you are having business dealing problems affect your opinions regarding the estate?" she questioned.

"No, what my brother is doing is hurting this family and that had nothing to do with our business dealings." Stacy was silent, calculating her next query.

"Were there any questions about your mother's mental capabilities up to her death?" My throat tightened and my eyes filled with tears. I could hear Steven muffling his own sniffles.

Don't you cry in front of her, I instructed myself, but I could not hold in the pain. "What do you mean by mental capabilities?" I finally was able to say.

"She bordered on paranoia, didn't she?" she skillfully continued.

314

I sat silent for a moment and then answered. "Yes, I think so."

We continued traveling down that dark version of memory lane, first discussing Mom's mental health and finishing off with questions about Mom's limited physical abilities. "When your mother spoke about the neediest, who do you think she was thinking about?"

"Shirley or Garth," I said quickly, not needing to think. "I never thought it was Steven."

"Why not Steven?" she asked.

"My mother wanted her children to have money so they could catch a spouse. Steven had a spouse. But Mom hated Brenda and since Mom couldn't go to the attorney lest she risk Dad finding out what she was about to do to him, she left the will as it stood, but I know in my heart after hearing her talk about Brenda, over and over again, that she wouldn't have left her one red cent of her money."

I sensed that Stacy was calculating her moves many steps ahead, much as a master chess player is really playing the game three plays ahead. Steven busily wrote things on his legal-sized yellow pad and continued to slide them over for Stacy's review. Shlomo was next, and then it was Nina's turn.

Nina in fact proved to be a formidable witness. She repeatedly challenged Stacy's questions and continually reiterated that this was her "pure speculation." She confirmed that Mom and Brenda had been archenemies and that everyone knew it, and spoke about her sincere effort to get Mom to ensure that any will she wrote would be equal and ironclad. "It'll be a legal nightmare," she remembered warning Mom. Nina next directed an answer to Steven, praying he would hear the hint. "Mom always thought that if Steven had money, his wife would run off with it."

We waited to hear when Shirley and Eric were going to Stacy's office, and were flabbergasted to learn that they were not being deposed. Shirley and Steven had either cut a deal, or Stacy had realized that they would make very bad witnesses for Steven; it would be much safer not to hear what they had to say at all.

For the next few weeks, Nina, Shlomo and I scrutinized what we had said during our time in that office. We each received copies of all the depositions, and Shirley and Eric demanded a copy of all the transcripts. Upon receiving them, they went over each sentence and every paragraph with a fine-tooth comb. Eric loved it. He filed it all into that steel trap he called a brain.

One evening, Shlomo received a call from Eric, who told him that he'd lied about one of his answers.

"What are you talking about?" Shlomo asked. He had not a clue what Eric was ranting on about.

"When Steven asked you if you had ever received money from your Mom, you didn't tell them about your house."

"My house, what about my house?" Shlomo asked.

"When Channa bought that house, she put down ten thousand dollars as a deposit, in essence giving you that money. You had *better* call Steven's attorney back and tell her the truth." His voice was almost threatening.

Shlomo was speechless. He, unlike the rest of the Poltzer children, had retained a semblance of a relationship with Shirley and Eric. "I've got family secrets," Eric tossed out for extra measure. Shlomo said nothing and hung up the phone. There had been no lies or omissions on his part; it just never came to his mind. His stomach turned. He quickly dialed my number and told me what had happened.

I was disgusted, but reassured Shlomo that Eric was just posturing as usual. There seemed to be no end to the drama.

After going through all these court actions for two years, it was apparent that family courts were fond of demanding mediation for battling siblings, and now our time for a second mediation had arrived. None of us had any faith it would work, but we went through the motions anyway.

This time, the court chose a frequently used mediation center that featured a suite designed to keep fighting foes divided. When I arrived, the receptionist directed me to the cubicle to which I, Shlomo and Nina were assigned. Shlomo was already seated when I walked in. Ken, our new lawyer, was next to enter. He was upbeat and why not – this was not his family tearing each other apart. A few moments later, Nina arrived and closed the door behind her. Shlomo was visibly down and I felt fatalistic. The mediator requested that we all come together in one room for a few moments to get started. We took a deep breath and walked down the hallway. It was terrible to feel such excruciating tension over seeing members of my own family. I asked myself once again how it had come to this. Mom, who had always held us all so close, had torn us apart. Shirley and Eric were already seated. Nina, Shlomo and I took our seats opposite them. Intermixed around the table in seats against the wall were Moshe Steinberg and a few others we knew, as well as a few faces we had not seen before. When Steven and his attorney made their grand entrance, they found it difficult to locate seats that were not beside a sibling. There was an open seat next to Shlomo, and Steven hesitated, but Ken quickly sat down, creating a buffer so Steven could sit down safely. Nina looked over at Steven and thought he looked dejected, but that was not what I saw. I saw a skillful foe who had donned a "pity me" face as easily as I pulled on my socks. His attorney stood directly behind him, guarding her benefactor as a cheetah does her prey. Shlomo had begun calling Moshe the sixth Poltzer child, but he was wrong, Steven's attorney stood to gain more than Steven's four siblings; she was really the newest Poltzer child.

At the head of the table sat the mediator, a meek-looking fellow who didn't look like he was up to the task that lay ahead. When everyone had arrived, he began his dissertation. I could tell that Shirley was not listening; she was scanning the room feeling uncomfortable with so many unknown faces in our midst. When there was a lull, she raised her hand and spoke up. "Who are all the unknown people in the room?"

In attendance, we learned, were Moshe Steinberg's malpractice insurance agent, Moshe's attorney, Mr. Klopman, and Mr. Korman, who stated that he was the one who long ago had generated Mom's will.

"Malpractice!" Shirley yelled, "Is that what we are here for? I didn't come for malpractice!" That was not why we had come either, but Steven was hedging his bets, just in case he lost his bid.

With introductions over, it was time to begin. Everyone returned to their respective rooms to discuss strategies. Ken explained to us the methodology of mediators, which sounded a lot like a game. "First, the mediator will listen very attentively as you speak," he said. "He will understand you and seemingly take your side, but then he'll move on to the next room and listen attentively, taking their side. When he finishes visiting all the rooms, he'll return, but now he will tell you that you have no case and that the others were right and that you will be lucky if you got anything so you'd better compromise."

"Don't tell the mediator you don't want to make up with Steven," Ken instructed us. "We want to create the illusion that we are above that." We argued with Ken about that for a while, but when a gentle rapping came on the door, we sat up straight and gathered our thoughts, just as children do when the teacher comes into the classroom. The mediator requested we provide him with a brief account of our family history with Steven and Shirley. It's difficult to condense a lifetime of history, but we each spoke briefly about our brother and sister and why we did not trust them. I had a little more to tell, as I had been screwed over more times, but I tried to keep it concise. We explained our position and told him what we would like in return.

"Steven is very interested in reconciliation. Is that something you are willing to consider?" the mediator asked us.

"NO!" Shlomo exploded. The mediator physically recoiled at Shlomo's outburst. Compared with Shlomo, Steven must have seemed like an obliging fellow, at least after a quick ten-minute meeting.

Nina sensed the need to perform disaster control. Given sufficient time, she was sure she could convince the mediator that Steven's views were based on untruths. She opened her notebook filled with red post-its and yellow highlighted areas. She was anxious to prove her points, but the mediator refused to give her the time or attention needed.

Shlomo then spoke again. His goal was to keep the mediator from being swayed by Steven and Eric and their ability to speak eloquently. "In my life I have been hurt by Steven and Eric, and although they look and speak well and seem kind, these two men are horrid creatures," he began.

When Shlomo was finished, I illuminated the mediator about my views and experiences with Steven. He seemed to listen and then brought up the subject of why Steven had offered Shirley and Eric a higher percentage of the house than the rest of us. "Steven is giving Shirley and Eric a little more to head off any problems," he claimed.

"No, they have some piece of information they are holding over Steven's head," I stated, correcting his obvious misinformation.

"That's not true," he said, rebutting me, but who was this man to make such an assertion? He had known Steven, Shirley and Eric mere hours; I had known them all my life. The mediator and I argued about whether or not it was true. "Thank you," he told us and left the room. The door closed and we were enraged, but more importantly, Ken was upset.

"Nina, stop interrupting the mediator with points of information, and Shlomo, don't get so angry! It looked as though you might climb on the table and punch him. We need to show that we are the room with good and logical people. Jaclyn, this man is a retired judge and you are to show more respect for the man!"

I have to admit that I was not nearly as impressed with the judge as he was with himself, and I guess I allowed that to show.

The mediation proceeded much more slowly than I had expected. I had hoped that the mediator would flit back and forth between rooms in short intervals. We had expected to cover many issues, but that was not happening. Nina, Shlomo and I sat in our overgrown closet for hours at a time with little to do. Nina decided to share her current reading material with us, which was Steven's deposition. The answers on the many pages appeared so practiced, so contrived. It was maddening to see how he altered events to suit his purposes.

The mediator returned. "Steven didn't like your offer of a five-way split, but there is another option for you to consider.

Steven's calls it Dad's Plan." The name alone infuriated us. It spelled out that each of us would get ten percent of La Jolla, while Steven got sixty percent. Lancer Street would be split evenly among the five of us, except the twenty-five percent Mom had already given to Steven and Nina via a deed written long ago.

Another proposed plan was that Steven, in all his magnanimousness, would keep as his inheritance all of La Jolla and we four would split up Lancer Street. Lancer Street was the property in which my father had a life estate and where he currently lived and would hopefully continue to live until he was a hundred. But again this was not about the money, but about La Jolla itself and what that family home represented.

The first thing we demanded the mediator do was to stop calling the first plan *Dad's plan,* as we found it offensive. "Call it something else, but not Dad's plan. And, we'd like to offer that we'd give him ALL of Lancer Street and we four will split up La Jolla." We had been there, stuck in that tiny room for hours and here we had offers which, to put it mildly, sucked. We were amazed. "Did he really think we would accept that ridiculous deal?" we asked almost in unison, but Ken kept repeating that this was the process and that we needed to be patient.

From under the doorway and through the walls we could hear Shirley and Eric yelling. We cracked the door open further so we could hear better. They had come out into the hallway and Eric was yelling at the mediator. "Shirley and I are being totally neglected during this entire mediation!" he stated. "You have only visited our room for a few minutes, one time. We have had no input in this process and our interests are not being considered." For once, he was correct – Shirley and Eric were a non-issue. The four of us had decided that if we could come to some sort of court-ordered decision, then Shirley and Eric would have to follow suit. It did not matter what they said or did; all that mattered was what Steven and the three of us agreed on. We were the ones named in the lawsuit. Shirley and Eric did not want to spend the money to hire their own attorney and we would not let them join us. I did not feel sorry for them. Here was a brief moment of justice, served up hot – the only shame was that we could not do the same to Steven.

The mediator returned once again to our room. It was late in the evening and the clock was ticking. "Steven didn't go for the Lancer Street instead of La Jolla offer," he stated.

"And that's a big surprise?" Nina joked.

"Here is what he is offering: He agrees to your offer of seventeen percent each of Lancer Street, but he then wants seventy-two percent of La Jolla." The mediator stopped and waited. Our three blood pressures must have gone off the charts. The counter offer was giving us virtually nothing.

"That's bullshit!" I spewed. "This mediation is a replay of the first one! I am out of here! Tell him we'll see him in court!" I was done. I began shoving my things into my briefcase. Shlomo was speechless. Nina did not even believe that Steven had made that offer; she thought that maybe the mediator had written it incorrectly or had devised it himself. She stayed lucid and quickly began doing the numbers while Ken and the mediator tried to get the situation back under control.

"All right, give me an offer and I will really press it on Steven," the mediator said, realizing he had to do something. We asked him to leave the room for a few moments so we could crunch the numbers without him, and he obliged. While Shlomo and I cursed under our breaths, Nina and Ken talked.

"If we go to court it will take a week, maybe two," Nina said. "The best we will get is the sixty-ten-ten-ten-ten for La Jolla. Let's offer that, and if he still is a greedy pig, we walk."

We all concurred. We told the mediator our offer and impressed upon him that if this did not work, we would leave.

The mediator returned a few minutes later. "Steven accepts your offer," he announced. He and Ken were thrilled while Nina, Shlomo and I were relieved, but forlorn. Paperwork was quickly drawn up and the mediator made sure that we three signed before he went on to Steven for his signature.

Now it was Shirley and Eric's turn to flex some muscle. "No, we're not going to sign anything!" they stated, having been made to feel ineffective in this proceeding. They left for the elevator. We were so close to resolving this and moving on with our lives, but once again, our plans had been foiled. This horrible fiasco would have to continue, with Shirley, as usual, responsible for complicating matters that we all just wanted desperately to put behind us. I felt so cursed at that moment, at the mercy of siblings who were blinded by greed. It was too late to back out, too late to do anything but dig ourselves in further.

Even though the first mediation ultimately proved fruitless, the court requested we try yet again. As before, we again did not see the mediator much, but then there came a rapping on our door. "Can your father come in? Stacy asked. Shlomo, Nina and I looked at each other and before we could say yes, she asked if Steven could come in also.

"What the hell." I said and we all nodded in agreement.

Steven, Dad, and Stacy came in the room and immediately began handing out copies of paperwork showing Moshe Steinberg's wrongdoings. He reminded me of a politician getting constituents properly papered with his version of the facts. "These are some of the papers I want to bring up in court when I go for my malpractice suit. If we all go in together, it will be a stronger front. It shows all the inconsistencies in Moshe Steinberg's deposition."

It was very important for him to come out of all this smelling like a rose. He so wanted to have his money and have no one be angry with him, but that could never be. I could only think he was delusional if he thought we were going to let him have it all and us too.

The door opened again and now Shirley stuck her head in. She asked if she could come inside also. It was a fair question – this was her inheritance, too – but we asked if we could have a moment to think about it.

"I don't want to see her!" Dad yelled, banging his hand on the table.

"But Dad, we are all in here; she should come in. We'll tell her not to yell at you."

Shlomo quickly went to get her and as she came into the room she slipped me a note: "*Amber wants to see the new baby.*

The children shouldn't pay for the problems that we are having."
My daughter, Laura, was expecting her first baby, my first
grandchild. I shook my head in astonishment. Shirley really did
not see the world through anyone's eyes but her own. Was it not
her who got my children involved in *our* problems when she
threw them out of school? I had never told Laura not to invite
Amber to any upcoming baby events. I folded up the note and
put it in my briefcase; now was not the time to address this, but
for the Poltzers legal, business, and family issues had always
been tangled together.

"Why don't you want me to have anything?" Dad asked
Shirley mere moments after she walked into the room. "Don't I
deserve to manage the property that I worked and slaved for?"

"Why don't you ask Steven to give you back the house
you worked for!" she snapped. "Why do you only yell at me and
never at your favorite, Steven, or can he do no wrong?"

Dad and Shirley continued yelling at each other until
Dad marched out into the hallway. I think that that is one of the
reasons Dad could not tolerate Shirley – she did not play the
forgive-Dad-his-wrongdoing game, like the rest of us did. We
rightly or wrongly turned our heads when he favored one of us or
behaved in a self-centered manner. She called him on his
wrongdoings, and he hated her for it.

Dad should have stood up for us against Steven. If it had
been Shirley who was fighting for one hundred percent, he
would have never rested until she gave it back, but it was Steven
and he did not fight nearly as hard. But Shirley was so
objectionable in her obvious disdain for Dad that we could not
feel a great deal of compassion for her. We knew that if she had
gotten the money, she too would be fighting tooth and nail to
keep every last penny of it.

"But what can we do about that now? What can we do
from this point on to settle this?" Shlomo asked. "What will
make you happy?" he asked Shirley, truly wanting peace.

"Happy?" she answered, "I can't be made happy after all
of this."

"But how can we go forward from all this?"

But she could not. She was stuck. Quickly she dove back into her childhood scoreboard and began recounting all the old inequities in which she had been involved or which she had witnessed. "Steven," she said, speaking directly to him, "it was because of me that Mom ever gave you anything! *I* told her that you needed help. She would have never thought of giving you a thing if I hadn't told her she needed to. And Nina, you wouldn't have gone to college if I hadn't told her to let you go. Jaclyn and I never went to college; we weren't even asked." She was right, but what good was it for her to dig up her past now?

In the midst of all this Steven remained undaunted – he still hoped for a family reconciliation. He knelt down, plugged in his laptop and turned the computer to face us as it began to play the Channa Poltzer memorial montage tape. Mom's tape only accentuated Steven's absurdity.

Within the walls of that mediation suite were the consequences of Adolf Hitler's handiwork. Although he had been dead for years, it was he who had been instrumental in shaping my parents and destroying this family. While almost of us had looked the other way when it came to Mom and Dad's shortcomings because we knew they were the result of what they had endured in the war, Shirley had never lowered her expectations for our parents. But again, this was not going to help us find any closure. It just confused matters further. Arguments raged back and forth, but by the end of the day, we were right where we started: angry, unresolved, defeated, and overwhelmed by the hatred that threatened to tear us all apart.

"Shlomo, I am so done. I'm thinking I don't want to continue with the case anymore." I told him on the phone once I made it home.

"What do you mean?" he asked, hoping I wasn't really talking about abandoning our little legal threesome.

"In my mind we've lost. It's over!" It was not kind to be so pessimistic and angry, when he'd done nothing wrong, but the pain was so intense and I wanted it to stop. I wanted to wake up the next day and think about something other than properties and inheritances. But now I felt worse than ever, so I called Nina.

"We have done all this for nothing, just more money thrown down the toilet," I told her. But Nina paid no attention to my whining; she simply pushed on to discuss what we would do next. "Nothing," I told her. "Let him have it. You can only try so long and then other things in your life take your attention away. For two years we have fought over this mess. Who really cares now? With the exception of Steven we aren't going to get very much after all the expenses. Can't we just put an end to this?"

"Relax, Jaclyn," Nina said and changed the subject to the note Shirley had slipped me.

"She has balls," I commented. "She doesn't mind keeping her kids from me, but heaven forbid I do that to hers."

"This really isn't about you or Shirley, this is about Amber and Laura," Nina explained with reason in her voice.

"I never told Laura not to invite her," I clarified.

"Well, can I talk to Laura about this? I don't want you to be angry at me," Nina asked.

"That's fine with me," I said, and I meant it. Amber had never done me any wrong – none of Shirley's children had.

I had barely hung up with Nina when Shirley called. She was not angry but wanted to talk. "Jaclyn, are you aware that if Steven wins he is going to give his attorney two hundred thousand dollars?"

"Yes, I knew that. Disgusting isn't it? He could have given us each fifty thousand plus the ten percent and we would have been almost whole, but I guess he'd rather give it to Stacy."

We were in agreement here. What Steven had done was beyond what I had thought him capable of.

"Why do you continue to forgive Dad when he didn't stand up for any of us? Doesn't his favoring Steven bother you?" she asked. I listened and her questions had validity and in fact she was right – Dad's bias did hurt, a lot. But then I had a moment of clarity.

"Shirley, I have watched Mom and Dad have favorites all my life and this isn't anything new or surprising to me. The only surprise was that you weren't the one." All my life I had watched Mom dote on Shirley. She loved her looks and admired the way she thought about life and people. Then there was the extra consideration Shirley always received because of having four children and Eric as a husband, so I had always thought she would be the recipient of the bulk of the money if it was not divided evenly.

She heard me and leveled with me, being totally honest. "You're right. I thought that also and it drives me crazy that it wasn't me."

"And now you want Dad to become the father he never was and stand up for us. He won't. Shirley, he can't. Mom and Dad were so messed up from the war, and because of them, we are all messed up."

"But that isn't the way it has to be! Some parents aren't so screwed up from the war. You watched Laura and Ian like a hawk; you were a good parent." And time stopped. It was a compliment, a nice compliment, the first I had received from Shirley in years and it felt wonderful.

"Shirley, I will tell you something that took me a lot of money and a lot of counseling to come to grips with: Dad isn't going to change, not for you or me or anyone. He likes the way he is. Dad is the most important person in Dad's life. You need to expect a whole lot less of him; otherwise he will let you down the rest of his life." It was true and it had taken me a long time to let that in – to accept the fact that my parents were so far from normal, healthy and supportive, and that I could still love them and still allow them a place in my life. But I had years of really good counseling and Shirley had none. We agreed to disagree. There was no fighting, just two sisters in pain, talking honestly and openly.

"What about Amber?" she asked.

"The baby isn't here yet," I explained.

"Why wasn't she invited to the shower?" Shirley asked.

"Laura couldn't invite Amber or Carol because she didn't know what to do about you and Brenda."

"I understand," she said, "but if you include Amber in the future I will simply drop her off and I won't be offended. Amber really wants to have Laura as a cousin."

"Then that's what we'll do," I told her. It was kind and good and we ended our phone call. When I hung up the phone, I smiled. The old Shirley had paid me a visit and I liked it.

The next day, Nina, the voice of reason, and I spoke. If we did not fight Steven when he went to court, he would get everything. Since the mediation was a bust and it appeared that he would not be getting the large settlement from a malpractice suit, the only route left to him was to go for the entire one hundred percent. Therefore we had to carry on and fight him in court. More emotions, more time, more money down the tube, but we had come this far and I was not going to jump ship and leave my brother and sister alone in this. Our hell would continue.

One day several weeks later, Shlomo was looking for a document in his safe deposit box. While he was searching through it, he came upon an old envelope. It was slightly yellowed and was in Mom's handwriting. He opened the paper and read it to himself. It was a letter written to Mom by the city regarding that 1971 deed, and attached to it was a copy of the deed. Mom had given it to Shlomo, but he had forgotten all about it. Shlomo had unearthed a piece of incredible evidence that would prove he had knowledge about the deed back in 1971. Since Steven's claim was based on the premise that none of the other children were aware of the deed, his grab was now in very serious jeopardy.

The three of us hurried to Ken's office with paperwork in hand. The attorney sat back in his chair. "Well?" Shlomo asked, "doesn't *this* change things!?"

Ken's smile grew large, "Yes, it does!" Those were three lovely words. "I will write everyone concerned and suggest strongly that we all just settle out of court and finish this."

While we felt better about our chances of not losing everything, we all knew that Steven would not settle with us until he got every last penny from the malpractice insurance company. With a little over a month to trial, Steven's response to the letter was that he would not settle. To make matters worse, Dad agreed with Steven.

Shlomo, Nina and I prepared ourselves for court the best we could, going over possible questions and problems. It was not something we were looking forward to. Shlomo was nervous; his testimony was pivotal and the weight felt significant on his shoulders. I was confident he would try his very best and that no matter what happened, my love for my brother would never change. He had always been a man of high integrity. I hoped that this would give him some peace of mind.

Nina's testimony would also be important because she had spent the most time with Mom and Dad when the wills and deeds were written, and she was more than ready to go on the witness stand and fight.

Now all of us just waited, waited for an impartial, uncaring stranger to render a judgment.

HER FIVE FINGERS

It was six o'clock on the morning of April 26, 2007, the first day of our trial. I had not slept well at all. I tried to understand how it had come to this. My life had been built as a house upon what I always felt was a strong concrete foundation, but now I discovered that my basis, my rules of living on this planet were not as solid as I'd thought. My most heartfelt belief—that family would always be there for you—was a fairytale, and I was left bare and naked in this world to figure it all out. Mom was gone, Dad was in his own selfish world, the sister that had meant the world to me was caustic and cruel, and my youngest brother would stab me as effortlessly as look at me.

Shirley and I drove to the courthouse together; it was a symbolic truce and as we waited in traffic it felt familiar and good to have her sitting beside me in the car. Nina called on my cell phone and reminded me to be careful and not tell Shirley too much of our plans. Shirley, after all was still Shirley. We walked to the tall City building and through the metal detectors. Our names were printed on an informal sheet of paper pinned to a board on the outside of a ninth-floor room. We pushed the double doors to make our entry.

The walls of our courtroom were completely covered with wooden panels and the floor was decked with the standard government-issue marbled vinyl tile. A long wooden conference table with six wooden chairs upholstered in black was set up for the attorneys and their assistants, and there was a wall clock to display the time. At the head of the room was an elevated judge's desk, which was flanked on both sides by flags, one for the United States and one for California. Filling in the balance of the room were permanently installed stadium seats with walking aisles on both sides and in the center.

The judge had not yet made his entry, but the stenographer sat by her machine ready to go.

Once inside, I found Shlomo already seated in the first row. He had devised his own method of handling frayed nerves by placing a large, thick rubber band around his hand which he planned on snapping when he felt the need to scream. I wished he had brought an extra one for me.

I threw my coat and purse down and sat behind him in the second row, while Shirley took a seat one row behind me. She watched the door for Eric, who was expected to arrive at any moment. Steven was also already seated in the room, but on the other side. He had brought many plastic containers filled with files and paperwork. His laptop was turned on, but at the moment he was busy reading some paper document with great concentration, his finger resting on his temple. His gray hair was thinning slightly, but still was as curly as when he was a baby.

Our attorney, Ken, walked in, exuding confidence. A few moments later, Moshe Steinberg and his attorney, Mr. Klopman, trudged in. Moshe, who was a defendant also, looked anything but confident, appearing exhausted and even a little frightened. Eventually, everyone was there and took their seats.

"All rise!" the bailiff announced, and Commissioner Jonathan Walkoff, wearing the obligatory black robe, walked in and took his seat. The judge was a balding, clean-shaven man and wore a pair of wire-framed reading glasses on his nose. He spoke clearly and loudly. "Is everybody ready?" he asked and court was in session.

The first order of business was to discuss whether Shirley would be allowed to testify. Although Stacy had Shirley subpoenaed, she now was requesting that Shirley be prohibited from testifying. "Mrs. Marlow refused to allow herself to be deposed, so she should not be permitted to testify now," Stacy stated.

Ken refuted that claim. "Mrs. Marlow has since provided proof that the reason she wasn't deposed was because the date for her deposition was changed often, and since she had no attorney she was never notified of when or where to arrive." The judge believed him; Shirley would be permitted to talk.

The next request from the judge was one we had heard before. "I'd like you all to go outside into the hall and try and see if you can work this out," he proposed.

"Again?" we all thought to ourselves, but we were not about to seem disobedient to the man in charge. I had been warned by Ken to behave. "No making faces at Steven, no making faces at the judge, no cursing, no mouthing words, no sighing, no sounds of any kind!" he had warned.

"I'll be good," I promised.

We all walked into the hallway. Calculators and pads of paper came out and numbers were volleyed about for a while. Steven continued harping on the idea of family counseling, so I walked down the hall in disgust. I took a seat on a marble bench. Steven handed Nina a yellow pad with an absurdly low figure scribbled on it, showing the amount for which he was willing to buy the La Jolla house from all of us, but the buyout number was unacceptable.

The percentage climbed to twelve-point-five, but Steven wanted us to carry some of the loan and he wanted us to give some of our portion to Dad. Steven wanted us to aid him in his quest to create the illusion that he had arranged the settlement single-handedly to protect Dad. I could not take it any longer and headed back to the room, quickly followed by the others.

Ken stopped us, not wanting us to go back inside. "You're all so fucking close!" he urged, but for us it was not close enough.

As I passed Steven, I said *Dianu* in his direction. In the Jewish Passover book, which dictates how we conduct our Passover Seder meal, there is a section that speaks of all the many hardships and plagues which befell the Jewish people. With each plague being recited, the congregation chants "Dianu." Translation: "sufficient" or "enough." Each year it was Steven's role to recite the plagues and we would all shout out "Dianu!" I hoped that he understood I felt he had wreaked enough havoc upon this family.

First on the witness stand was Moshe Steinberg. Microphones were positioned on both sides of him, and three large notebooks filled with numbered pieces of evidence rested on the slender shelf that sat before him. The questioning began and we listened. He rambled on for a while, and finally zeroed in on Mom.

"Can you tell me about the first time you met Channa Poltzer?" Ken asked.

"Mrs. Poltzer was a very unsophisticated woman," Moshe began. My eyes welled up. It was one thing for me to know it, but now it was different to have it said aloud in public. He talked about how she feared Dad, but he failed to mention how she equally adored him. He failed to explain that had she had to do it all again she would have married the tall dark Nathan in a heartbeat. As Ken questioned Moshe further, Nina highlighted statements and jotted down questions on a notepad. She then slid the pad over to Ken, who read the questions and continued his examination. After a short while, he finished with Moshe and handed him over to Stacy for cross-examination.

Stacy's questioning was lengthy and repetitive. We could not understand why she needed to ask the same questions over and over again. At the end of day one of what was scheduled to be a two-day trial, we had not even finished with our very first witness. We knew the trial was going to take much longer than two days, so Nina decided to try to effect a change and approached Steven. "Would you like to discuss a settlement?" she asked.

"No!" he answered and turned his back on her. Nina shook her head and walked off to join us as we headed for our cars.

The next morning, we reassumed our seating arrangements from the prior day. While Stacy finished grilling Moshe, I re-read my deposition, having been warned by Nina that my court testimony should not differ in any way from my deposition.

"I call Shlomo Poltzer!" Ken said aloud.

All eyes turned to him. He turned around, looked us in the eyes and walked up. His shoulders were straight and he was almost coming out of his skin, but with the rubber band firmly in place on his hand he walked towards the witness stand. He raised his right hand and swore to tell the truth, the whole truth and nothing but the truth, and sat down. He put on a pair of reading glasses and listened attentively as Ken questioned him. I could not have been prouder of Shlomo at that moment. He was the first of us to be up there, on the witness stand, and by my account he was doing a great job. He answered each question with clarity of thought and a pure honesty that had the judge spellbound.

Stacy then began her cross-examination. Shlomo's persona quickly changed – he was no longer quiet or subdued, but a new, adversarial man who was up to anything Stacy threw his way. He made sure to make eye contact with her and addressed her as "counselor" many times. At times he spoke directly to the judge, addressing him as "Your Honor" and seeming very much at ease, almost relaxed. After answering one of Stacy's inane questions, he decided to digress and defend Mom and her *lack of sophistication.* "In response to your statement that my mother was penurious, my parents were survivors of the Holocaust! My mother lost almost everyone in her family and was chased through the forest by Nazis with guns. When she came to this country it was because of her *cheapness* that she could afford this house that her five children are now fighting over!" He made that statement with such humility and force that we all cried, and even the judge had to wipe away tears. But Shlomo was not yet finished; he had more to say. He spoke about Mom and Dad and about their relationship, admitting that, "Yes, I've seen wounds on Mom's legs from time to time as a result of her driving Dad insane." Then he stated, looking directly at Steven, "The only reason Mom might have written the will the way she did was because back in 1983, Steven, you were unemployed with no work prospects and she was afraid you'd end up homeless and forced to live under a bridge!"

In an attempt to soil Shlomo's excellent testimony, Stacy decided that now was a good time to voice an objection to his new-found evidence. "I question the authenticity of the paperwork which has recently been presented and I move to have it tossed out as hearsay." We were all shocked. Stacy was actually suggesting that Shlomo was bringing in some questionable evidence.

The judge went over each of the three pieces of Shlomo's documentation – the slightly yellowed envelope, the letter from the city to Mom and the 1971 deed. He asked what Stacy found so suspicious, but try as she might, she could not convince the judge of any inappropriateness. So Shlomo's evidence and good name were maintained. Shlomo then continued with his recollections of the Poltzer's past.

"Objection!" Stacy called out.

"Overruled!" the judge told her.

"Why was your mother so frightened in regards to your father?" Stacy asked, trying her best to regain control of Shlomo's testimony.

"Because Mom was positive that Dad would abandon her, start a new family and leave her and her five children alone and destitute." Then Shlomo raised his hand and spread out his fingers wide. "Five fingers and equality is what my mother would have wanted for us kids!" he said.

"A betrayal by your Mom?" Stacy asked.

"And by my brother!" he corrected her, staring at Steven with such force that it might have knocked Steven to the ground if he had been standing.

Stacy went on to ask Shlomo about a cardboard box in which he had kept important papers. "Where in your room did you keep this box throughout the years you lived in La Jolla?" Shlomo's face changed to one of confusion and all of us other children shook our heads. We had never heard about a cardboard box. The question seemed trite and irritating, but Shlomo tried his best to remember.

"Are you talking about the cardboard box I kept in my room on the floor?" Shlomo asked, not understanding what importance that box could possibly have here.

The judge looked at his watch. It was nearing noontime and rather than stop in the middle of something important he decided to interrupt Shlomo's questioning "We'll break for lunch," he announced and with that, we left the courtroom.

Nina, Shirley, Eric, Shlomo and I walked out into the hall. Our compliments to Shlomo seemed so insufficient for the brilliant work he had done. He felt really good about how he had done. "I am ready, willing and a little anxious to continue for as long as Stacy wants to do this," he said. "I'm not afraid of her."

It was Steven this time who came running over to our happy little sewing circle and pulled Nina aside. They spoke and moments later, Nina told us that Steven wanted to meet with all of us upstairs in the cafeteria, without the attorneys, to talk settlement. Shlomo's brilliance had not gone unnoticed by Steven. There was much number crunching around a cafeteria table, but no agreement was reached.

We were just outside the courtroom double doors when Steven turned to me. "Jaclyn," he began, "you don't need the money…you're rich."

What was that all about? Why was this coming up now? With my teeth clenched, I said, "I work fucking hard!" and walked away.

Shlomo returned to the witness stand and retook his seat. The judge looked at him and smiled, "Shlomo, you don't need to finish your testimony; they're settling."

"But what about my box?" Shlomo asked in a moment of pure perfected comedy, except he wasn't joking.

The verdict was finally in.

"Steven gets the house on La Jolla for a value of $1,200,000," the judge explained. "You'll each get twelve percent, or $144.000, $94,000 of which he will pay you within sixty days. But," the judge continued, "you'll each need to carry the balance of $50,000 worth of paper for three years." Steven was planning to refinance La Jolla in order to pay us and his attorney.

I quickly scribbled the numbers on my note pad. After Steven paid Stacy her $200,000 legal bill, which was sadly more than Mom's four legitimate children were about to get, Steven would walk away with $424,000. The actual difference between what Steven would be getting now versus what he would have gotten had he been a *Mench* ("decent human being" in Yiddish), would be a whopping $184,000. It was sad to think that my own brother was willing to trade his brothers and sisters for $46,000 each.

"Alright," we sadly informed the judge. We stepped back into the courtroom waiting area and took our seats. We went over the numbers, hoping that if we kept writing them out they would somehow magically change in our favor, to no avail. Before leaving, I looked down at my notebook, on which I'd jotted notes to Shlomo during the past two days. My feelings were summed up in an earlier note to him: "There is no justice here."

MACARONI AND CHEESE

We stepped out into the cool evening air, feeling somewhat upbeat because Steven had not gotten it all. Nina, Shlomo, Shirley, Eric and I walked down the courtroom steps. The boulevard before us was crowded with cars on their way out of downtown and heading home; traffic would be a bear. "Let's all go out to dinner together," we said almost in unison, and we knew exactly where we would go. When we were young, Mom used to take us to the Clifton Cafeteria which happened to be only a mile or so away. The eatery's menu could never be confused with *haute cuisine*, but the Poltzer family had always enjoyed the selection of salads, vegetables, hot turkey plates and creamy desserts. We had not been there in years, but today it was time to return.

Shirley's car was the largest, so we all hopped in.

We stood in line with our trays at the ready, as we had done over forty years ago, each searching for his or her own childhood favorite. I headed straight for the macaroni and cheese. It still appeared to be made that same old way – a layer of cheddar cheese on top, melted not too much, but just enough to hold back the molten cheddar beneath. Shlomo went for the strawberry shortcake slices, Shirley revisited the turkey plate, Nina got the pot roast and soon our trays were filled. We all laughed, remembering what it was like when we were young, trying to talk Mom into letting us get everything our "big eyes" wanted.

As we shared each other's dishes we never once brought up the court case, but reminisced about our youth and the happy memories we had of this establishment. "Oh my god," I said, seeing the tiny in-house chapel the restaurant had built for spiritual enrichment. "Remember how we used to go inside and hide from Mom?"

The chapel was tucked away behind some tables but visible to us. We hurried over, leaving our cups and plates on the table. Eric remained outside the chapel, understanding that this was a Poltzer memory he did not share. In the course of these past forty years the door had been permanently wired open because, we had heard, heroin addicts would go in and shoot up behind the safety of the closed door. The four of us squeezed into that tiny little structure, barely able to stand upright, and faced the glass display that showed a lovely forest scene with miniature spruce trees and a pair of plastic deer grazing in the artificial, tall grass. I pressed a button and we listened to an old familiar voice come on over the single speaker. I wonder if any of us had ever noticed before that the calm voice recited an uplifting, but religious statement about God and the world. We all had to laugh.

We left the chapel and continued reminiscing as we checked out the rest of the restaurant. The next area was cordoned off with red velvet ropes, but we would not be deterred. We had come to see our favorite red and white dining room. We never really understood why this room was so dolled up or what its purpose was, but we loved the flocked wallpaper and coordinating window treatments. In the corner sat a sealed, commemorative box full of toys we remembered well. Above it was a plaque that explained how these toys were once given out to satisfied customers who were under the age of ten once they had finished their meals. How many times had we all fought over those toys? Being there in that room all together, even if it was not to occur ever again, felt good because for a brief moment in time, we were all Poltzer siblings again.

OTTA BIST MEIN JACLYN

Three long, painful, life-changing years have passed and I am saddened by the loss of a fantasy about my family I had always held dear. I am heartbroken that my family will not continue as I had dreamed it would. I am mournful that there is nothing anyone can do to undo the past and restore my family to the cohesive unit I once fantasized it was. And I will grieve the fact that I will never again sit at a dining-room table, sharing warm vichyssoise soup and chilled gefilte fish balls with Mom, Dad and *all* my brothers and sisters around me.

My mother perpetuated many wrongs, but I still adore and idolize that broken bird I knew as my Mom. I miss the feel of her hand and the coolness of her lips when she placed them upon my forehead. I miss the sound of her voice. I miss hearing her say, "Otta bist mein Jaclyn" (Here is my Jaclyn), when she would answer my daily five o'clock phone call, and I miss the woman she was when she was not getting in her own way. I just miss my Mom.

On November 17, 2006, the next generation arrived with the birth of my first grandchild, Tyler. I wondered, as I held him in my arms that first time, how his life would differ from mine, never having the chance to meet that Mom of mine. He would never know the Poltzers as I had once known them, which made me a little sad. But he would know love and support and healthy family relationships.

During the war, Dad and Mom had experienced the untimely loss of their families and suffered atrocities that corrupted their souls. They carried all those distorted thoughts with them as if in a large bag of soiled clothes and passed them along to their five children. We, then, were to suffer our own disillusionment and sadness at the destruction and loss of a family – a loss not caused by strangers as Mom had always feared, but by ourselves, the broken birds we had all become.

THE END

EPILOGUE

It has been four and a half years since Mom died. Many fears and fantasies have been dispelled in that time.

I have come to terms with the fact that Steven got the family house, but in doing so, he lost Shlomo, Nina and myself.

We don't speak with him and can't see any reason to bring him back into our lives.

Shirley also has been cut loose from the family fold, although she continues to wonder why.

I understand Garth has a daughter, but I know in my heart I will never know the little girl who is my great niece and I am sad for the loss.

Dad is well. Tovah is good to him and he is happy and we are happy for him.

The Polzer family is forever changed, it's lonely without the others, but Shlomo, Nina and I continue to grow ever closer. They, along with my husband and children, prove to me that family can be everything I always hoped it could be.

The photo in Channa's Pocket